UNDERSTANDING SOUTH AFRICA

T0322654

MARTIN PLAUT
CARIEN DU PLESSIS

Understanding South Africa

HURST & COMPANY, LONDON

First published in the United Kingdom in 2019 by
C. Hurst & Co. (Publishers) Ltd.,
41 Great Russell Street, London, WC1B 3PL
© Martin Plaut and Carien du Plessis, 2019
All rights reserved.
Printed in Great Britain by Bell and Bain Ltd, Glasgow

Distributed in the United States, Canada and Latin America by
Oxford University Press, 198 Madison Avenue, New York, NY 10016,
United States of America.

A Cataloguing-in-Publication data record for this book
is available from the British Library.

ISBN: 9781787382046

This book is printed using paper from registered sustainable
and managed sources.

www.hurstpublishers.com

CONTENTS

ABBREVIATIONS

ACDP	African Christian Democratic Party
ASGISA	Accelerated and Shared Growth Initiative for South Africa
Azapo	Azanian People's Organisation
B-BBEE	Broad-Based Black Economic Empowerment
BEE	Black Economic Empowerment
BLF	Black First Land First
CALS	Centre for Applied Legal Studies
Cope	Congress of the People
Cosatu	Congress of South African Trade Unions
CSDA	Centre for Social Development in Africa
DA	Democratic Alliance
EFF	Economic Freedom Fighters
ESG	Environmental, Social and Governance
FF Plus	Freedom Front Plus
FOSATU	Federation of South African Trade Unions
GEAR	Growth, Employment and Redistribution
ICU	Industrial and Commercial Workers' Union
IEC	Independent Electoral Commission
IFP	Inkatha Freedom Party
MK	Umkhonto we Sizwe
NDP	National Development Plan

ABBREVIATIONS

NP	National Party
PAC	Pan Africanist Congress
PBF	Progressive Business Forum
RDP	Reconstruction and Development Programme
SABC	South African Broadcasting Corporation
SACP	Communist Party of South Africa
SADTU	South African Democratic Teachers' Union
SANNC	South African Native National Congress
TAC	Treatment Action Campaign
UDF	United Democratic Front
UDM	United Democratic Movement

1

INTRODUCTION

EXTRAORDINARY COUNTRY, CONTRASTING LIVES

Extraordinary country, contrasting lives

Two women stand with their faces inches apart. 'Fuck you, fuck you, fuck you,' the younger black woman yells at her white compatriot. All around them spectators film the confrontation on their mobile phones.

The scene is Clifton—probably the most exclusive beach in the whole of South Africa. Above its white sands tower blocks of flats that are home to some of the richest people in the country, almost all of them white. A group of black Capetonians has 'invaded' their space—slaughtering a sheep in a traditional ritual to 'avenge our trauma at the hands of white people over the years,' as an activist explains. The white residents furiously denounce the slaughter as a violation of animal rights.

No meeting of minds is even remotely possible. The scenes are broadcast around the world—a blot on Cape Town's reputation as the top holiday destination of 2019.

A few hundred miles further north another scene is being played out. A trade union leader lies dying in his home. Ronald

Mani—a regional leader of the municipal workers union—has been shot in the village of Tshisahulu.

Tshisahulu is in Limpopo, north of South Africa's executive capital, Pretoria. The village has been the scene of many murders over the years. Few cases have ever been resolved, or the suspects arrested.[1] A week later, another political leader is killed.[2] The latest murders are believed to have been intended to silence anyone who spoke out against the looting of South Africa's VBS Mutual Bank. Yet even though the international auditing firm KPMG is named in an official report into the fraud, the world has no interest.[3]

The lives of men like Ronald Mani are cheap. The pristine sands of Clifton, defiled by a sheep's blood, are expensive.

Yet there is another side to this extraordinary country that is seldom remarked on. From time to time its people forget their terrible past and their racial divisions and unite for a common cause.

Faced with the prospect of an unprecedented drought, the people of Cape Town did something that no other city has ever done: in three years, residents more than halved their use of water. Consumption fell from 1.2 billion litres a day in 2015 to just over 500 million litres at the start of 2018—a record-breaking achievement.[4] And it was accomplished by exempting the poorest communities, living in shanty towns around the city, from any of the cuts. By naming and shaming those who broke tight controls, removing taps in some of the top hotels and banning Capetonians from washing cars or filling swimming pools, the city met its target. Catastrophe was averted.

There are also many stories of *ubuntu*—people reaching out across racial and other divisions to help each other.

In the late 1970s in the small KwaZulu-Natal town of Ixopo, a bright young Zulu man was awarded a bursary to study law. This presented him with a dilemma. He was needed at home to look after his mother, who had lost her job two years earlier, and his younger siblings. A local Indian shopkeeper agreed to provide the family with groceries until the young man finished his studies. After he graduated, the shopkeeper refused to take money, simply telling him to pay it later. The young man, Raymond Zondo, went on to become Deputy Chief Justice. He heads the critical Commission of Inquiry into State Capture inquiring into government corruption, or 'state capture', by the African National Congress (ANC). Four decades later, Justice Zondo and the aged shopkeeper established a trust to help other young people who were in the same position as Zondo had been.[5]

South Africans—as renowned for their confrontational politics as their exquisite wines—were seared by the policy of apartheid. But that was abandoned more than a quarter of a century ago. Since then the country has travelled from the healing magic of Nelson Mandela to the slough of corruption heralded by Jacob Zuma.

This book is an attempt to describe and explain this extraordinary land and its many peoples. It is a Janus-faced nation—diverse and divided; harmonious and confrontational—that defies simple explanations.

2

A BRIEF HISTORY

Approaching doom

Driving north from Cape Town the flat top of Table Mountain gradually recedes in your rear-view mirror. Wheat fields and vineyards turn to scrub as the terrain becomes increasingly arid. The Cederberg Mountains—rock-strewn massifs of yellow, orange and sage green—rise around the road. Finally, after 155 kilometres, one arrives at Porterville, a nondescript town of some 9,000 people at the foot of the Olifants River Mountains. There is little to detain even an inquisitive visitor in the town, but in the mountains above Porterville is one of the most remarkable works of art in all of southern Africa.

Painted in red ochre on the walls of a rock shelter is a four-masted European galleon in full sail, with flags flying. Probably painted in the eighteenth century, it is the work of a member of the Khoisan.[1] The Khoisan were the original inhabitants of southern Africa: the region's 'first nations', once called 'Bushmen' or 'Hottentots'. For the artist who saw the vessel it must have seemed like something from outer space. The image made such an impression that, although Porterville is more than 100 kilometres inland, it had to be captured on the walls of the shelter. It was, in reality, a vision of impending doom.

Southern Africa has been inhabited for around 10,000 years, first by hunter-gatherers and then by people who cultivated crops and herded their animals—mostly sheep. Their legacy lies in the paintings and engravings which are found in almost every district in South Africa; there are at least 20,000 sites and over a million images.[2] Around 2,000 years ago other peoples arrived from central Africa. They were the Bantu-speaking peoples and—like most arriving settlers—they lived alongside, fought with, traded with and married the original inhabitants.[3] Gradually the Khoisan found themselves relegated to the southern fringes of the region and its arid interior.

White settlement

By 1488, when Portuguese explorer Bartolomeu Dias rounded the Cape—the first to do so—most of the peoples of southern Africa lived in the interior. To the rest of the world they were of little interest, and so they remained until 1652 when the first permanent European settlement began. This was to be a refreshment station, and not a colony, on the way to the lucrative Dutch colonies in the East Indies which provided the spices sold at exorbitant prices on European markets. When the Dutch East India Company, which controlled this trade, decided to send Jan van Riebeeck to lead an expedition to Cape Town he was under strict instructions to establish a fort, a place to berth vessels and plant gardens for fresh produce—nothing more. The South African interior—from the Company's point of view—was an irrelevance. On his arrival van Riebeeck encountered the Khoisan. Soon he was planting a thick hedge of wild almonds in an attempt to keep them from the well-watered fields on which he planted the Company gardens.

Just seven years after van Riebeeck arrived the first clash took place between the two communities, over crops and livestock. The Khoisan leaders explained their anger at the appropriation of increasing parcels of their land, as recorded in van Riebeeck's own journal in April 1660:

> They asked if they would be allowed to do such a thing supposing they went to Holland, and they added: 'it would be of little consequence if you people stayed here at the fort, but you come right into the interior and select the best land for yourselves, without even asking whether we mind or whether it will cause us any inconvenience ...'[4]

A pattern had been established: expanding colonial settlement leading to war and trade between the settlers and the indigenous communities.

Gradually, supplemented by imported slaves from the Dutch colonies in the East, the settlement expanded. Some left the Company's employment and became 'free burghers'—citizen farmers. These Dutch farmers gradually intermarried with local peoples and with others—including French Huguenots—who arrived to escape religious persecution. If they were itinerant they were called 'Trek Boers', and later Afrikaners. Their actions had little impact on the rest of the world. As the historians Richard Elphick and Hermann Giliomee put it, 'Three hundred years ago the Cape Colony was a poor, underpopulated territory of interest to no one but its rulers, its inhabitants, its neighbours and a few inquisitive travellers.'[5]

The Bantu-speaking peoples, who had arrived centuries before the whites, split broadly into two groups: the Tswana and Sotho, who settled in the northern and central areas of what is today South Africa and Botswana, and the Nguni peoples of the Eastern Cape, Swaziland and KwaZulu-Natal, today known as the Zulu and Xhosa. The Drakensberg Mountains formed a rough division between these groups, although there was considerable exchange between them.[6] At first, whites—whether farmers, missionaries or traders—had little contact with these peoples. But contact was inevitable as the Cape Colony's frontier gradually expanded, with itinerant farmers moving away from Cape Town in search of grazing for their flocks.

Giliomee provides a graphic account of how this took place:

> During the eighteenth century the line moved more than 800 km further as hunters, traders, raiders and, finally, cattle farmers pushed eastward into the interior. During the same period, along the southeastern coast, the limits of Xhosa settlement were slowly moving westward. In about 1770 the vanguard of white settlement reached the outlying Xhosa chiefdoms, and the so-called Eastern Frontier opened. Here European and black pastoralists dispossessed and finally subjugated the last of the eastern Khoikhoi ('Hottentot') clans. Here, too, began the process of interaction between white and black which has dominated South African history. For four decades trekboers and Xhosa, both aided at various times by Khoikhoi, jostled each other, neither succeeding in establishing supremacy, until in 1812 a combined colonist-Khoikhoi force under British military leadership finally pushed the Xhosa over the Fish River.[7]

There then followed a series of brutal wars between the whites and the Xhosa that continued, sporadically, for a century between 1779 and 1879. What had begun as border skirmishes ended with the conquest of the territory by the British.

If the eighteenth century had seen the gradual expansion of white settlement at the Cape, the nineteenth century was to see a transformation in the territory that became South Africa.

The first major event took place soon after the British seized the Cape in 1795, ending Dutch rule. In 1807 the British government outlawed the slave trade, but not slavery itself. This threatened the farming practices of the whites, many of whom relied on slave labour. Shiploads of slaves had been imported from India, Sri Lanka (then Ceylon), Indonesia, Madagascar and

Mozambique—some 63,000 slaves in total.[8] Wealthy farmers owned as many as twenty slaves. Farmers who had bought slaves on credit faced ruin, and there was anger at British interference in local affairs. Despite this opposition, the movement for emancipation, driven in Britain by men such as William Wilberforce and his friends among the Cape missionaries, was unstoppable. In 1833, the British parliament banned slavery across the Empire. Dr John Phillips, the leading missionary at the Cape, went to London and mounted a vigorous campaign for black rights, supported by the most effective campaigning organisation of the time, the Anti-Slavery Society.[9]

As a result, a series of laws was passed guaranteeing the political rights of the African and Coloured peoples of the Cape.[10] These were strengthened by the Privy Council, which ruled on 15 January 1829 'that all Hottentots and other free persons of colour lawfully residing in the Colony, are, and shall be, in most full and ample manner, entitled to all and every, the rights, privileges and benefits of the law to which any other of His Majesty's subjects are, or can be, entitled'.[11] The equality of all people—black or white—appeared to be assured.

In 1836 the Cape's Legislative Council created municipal boards for the colony's towns and villages. The vote was given to any man as long as he had property worth £1,000, or paid a yearly rent of not less than £10 per annum. Any qualified man could stand for election.[12] From the very beginning, people of colour participated in these elections. The Cape had established a limited non-racial franchise. In Natal (proclaimed a British colony in 1843) there was a similar right, but it was so proscribed by regulations that very few Africans, Coloureds or Indians ever qualified for the vote. In the rest of South Africa the franchise was exclusively restricted to white men, although there was no property qualification.

The extension of political rights was deeply resented by the white farmers of the Cape, some of whom could trace their roots back to the first colonisation of the country in April 1652. Many were itinerant farmers who moved across the vast open spaces of the Cape. Their livelihoods were dependent on the availability of cheap labour. To them it appeared that the British were determined to undermine the Afrikaner way of life.[13] Starting in 1834 these farmers set out on one of the defining events of white history—the movement of 12,000 Afrikaners out of the Cape and over the Orange River, to escape London's grasp. It became known as the 'Great Trek'. The Afrikaners moved away from the Cape in the hope of leaving British dominance behind them. They carved out an independent existence, cultivating their farms and clashing with the African peoples in whose midst they had arrived. Britain, somewhat reluctantly, granted them independence in the South African Republic (or, more colloquially, the Transvaal) and the Orange Free State.[14]

The arrival of the trekkers was by no means the only blow that African communities experienced. Many of them had already been severely displaced and weakened by the *Mfecane* (meaning 'crushing' or 'scattering'), a series of events that are still controversial today. These conflicts convulsed southern Africa between 1815 and 1840. They involved the rise of the Zulu kingdom under their leader, Shaka. Using novel tactics and instilling discipline in young men grouped into 'age regiments', Shaka succeeded in dominating the region, brutally crushing those that failed to surrender.[15] The resulting instability forced the flight of vast numbers of people—perhaps as many as 1 million or even 2 million. Some, like the Ndebele, ended up in what is today Zimbabwe; others in Swaziland or Mozambique and even further afield. The Basotho, under Moshoeshoe, clustered together in the mountain kingdom of Lesotho. Refugees from the *Mfecane* were forced into isiXhosa-speaking areas of the Cape. 'In the seventy years or so after 1760, the political face of the region north of the Orange (River) and east of the Kalahari was profoundly changed,' John Wright concludes.[16] Out of several hundred small, decentralised chiefdoms came large, centralised kingdoms, of which the Zulu in the East and the Ndebele in the West were the best known.

The Zulu nation soon also received a crushing blow. Conflict with the Boers had continued on and off ever since the murder of Piet Retief and his party during negotiations with the Zulu over land in February 1838. The British declared Natal a colony in 1843 and expanded their influence beyond the coast. In 1879 they attacked the Zulu, who were this time led by Cetshwayo. An initial Zulu victory at Isandlwana astonished the British, but they soon recovered and brought in reinforcements. Cetshwayo's army was decisively defeated at his capital of Ulundi on 4 July 1879. The Zulu kingdom was split into thirteen territories and divided among chiefs loyal to the British Crown.

Gold and diamonds

Important as these events had been, they were eclipsed by the discovery of first diamonds and then gold, which transformed the region profoundly. There had long been an interest in commercial mining, and in 1866 diamonds were discovered around Kimberley. It was here that Cecil Rhodes, a mining magnate and passionate advocate of imperialism, made his fortune. African miners were controlled severely. From 1856 it had been a crime in the Cape to break a labour contract, and this measure was soon adopted by the Natal and the Boer republics.[17] On the diamond fields black labourers were forced to live in compounds, conditions which white workers refused to accept for themselves.[18] The outlines of what was to be formalised as apartheid many years hence were beginning to take shape.

Then, in 1884, gold was found in the Eastern Transvaal and on the Witwatersrand—the area around what is today the city of

Johannesburg. White prospectors poured into South Africa from across the globe.[19] In the Transvaal the 'uitlanders', as the foreigners were known in Afrikaans, soon outnumbered the burghers, or citizens.[20] By the outbreak of the Anglo-Boer War in 1899 it was estimated that there were some 76,000 Boers in the Transvaal and around 225,000 'uitlanders'.[21] The Boer republics of the Orange Free State and the Transvaal resented this influx, but the development of an industrialised and commercial economy also tipped the scales decisively against the black societies of southern Africa.

The mines required vast quantities of labour. There was plenty of gold, but the mines were deep and the percentage of gold in each tonne of rock mined was low, so the wages had to be kept down if the operations were to be profitable.[22] Further restrictions followed controlling the movement of Africans—these became known as the 'pass laws'. In 1897 George Albu, chairman of the Association of Mines, explained to a government commission of inquiry that he proposed to reduce the cost of his labour by 'simply telling the boys [African labourers] that their wages are reduced'. Asked whether he believed that the men should be forced to leave the rural areas to work he replied: 'I think a kaffir should be compelled to work in order to earn a living.'[23]

These events transformed South Africa. Its heartland moved from the ports of Cape Town and Durban to the Transvaal and the Witwatersrand. Within ten years of its foundation, Johannesburg, as the centre of the gold industry, had a population of 102,000.[24] Mining, rather than agriculture, became the core of the economy.[25]

The rise of 'school people'

Colonial expansion and the consequent destruction of African societies took place throughout the nineteenth century, but there was another side to the story. African peoples adapted and began to come to terms with the whites they found among their midst. They became market farmers, competing effectively with white farmers. Missionary schools were established, and taught the gospel and rudiments of education. Gradually a stratum of educated, prosperous Africans emerged.

By the 1860s, missionary education had given rise to a class of 'school people' who had 'emerged as a distinct stratum of society in the Eastern Cape and started to make their voices heard'.[26] Among these 'school people' were the young leaders of the future. Walter Rubusana, a future leader of the African National Congress (ANC), received his education at the Lovedale Missionary Institute in the Eastern Cape. Sol Plaatje, who chronicled the experience of Africans in the Siege of Mafeking during the Anglo-Boer War before helping to found the ANC in 1912, was taught by missionaries in the Northern Cape.[27] John Langalibalele Dube, the first president of the ANC, studied at Adams College near Durban.[28] In a few decades the missionaries had produced a class of well-educated young men who had the skills and the confidence to lead their people.

Britain granted the Cape Colony the power to govern its own internal affairs in 1872, ushering in a new political consciousness and the growth of political parties. African voters took advantage of this and in 1873 a group of 100 voters registered in the Queenstown district, accounting for over 10 per cent of the electorate in the constituency.[29] African voters were becoming a force to be reckoned with. By 1886 Africans made up 43 per cent of the vote in six constituencies of the Eastern Cape.[30] This was recognised—particularly by the defeated candidates, who attacked the missionaries for 'manipulating' the election by encouraging African voters and called for the Africans to be removed from the voters' roll.[31] It was a theme to which white racists were to return time and again in the years ahead.

For the newly enfranchised, the ballot box was beginning to prove an effective means of making one's voice heard. This view was expressed by Isaac Wauchope, an interpreter at the Port Elizabeth magistrates' court:

> Your cattle are gone, my countrymen!
> Go rescue them! Go rescue them!
> Leave the breechloader alone
> And turn to the pen.
> Take paper and ink,
> For that is your shield.
> Your rights are going!
> So pick up your pen.
> Load it, load it with ink.
> Sit on a chair.
> Repair not to Hoho [a mountain fortress],
> But fire with your pen.[32]

By the close of the nineteenth century the country had been utterly transformed. Most of the African peoples had been conquered, but a new wave of 'school people' were beginning to organise to improve their lot. The economy had taken off, with mining replacing agriculture as its central wealth generator. Cities had sprung up in the centre of the country, where none had existed before. Indians had arrived in Natal as indentured labourers to harvest its giant sugar plantations and to mine its coal. While the Cape and Natal were under British control, London was greedily eyeing the riches of the Boer republics of the Transvaal and the Orange Free State. It was the contest to win control over the gold and diamonds that was to plunge the British and the Boers back into their second—and far bloodier—conflict.

The Anglo-Boer War (1899–1902)

Cecil Rhodes and other mining magnates had long chafed under Afrikaner rule. They argued that they were being scalped by the

Transvaal. Living under its complex and truculent president, Paul Kruger, they complained that they were deprived of a right to citizenship, while being heavily taxed. Rhodes claimed that the industry could save £2,500,000 a year if the Transvaal had a sympathetic government.[33] Impatient with the British government, he plotted to overthrow Kruger by launching a raid from Bechuanaland (today Botswana) with troops from Rhodesia (today Zimbabwe). The attack, which became known as the 'Jameson Raid', took place between 29 December 1895 and 2 January 1896. Kruger easily thwarted the raid when a planned uprising in Johannesburg failed to materialise. The raid was a catastrophe for Rhodes and the British, but the issue of the Transvaal would not go away.

The Queen's subjects in the Transvaal petitioned her for protection. On 4 May 1899, Sir Alfred Milner, High Commissioner for Southern Africa, sent London an urgent dispatch. 'The case for intervention is overwhelming,' Milner wrote. 'The spectre of thousands of British subjects kept permanently in the position of helots, constantly chafing under undoubted grievances, and calling vainly to Her Majesty's Government for redress, does steadily undermine the influence and reputation of Great Britain and respect for the British Government within its own dominions.'[34] This position was summed up by the poet laureate, Alfred Austin:

> There are girls in the gold-reef city,
> There are mothers and children too!
> And they cry, 'Hurry up! For pity!'
> So what can a brave man do?[35]

Relations between Pretoria and London went from bad to worse, but Britain was supremely confident. On the one side stood Britain and all its imperial possessions. On the other side stood the two Boer republics, whose total population was tiny by comparison.[36] Despite this, at the outbreak of the war the two Boer republics managed to field some 50,000 well-armed and well-provisioned men, while the British (who had not really prepared for the conflict) had barely 20,000 troops at their disposal.[37] The Afrikaners had used their gold to purchase fine German Mauser rifles and modern, rapid-firing artillery.[38] By comparison the British army was deficient in tactics, leadership, uniforms and manpower.[39] It was unprofessionally led, and lacked the means to organise its forces.

Within weeks the Boers had routed their enemies, driving deep into the British colonies of Natal and the Cape. But Britain overcame her initial hesitancy and began mobilising her forces, drawing on soldiers from Australia, Canada, New Zealand and India. Gradually the weight of numbers, together with fresh tactics, wore down the Boers. They lost the territory they had captured, and some Boers drifted away from the battlefield and returned to their farms. On 5 June 1900 Kruger's capital, Pretoria, fell. The Boer forces were close to disintegration and the conflict was all but at an end. On 30 May 1900 Milner had declared to a friend that the war was over: 'I have saved the British position in South Africa, and I have knocked the bottom out of "the great Afrikaander nation" forever and ever.'[40] He could hardly have been more wrong.

Deprived of the cities, the Boers adopted guerrilla tactics. Boer commandos fanned out across the open veld, attacking British lines of communication. In retaliation, and to deprive their fighters of supplies, the British burnt their farms to the ground. In the Orange Free State alone, 600 farms were destroyed within the first six months of 1900.[41] The scenes were heartbreaking. Captain L. March Phillipps provided a moving description of what took place:

> The worst moment is when you first come to the house. The people thought we had called for refreshments, and one of the women went to get milk. Then we had to tell them that we had come to burn the place down. I simply didn't know which way to look ... We can't

exterminate the Dutch or seriously reduce their numbers. We can do enough to make hatred of England and thirst for revenge the first duty of every Dutchman, and we can't effectively reduce the numbers of the men who will carry that duty out. Of course it is not a question of the war only. It is a question of governing the country afterwards.[42]

Having destroyed their homes, the British consigned Boer women and children to concentration camps, in which they languished. Their African servants, imprisoned nearby, were even more harshly treated. The camps became a byword for oppression and thousands died of disease and malnutrition.[43] Under unrelenting pressure, Boer fighters became exhausted and dispirited. The rebels gradually drifted away from their commandos. Some went over to their British foes. By the end of the war 5,000 Boers had joined the British (more than a quarter of the Afrikaners then in the field) and Boer leaders feared that their forces might surrender en masse.[44]

The time had finally come to sue for peace. In March 1902 both sides agreed to further talks. Boer leaders gathered in the Transvaal town of Vereeniging to discuss their terms, among them Jan Christian Smuts. Once a bookish and sometimes sickly child, but later a lawyer and philosopher, he had been transformed by the war into a tough, resolute guerrilla commander.[45] Smuts had fought behind British lines, and was in the Northern Cape when negotiations began. He held a meeting with General Kitchener, the British military commander.[46] Kitchener, who had ruthlessly prosecuted the war, was by this stage convinced of the need to strike a deal with the Boers.[47] The meeting was a turning point, for it addressed the key issues that separated the two sides: among them the question of the treatment of Africans. Although the war had not been fought over this, it was the first issue that Smuts raised. The record in his notebook began: 'Natives to be disarmed and no franchise until after self-government.' At

Smuts's insistence the British abandoned suggestions that Africans should be given the vote in the Transvaal and the Orange Free State. As Smuts's biographer noted wryly: 'Surrender was not all on the Boer side.'[48]

There were still Afrikaners who believed they should fight on to the 'bitter end', but the leadership, including generals Louis Botha and Smuts, felt the game was over. On 16 May 1902 Smuts made a passionate plea to the assembled Boers at Vereeniging:

> We have still 18,000 men in the field, veterans, with whom you can do almost any work. We can thus push our cause, from a military point of view, still further. But we are not here as an army, but as a people ... We represent, not only ourselves, but also the thousands who are dead ... and the men and women who are dying by their thousands in the Concentration Camps of the enemy; we represent the blood and tears of an entire nation.[49]

On 31 May 1902, after much debate, the peace terms were finally put to the assembled Boer leaders. Of the sixty who were present all but six voted for the motion, but not all Boers accepted the terms, which required them to sign an oath of allegiance to Britain. The division of the Boers, between those who decided to come to terms with living under the British Empire and those who saw this as a betrayal, was to haunt Afrikaner politics for the rest of the century. While Botha and Smuts made their peace with London, others did not.

White South Africans make peace with Britain

The war left South Africa terribly scarred. The losses among the Boer troops stood at over 7,000. Between 18,000 and 28,000 of white women and children died in the concentration camps, as did many thousands of Africans, who had even poorer conditions. The exact number of Africans who died was not recorded.[50] Hardly a farm remained unscathed; their roofs were destroyed, their windows and doors were burnt for firewood and their live-stock was butchered. In due course, £3 million was provided by the British to rebuild the country, but most went to those who surrendered early rather than those who held out to the end.

It was a bitter peace indeed, but the fate of the black popula-tion was more bitter still. The British had promised to safeguard their rights, but when the war ended London had other priori-ties, foremost among them a settlement with the Afrikaners. Africans and Coloureds who attempted to assert their rights were forced off white farms they had taken during the war and were driven back to work, sometimes by British troops they had wel-comed only months earlier as their liberators. It dawned on all concerned that the price of reconciliation between Briton and Boer would be paid by black people.

In 1906 the Transvaal was granted self-government, and the following year so too was the Orange Free State. White politi-cians began to discuss unity between the two Boer republics and the English-speaking Cape and Natal. A National Convention took place in Durban in October 1908, bringing together politi-cians from the four South African colonies as well as Rhodesia. The aim was to draw up a Union constitution. Africans peti-tioned London for a say, but this was not granted. The future of the country would be decided by whites alone, even though by 1909 there were 14,388 Coloured voters and 6,633 Africans in the Cape, making up 14.8 per cent of the electorate. In the end, the white politicians arrived at a compromise: men of colour would retain their votes in the Cape, but only white men would vote in the rest of the country.

It was this compromise—unsatisfactory as it was for most South Africans—that the white leaders took to London in June 1909 for ratification. A second delegation also made the journey. This delegation represented, for the very first time, a group of politicians of all races. Only Gandhi and the Indians remained aloof, sending their own delegation.[51] Led by the most liberal white politician of his day, William Schreiner, they included the brightest and best of their generation. The preacher and author Walter Rubusana, the newspaper editor John Tengo Jabavu and the educationalist John Langalibalele Dube were among them.

The official delegates, including Botha and Smuts, were royally treated. They were feted in parliament and had an audience with the king. The unofficial delegation led by Schreiner were politely received by government officials, but were promised nothing. They went to parliament, but only at the invitation of their supporters—including the newly-formed Labour Party, led by Keir Hardie. Hardie and his colleagues argued passionately for the Cape's non-racial vote to be extended to all South Africans, but with little success. In the end, Botha, Smuts and their colleagues got their way and the Union Constitution they had brought with them was endorsed by the Liberal government almost unchanged. Only on one point did the British hold firm: the right of people of colour to vote in the Cape would be enshrined in the Royal Instructions that accompanied the new Constitution. The king would effectively exercise a veto over any attempts to remove it, the House of Commons was told.[52]

This was not the only outcome of the long voyage to Britain. The formal negotiations over the Constitution had taken less than two days, but a second conference followed. 'The business that has brought these distinguished visitors to London is twofold,' explained the *Daily Mail*, reporting the opening of the South African Conference at the Foreign Office.[53] 'They have to consider with the Government the final form of the Act of Union, and later to discuss with the Imperial and Colonial authorities the important question of imperial defence.' The defence conference brought together senior politicians from Australia, Canada, Newfoundland (still a separate territory), New Zealand and the four South African self-governing colonies.

They met from 29 July until 19 August 1909 and finally agreed that the white dominions would share in Britain's burden of defending the Empire.[54]

The defence agreement came at a price.[55] On key issues like 'native rights' Britain promised it would not interfere in the domestic affairs of South Africa. It was an agreement that both sides would honour, to the intense frustration of black South Africans, whose petitions to the British were henceforth politely, but routinely, ignored. All such questions were henceforth to be settled in Pretoria, not in London.

The Africans on the Schreiner delegation, such as Rubusana, Dube and Jabavu, used their time in London to meet African students who were already living there. They discussed the situation back home, agreeing on the urgent need for a national organisation to represent all African opinion. ANC founding member Thomas Mapikela later recalled that 'the conversations which took place then had reference to the starting of the great African National Congress'.[56] On their return to South Africa the delegates were gradually reinforced by the students they had met in London. Pixley Seme was among this group of young, ambitious South Africans who had completed their legal studies abroad.[57]

This group of young, brilliant and well-educated men set about establishing themselves back home. They were determined to establish a united organisation to confront the emerging menace represented by white racism. Chapter Three will discuss how they came to found the African National Congress.

In 1913, on the eve of the First World War, the rights of Africans were severely undermined by a fresh law: the Natives Land Act. This reserved only 7 per cent of all land for Africans (later increased to 13 per cent). Although welcomed by some as a means of halting a land-grab by commercial farmers, it became one of the most notorious pieces of legislation in South Africa. The significance of the Land Act was immediately grasped by Sol Plaatje, the ANC's secretary general: 'Awakening on Friday morning, June 20, 1913, the South African native found himself, not actually a slave, but a pariah in the land of his birth.'[58] Plaatje toured the country, coming across families driven from the farms they had worked, travelling on the roads in the hope of finding new homes. There were suggestions of some form of strike action, but this received little support in the ANC and was voted down.

The erosion of black rights

As the First World War loomed on the horizon, Afrikaners had to decide whether they should join their old enemy (Britain) in attacking their former allies during the Anglo-Boer War (Germany). Some Boer War generals, like Botha and Smuts, argued that they had made their peace with London; others were less forgiving. When the First World War erupted, Botha, by this time prime minister, immediately telegraphed to London his willingness to take on the burden of his country's defence, allowing British troops to be redeployed to the war front. On 7 August 1914 the Colonial Secretary, Lord Harcourt, accepted Botha's offer and enquired whether South African forces could seize ports in the neighbouring German colony of South West Africa (today's Namibia).[59]

The South African cabinet met the same day to consider the request. Acceding to London's wishes was not going to be easy. It took the prime minister three days of persuasion to achieve a unanimous vote in cabinet in favour of going to war—and even then, only by promising that the army would be composed solely of volunteers. Outside government the opposition was led by another Boer War general, James Barry Hertzog. He had refused to accept Botha's policy of reconciliation between English- and Afrikaans-speaking whites and had been excluded from the cabinet. Then, in January 1914, he had broken with Botha to form the National Party.

When South Africa joined the British in August that year and Botha announced that forces would be sent into South West Africa, there was a mutiny. General Manie Maritz, a fiercely anti-British officer who commanded an area just south of the border, abandoned his post and led his troops to join the Germans—much to the amazement of the German commander. There was a full-scale rebellion in the Orange Free State and the Transvaal, with troops led by mutinous army officers. Some 13,000 Afrikaners took up arms against their own government. It took hard marches and sporadic fighting before the rebels conceded defeat.

By 1915, Botha was free to take command of the South West Africa campaign and lead his troops into the territory. After six months of hard fighting the Germans capitulated and Smuts led an attack on German forces in Tanganyika—now Tanzania. South African troops were dispatched to join the war in Europe. African volunteers on board the *SS Mendi* were sent to dig trenches, but were accidentally rammed off the Isle of Wight in February 1917. More than 600 men drowned.[60] On hearing of the tragedy, Botha led the House of Parliament in standing to pay tribute to their courage and sacrifice.

Botha died in 1919 and was succeeded by Smuts, who became one of the most senior politicians in the Imperial system, serving on the British cabinet in the First and then the Second World War. Smuts held the office of prime minister until he was ousted by Hertzog, his much more hard-line opponent, in June 1924. It was only in 1939 that Smuts managed to win the premiership once more—a post he held throughout the Second World War, before finally losing office to the National Party in 1948.

When the First World War was over, and the troops returned home, there were pressing issues to be faced. Afrikaners, many of them destitute, had flocked to the towns following the Anglo-

Boer War. There they competed for jobs with African, Indian and Coloured labourers. Some joined unions to improve their lot. The interwar years saw fierce conflicts between labour and capital on the mines, leading to a full-scale uprising in Johannesburg in 1922. White miners fought for their rights, with one banner proclaiming: 'Workers of the World Unite, for a White South Africa.' The Smuts government crushed them ruthlessly, using troops, tanks, heavy artillery and aircraft.

The miners were defeated but two years later they had their revenge, inflicting a political defeat on Smuts. In 1924, a coalition led by Hertzog won the election, backed by the union's political representatives in the Labour Party. Henceforth the rights of whites would predominate in employment, as they did in politics. Legislation was introduced which strengthened the position of whites by enshrining differential pay and job protection. Hertzog introduced a 'civilized labour' policy in 1924, reserving categories of work on everything from the mines to the railways for whites. This was a bitter blow for the black population. Historian Phil Bonner sums up their plight: 'This left teaching and preaching as virtually the only avenues of white-collar employment open to educated Africans.'[61]

The political rights of Africans, limited though they were, were also under attack. In 1936, after a decade of agitating for the change, Hertzog managed to end the rights of African men to vote in the Cape. On 6 April, he persuaded the South African parliament—to the loud cheers of the white MPs—to abolish the Cape franchise.[62] For the first time since 1836, no African in any part of South Africa had the vote. Africans were instead presented with a limited form of parliamentary representation through special white parliamentarians. Political rights, cherished and protected for a century, were extinguished. British assurances that their rights would be protected by the king had proved worthless.

By the late 1930s the shadow of war was looming over the world again. Would South Africa join Britain's defence once more? For Smuts there was no question, but Hertzog (who headed a coalition government) argued that the country should remain neutral towards Nazi Germany. It was an argument Smuts won. Hertzog resigned in September 1939, and Smuts once again became prime minister. South African troops fought, with distinction, in Ethiopia, the Western Desert and Italy. Some Afrikaners saw this as a betrayal: an alliance with the old adversary. The bitter legacy of the Anglo-Boer War still lingered. A neo-fascist movement, the Ossewabrandwag, was formed with a mission of resisting the British Empire, Jews and capitalists. Among its members were young men who would go on to become leaders of the country: B. J. Vorster (1966–78) and P. W. Botha (1978–89).[63]

Apartheid

South Africans, black as well as white, participated in the Second World War. In total 334,000 joined up, including some 211,000 whites, 77,000 Africans and 46,000 Coloureds and Indians. Just over 11,000 lost their lives. As in the previous world war, the majority of whites who served were English-speaking. The black troops hoped, once more, that their loyalty would be rewarded, but once more they were disappointed.

When the war ended, the scene was set for a political transformation. Afrikaner nationalism, which had been on the rise for half a century, came to fruition. Afrikaners had taken measures to strengthen their positions. Some were economic—such as a range of mutual organisations that dealt with everything from insurance to burial societies. Others were directly political, including the formation of a secret society—the Broederbond (Brotherhood)—which co-ordinated strategy behind the scenes.

Some left-wing servicemen, horrified that the fascism they had fought during the war was rearing its head back home, joined the 'Springbok Legion'. They resisted for a while, but their movement gradually petered out.[64]

In 1948, Smuts narrowly lost a general election to the predominantly Afrikaner National Party. These Afrikaners, determined to oust the English-speaking elite who controlled the economy and ran much of the civil service, believed their day had come. The programme they launched was designed to put whites in control, in perpetuity. Building on the many existing racist laws, they introduced a more formal system of discrimination: apartheid.

The term apartheid dated back to 1929, when it suggested that each race should go its separate way.[65] By the 1940s it had taken on a far more repressive meaning:

> It started from the premise that black and coloured people were different, not because they were poor but because they were racially different. The message that apartheid as a system conveyed, offensively and obscenely, was that black and coloured people were socially inferior, morally inadequate, intellectually underdeveloped and sexually unfit for intimate relationships.[66]

Although the slogans were not used during the 1948 election, Nelson Mandela had the measure of apartheid when he declared that the aim of the National Party was 'the nigger in his place' and 'the coolies [Indians] out of the country'.[67]

The ANC had maintained a powerful, but constitutional, opposition to the rising tide of racism. Now it adopted new forms of resistance. During the war a number of young men had joined the party, including Nelson Mandela, Oliver Tambo and Walter Sisulu. They formed the Congress Youth League in 1944, taking a more radical stand than their elders. Calling for pan-African unity 'from the Mediterranean to the Indian and Atlantic Oceans', they were sharply critical of what they perceived as the timidity of the ANC's previous leadership.[68] When the National

Party won the 1948 election Mandela was 'stunned and dismayed', but Oliver Tambo reacted coolly: 'now we know exactly who our enemies are,' he said.[69] The Youth League began drawing up a 'programme of action' committing the ANC to militant tactics—strikes, boycotts and civil disobedience.

By 1950 Mandela was co-opted onto the party's National Executive. At first, he and others in the Youth League were opposed to working with other movements, including Indian groups and the Communist Party. Gradually their position softened. On 1 May 1950 the police killed eighteen people during a Communist Party 'Freedom Day' meeting. By 1951 Mandela had changed his stand and was using Marxist phrases in his speeches. Although he always denied becoming a Communist, he certainly came to work closely with the party and may indeed have taken membership.[70] The Communist Party (founded in 1921) was banned in 1950 and dissolved itself. Many members went into exile, some finding a home in Britain, where they were to become the backbone of the Anti-Apartheid Movement. Others remained in South Africa, and in 1953 the party was revived as an underground organisation.

Despite opposition, the National Party rolled out apartheid legislation until it regulated every aspect of life. The very first law was the 1950 Immorality Amendment Act, which prohibited every sexual act between black and white people. It tore people apart, with police raiding bedrooms late at night. It even led to a regulation preventing 'non-white' women from sitting in the front seats of cars driven by white men, in case 'immoral' acts took place. By the 1960s there was not a park bench that was not designated 'black' or 'white'; not an entrance to a station, lavatory or swimming pool that was not racially segregated. The aim was to separate, as far as possible, the country's 'races' in every possible sphere of life. This was termed 'petty apartheid'.

Severe as these measures were, more devastating still was what was termed 'grand apartheid'. This took the scraps of land reserved for Africans in 1913 and renamed them 'homelands'. Poor and economically stagnant backwaters, the homelands were meant to become 'independent states' within South Africa. All Africans were assigned to a 'homeland', regardless of where they might actually have lived. Africans, who made up 70 per cent of the population, were deemed to be citizens of these states, although only 11 million of the 23 million black Africans in South Africa lived in the 'homelands'. Influx control laws regulated the movement of black people, requiring anyone over the age of sixteen to be fingerprinted and to carry a 'passbook' containing their identity card and employment record. A policeman could demand a pass at any time. Black townships were routinely raided. Anyone without the correct documentation was imprisoned or 'returned' to their designated homeland.

South Africans were left under no illusions about what apartheid was designed to achieve. Prime Minister Hans Strijdom (1954–58) spelled it out with brutal clarity:

> I say that the White man today has baasskap [supremacy], paramountcy and domination because the franchise laws of the country put the vote into his hands ... The franchise laws do not give the Natives the slightest chance of ever gaining power, not on merit or on any other grounds ... That power is vested in the White man and for that reason the White man is master.[71]

The resurgent ANC refused to accept such a policy. During the 1950s, the party developed a Defiance Campaign to confront apartheid. Launched on 26 June 1952, its volunteers pledged to defy all unjust laws. The campaign linked the ANC with other political parties. These included the Congress of Democrats (many of whom were secret members of the Communist Party), as well as Indian and Coloured allies. By December there had been more than 8,000 arrests.[72] In 1955 a Congress of the People was held to unite this disparate movement. It gathered ideas from across the country, finally adopted as the Freedom Charter.

Committing the country to basic freedoms, the charter opened with a famous pledge: 'We, the People of South Africa, declare for all our country and the world to know: that South Africa belongs to all who live in it, black and white ...' It contained the core principles of the ANC and remains its defining philosophy.

The government's response was not long delayed. The police arrested 156 Congress leaders, who were charged with treason. The case became a cause celebre, yet after a lengthy trial all the defendants were found not guilty on 29 March 1961. The judge concluded:

> it is impossible for this court to come to the conclusion that the African National Congress has acquired or adopted a policy to overthrow the state by violence, that is, in the sense that the masses had to be prepared or conditioned to commit direct acts of violence against the state.[73]

The judge was further from the truth than he knew. By July 1960, members of the Communist Party had already travelled to Moscow and then Beijing.[74] They met Mao Zedong and received his support for launching an armed struggle. On 25 December 1960, a meeting was held by the Communist Party in a suburb of Johannesburg. Twenty-five people attended, including ANC leaders Mandela, Sisulu and Govan Mbeki. They voted unanimously to move from nonviolence to armed resistance, burning the resolution after it was adopted. At a meeting in June 1961, the ANC National Executive agreed to form a military organisation, Umkhonto we Sizwe ('the spear of the nation'), along the lines adopted by the Communist Party six months earlier. A series of attacks on economic and symbolic targets, without risk to human life, began in December 1961. In the next two years, nearly 200 targets were hit.

By this time another event had taken place, led by a different party: the Pan Africanist Congress (PAC). The PAC had broken away from the ANC in protest against the influence of the

Communist Party, as well as ideological elements of the Freedom Charter. Led by the charismatic Robert Sobukwe, they decided to protest against the hated passbooks that all Africans had to carry. On 21 March 1960, thousands gathered at the police station in Sharpeville. After a standoff, a shot was fired from the crowd. The police opened fire with automatic weapons. The fields around the police station were strewn with bodies: sixty-nine died and nearly 200 were injured. The massacre provoked an outcry around the world: thousands of Londoners filled Trafalgar Square. The South African government responded by outlawing the ANC and the PAC. Like the Communist Party before them, the groups went underground and into exile, attempting to continue the fight from surrounding states. Camps were established in Tanzania and Angola at which training was given to turn militants into fighters. The Organisation of African Unity did what it could to bolster the resistance; the Soviet Union and East Germany provided arms and training; and the Swedes provided finance. What had begun as a nonviolent resistance had been transformed into a guerrilla war. The South African government responded by launching raids across southern Africa, hitting rebel bases and assassinating leaders.

Inside South Africa the ANC was struggling to survive. Nelson Mandela went on the run but was arrested on 5 August 1962. On 11 July 1963, police arrested a number of others during a raid on the ANC's headquarters at Rivonia, on the outskirts of Johannesburg. Based on evidence from this raid, Mandela was charged with sabotage and brought to court. It was in his speech from the dock that he famously declared:

> During my lifetime I have dedicated myself to this struggle of the African people. I have fought against white domination, and I have fought against black domination. I have cherished the ideal of a democratic and free society in which all persons live together in harmony and with equal opportunities. It is an ideal which I hope to

live for and to achieve. But if needs be, it is an ideal for which I am prepared to die.[75]

The prosecution had called for the death penalty, but the judge turned this down, to the surprise of the defendants. Mandela and his co-accused were found guilty and sentenced to life imprisonment.

Mandela was to spend the next twenty-seven years in jail—most of them on Robben Island, within view of Cape Town. With the ANC and other movements banned, the apartheid government was at its zenith. During the 1960s there seemed to be few clouds on the horizon for white rule. Yet the forces that would finally lead to the demise of apartheid were already form-ing. The first was the re-emergence of a black trade union move-ment. This began in 1973, when workers in the Durban area launched a spontaneous wave of strikes. Workers began pressing management for a living wage. Successful strikes won economic benefits and trade union recognition. Gradually hope was rekin-dled in the black, Coloured and Indian communities. There were calls for wider political demands.

The second development was the emergence of anti-colonial movements in the white-ruled states surrounding South Africa, which had previously acted as a buffer for Pretoria. Rebellions in Angola, Mozambique and Rhodesia gradually grew in strength. South Africa attempted to counter this by launching raids across southern Africa. This succeeded in limiting the ability of the ANC to develop its armed struggle, with most of its fighters languishing in camps rather than marching on Pretoria. By the late 1980s, the ANC admitted it was unable to step up the mili-tary offensive against apartheid. As Alfred Nzo, secretary general of the ANC, admitted publicly in 1989, 'we do not have the capacity to intensify the armed struggle in any meaningful way'.[76]

Although the guerrilla offensive made little progress against the South African military, it was successful against the sur-

rounding white states. In 1974 Angolan and Mozambiquan fighters had sapped the Portuguese government's will to continue
with the conflict. The Portuguese military decided to launch a
coup, in the wake of which the colonies won independence.
Despite this, both Angola and Mozambique continued to suffer
due to South African aggression. These attacks culminated in
battles in southern Angola around the town of Cuito Cuanavale
in 1987–88. Cuban forces, supporting the Angolans, managed to
bog the South Africans down, preventing Pretoria from achieving a decisive victory. Losing irreplaceable equipment including
aircraft and tanks, the South Africans withdrew to Namibia. The
limits of South African military power had been revealed.

In Zimbabwe the two major liberation movements, led by
Joshua Ŋkomo and Robert Mugabe, were fighting white rule. By
1979 the prime minister, Ian Smith, was finally convinced he
could not win the war. After lengthy negotiations in London, a
deal was reached and elections were held in 1979 and 1980;
Mugabe went on to win the latter. There were now independent
African states on the borders of South Africa. The South African
government sent its intelligence staff to Harare, to see what lessons could be learnt. Their report made it clear that although
white rule could last in South Africa for the next fifteen or
twenty years, it could not last indefinitely. Far better, the security
officers argued, to open talks with the ANC to see whether a
deal could be made. Between 1984 and 1989, secret meetings
aimed at ending apartheid took place between the ANC and the
government. Most were outside of the country. Some involved
ANC prisoners, including Mandela, and early initiatives were
facilitated by businessmen. Together they paved the way towards
a settlement.

The third strand of the pressure on South Africa was the
growing strength of the international Anti-Apartheid Movement.
Although it began as a British organisation, it took on an inter-

national dimension. It lobbied, with increasing success, the Organisation of African Unity, the Non-Aligned Movement and the United Nations. By the 1970s and 1980s it had sufficient recognition to make it increasingly difficult for the South African government to appear in international forums. In the USA, there was a growing movement to prevent the pension funds of universities, trade unions and cities from investing in South African companies or making loans to the South African government.

Finally, and most importantly, there was the resumption of open opposition inside the country. This began in 1976, when school children in Soweto, a black township on the outskirts of Johannesburg, took to the streets to protest against enforced teaching in Afrikaans. Their peaceful protest was confronted by the police, who opened fire. More than 100, and perhaps as many as 200, children were mown down. Survivors left the country or regrouped to continue the resistance. Civil organisations, church groups and students made common cause with the emerging trade union movement. Together they began confronting the authorities. These organisations came together to found the United Democratic Front on 20 August 1983. 10,000 people, from some 500 organisations, met on the outskirts of Cape Town. Initially non-partisan, they became the ANC's unofficial representatives inside the country.

In the early 1980s, faced with these pressures, the government decided to open secret talks with the ANC. The party's precondition for any resolution was the unbanning of political parties and the release of political prisoners. Eventually, the authorities agreed. On 2 February 1990, President F. W. de Klerk spoke at the opening of parliament. 'The hopes of millions of South Africans are centred around us,' he said. 'The future of Southern Africa depends on us. We dare not falter or fail.'[77] And, with that, he declared that Mandela would be unconditionally released. A week later Mandela was free, speaking from the steps of the Cape Town City Hall. Raising his fist, he greeted a vast crowd that had waited for hours in the sun.[78] 'My friends, comrades and fellow South Africans,' he said to huge cheers. 'I greet you all in the name of peace, democracy and freedom for all. I stand here before you not as a prophet but as a humble servant of you, the people.'[79]

Apartheid was effectively at an end. Although there were to be many months of difficult negotiations to thrash out a formal settlement and draw up a new Constitution, the mantle of legitimate government had been passed on. President de Klerk formally handed power to Mandela after a bitterly contested, and sometimes bloody, election in 1994; the era of white rule was at an end. South Africa had finally emerged as a fully-fledged democracy, shared between all its people. The political oppression of centuries had been removed; the legacy remained.

3

THE AFRICAN NATIONAL CONGRESS

President Jacob Zuma steadied himself at his table as the election official read out the numbers. For once, the man whose middle name, Gedleyihlekisa, means 'someone who laughs with you while he is doing you harm' couldn't muster a smile, nor could he applaud.[1] He'd been outmanoeuvred. It was exactly a week before Christmas 2017, and Cyril Ramaphosa had just unseated Zuma as the party's president. He had run on a ticket of cleaning up the graft that had sullied the incumbent's reign, and this could mean jail.

Ramaphosa won by a mere sliver. His 2,440 supporters numbered just 179 more than those who voted for Zuma's first choice, former African Union Commission chairperson Nkosazana Dlamini Zuma—his ex-wife, and mother of four of his roughly two dozen children. More graceful in defeat than him, she stepped onto the stage and congratulated Ramaphosa with a hug and a smile. Two months later she was absorbed into his cabinet as minister in the presidency, tasked with the unpopular job of streamlining the government.

Ramaphosa would need all the help he could get. The party's new leadership structure—the top six officials as well as the powerful eighty-strong National Executive Committee—was only marginally skewed in his favour, and asserting his authority to accomplish the clean-up he envisaged would not be easy.

Contestation and intrigue were always part of the oldest liberation movement in Africa, but the benefits of rising to the top since the ANC came to power in 1994 have become roughly as great as the risks of supporting the movement before that. Backing the party could cost you your life back then. Now, it could reward you with riches. The number of party positions in government has, however, reduced because the party got fewer votes in 2016, and contestation has become fiercer. The ANC has lost power in three of the country's nine metropolitan areas, and no longer has unfettered access to these budgets, from which money was often amply allocated to party activities and patronage networks.

Ideological battles, too, have always raged in the organisation, which rose as a motley mixture of Marxists and capitalists drawn together by the common goal of fighting apartheid. It still calls itself a 'broad church', but it often finds itself preaching contradictions, and its congregants are frequently at odds. The party—which nostalgically still thinks of itself as a liberation movement—is constantly in renewal after a succession of crises. The cure often called upon is a return to the party's roots and traditions, but the truth is that the cupboards of its history are laden with skeletons as well as glory.

The ANC has managed, though, to airbrush its history to perfection, and the stories its leaders tell contribute to a mythology of common struggle. The ANC has, for instance, managed to convince the world—and most South Africans—that it was the party that brought liberation to South Africa. History, however, is much more complex than that.

The ANC styles itself as a champion of the poor, and there is much commitment in the rhetoric of its leaders. Its founders and leaders, even to date, are elites. In the 1920s and 1930s the party was somewhat moribund, but it became an increasingly radical actor in the struggle for political rights and justice in the 1940s. In the 1950s it was a mobilising force behind the campaign of defiance against apartheid, but it operated from exile and prison in the 1960s and 1970s, when the armed struggle grew. In the 1990s, it was unbanned and operated as a mass-based party before becoming a troubled party of government after 1994.[2]

The founding of a liberation movement: 1912–1937

As the clock struck midnight on 8 January 2012 an A-list group of chieftains and South African and African leaders packed out the tiny Waaihoek Wesleyan Church in Bloemfontein. Exactly a century before, chiefs and community leaders from across the country had gathered in the same place to establish the South African Native National Congress (SANNC), and this was celebrated with a ceremony that included the lighting of a candle by Zuma.

While the ANC had grown into a major force over the past century, the church had been neglected, becoming a panel beating establishment in the industrial part of town before it was bought by the government and fixed up for the centenary. Giant banners bearing the faces of past ANC presidents—as well as Zuma, the leader at the time of the centenary—decorated the three large cooling towers from the nearby power station that the church nestled up to. Soon after the celebrations they, too, were forgotten and in tatters.

The ANC was founded in direct response to the formation of the Union of South Africa in 1910, which united the British and the Afrikaners but granted black people scant rights. It was preceded by a long history of black resistance against colonialism, starting with the Dutch settlement in 1652.[3]

Pixley ka Isaka Seme, a 30-year-old lawyer born in KwaZulu-Natal, issued a rallying call for African unity soon after his return in 1911 from twelve years of study in the United Kingdom and the United States. He declared that the 'dark races of this sub-continent' had to face their historic divisions:

> The demon of racialism, the aberrations of the Xosa-Fingo feud, the animosity that exists between the Zulus and the Tongaas [sic], between the Basutos and every other native must be buried and forgotten; it has shed among us sufficient blood! We are one people. Those divisions, those jealousies are the cause of all our woes and of all our backwardness and ignorance today.[4]

A few months later the SANNC was founded, initially an elite club for black men only.[5] John Langalibalele Dube, a teacher, journalist and reverend from KwaZulu-Natal, was the first president, and for his first major campaign he sent a deputation to London in 1914 to protest against the now-notorious 1913 Natives Land Act, which assigned 93 per cent of land to white people and forced black people into reserves. This was met with inaction from the British government.[6]

Dube's apparent acceptance of segregation in a petition against the act presented to Prime Minister Louis Botha cost him his position. In 1917 he was replaced as leader by Sefako Mapogo Makgatho, a teacher, journalist and lay preacher from Limpopo.[7]

At that time there were also women leaders who sympathised with the SANNC cause, but they were only recognised much later. One of the most well-known of these was Charlotte Maxeke, who led 800 women on a march in the Free State in 1913 that led to the withdrawal of pass laws for women in that province, and organised the Bantu Women's League in 1918.[8]

In 1923 the SANNC changed its name to the African National Congress and adopted its earliest Bill of Rights, stating that 'the Bantu inhabitants of the Union have, as human beings, the indisputable right to a place of abode in this land of their fathers'.[9] The year after, the breakaway white Afrikaner National Party came to power, and the ANC launched ineffectual protests against a number of its racist laws.[10]

Trade unions like Clements Kadalie's Industrial and Commercial Workers' Union (ICU) were more successful in rallying people around the working class causes of inflation and low wages after the First World War.[11] Amidst the strikes, in 1921, the Communist Party of South Africa (SACP)—later an important ANC ally—was founded. It was among the first non-racial political organisations in South Africa.[12]

Lack of political success meant the ANC chose a more radical president in 1927. Josiah Tshangana Gumede, teacher, business-person and journalist, had spent time in the Soviet Union, where he saw 'the new world to come', but his closer cooperation with the Communist Party of South Africa didn't gain much traction in the ANC, and in 1930 the moderate Seme took over.[13] The ANC declined 'into almost total moribundancy', Chief Albert Luthuli later commented.[14]

Move to action and the inclusion of women: the 1940s to the 1960s

Women were finally welcomed into the fray under the party's 1943 constitution, and Ida Mntwana, a dressmaker who joined the ICU in 1927, became the ANC Women's League's first president.[15] Under Alfred Xuma, a teacher and medical doctor from the former Transkei, the ANC took a more radical turn. Still a moderate, Xuma brought radicals like Nelson Mandela, Walter Sisulu and Oliver Tambo into the fray. They formed the ANC Youth League in 1944, and shunned polite methods of protest such as petitions.[16] The new crowd believed Africans could be freed only by their own efforts.

The ANC stepped up its resistance politics after the National Party got into power with its segregationist policy of apartheid in

1948. In 1949, with James Moroka as president, it adopted the Youth League's programme of action, which prompted open defiance against the government.[17]

Chief Albert Luthuli, a teacher from Groutville, KwaZulu-Natal, became ANC president in 1952, the same year that saw the Defiance Campaign organised. He was banned early in 1953 under the Suppression of Communism Act as the government enacted tougher security laws.[18]

On 26 June 1955, an assembly of 3,000 people produced the Freedom Charter. This document was a crude forerunner to South Africa's modern constitution, which dropped the charter's references to nationalisation of industry and the redistribution of land; this adjustment is still frequently cited in debates by those who believe the ANC made too many concessions for a democratic South Africa. The ANC was severely disrupted by the arrest—and subsequent acquittal—of 156 of its ranks for 'high treason'.[19]

Women's groups also played an active role in the campaigns of the 1950s. Mntwana declared: 'Gone are the days when the place of women was in the kitchen and looking after the children. Today, they are marching side by side with men on the road to freedom.'[20] In 1956 the ANC Women's League was amongst those leading the Women's March against the pass laws, with 20,000 women singing 'wathint' abafazi, wathint' imbokodo' ('you strike the women, you strike a rock'). This march is commemorated on 9 August as Women's Day.

In 1959, internal differences over the multi-racial approach of the Freedom Charter and the role of the SACP caused the Pan Africanist Congress (PAC) to break away from the ANC. The PAC took the lead in organising the anti-passbook protests that led to the massacre of sixty-nine people in Sharpeville on 21 March 1960, and played a significant role in the Soweto youth uprisings on 16 June 1976. Both were turning points in the struggle against apartheid. The ANC and PAC were both banned after Sharpeville and were driven underground into an armed struggle.[21] In the ANC this was a time of much demoralisation and confusion, as a number of organisations sprung up to fill the vacuum that it had left in the country.[22]

Going underground: the 1960s

Anti-apartheid activists emerged from the Defiance Campaign emboldened. 'It was the beginning of a new situation, which led even to a person facing the death penalty with confidence,' Walter Sisulu said.[23]

On 16 December 1961 the ANC's armed wing, Umkhonto we Sizwe (MK), was formed with Mandela as its first commander-in-chief. Some ANC leaders such as Luthuli, who was awarded the Nobel Peace Prize in 1960, remained committed to nonviolence, but this stance saw him sidelined in the ANC.[24]

MK carried out 200 acts of sabotage in the next eighteen months (a further 200 acts of sabotage were carried out by other groups at this time), and members went for military training abroad in places like China, the USSR, East Germany and Tanzania.[25] The ANC proclaimed MK's might with songs, slogans and symbols, but in reality it wasn't that well-equipped or successful, and human rights abuses and tribalism flourished in some of its exile training camps.[26]

Mandela was arrested in 1962, shortly after his return from a trip abroad to garner support for MK, and together with a host of other ANC leaders was charged with sabotage. They faced the death penalty, but were instead sentenced to life imprisonment. The Rivonia Trial gave the men a great political platform, but left the ANC's underground structures severely weakened.[27]

Not many records exist about the secret underground but it is known that operations were planned and supplied from exile.[28] Life was far from normal, and both noble deeds and abuse occurred under the cloak of secrecy.[29] For instance, there were incidents of poor discipline and corruption even within the top command, and donor money was misappropriated. Illicit car trading, drug smuggling and diamond deals became commonplace in some ANC camps.[30] The fight against apartheid was, after all, in itself a crime.

The ANC used culture and image to keep itself alive in people's minds during this time, and this sense of identification with the party endures even to this day.[31] The ANC presented itself as a people's liberation movement which identified closely with the aspirations of the black majority.[32]

Media like Radio Freedom, operating from outside the country, and *Sechaba*, the party's regular journal, carried messages from the ANC to counter apartheid propaganda and rumours.[33] Prisons like Robben Island, off the coast of Cape Town, turned into informal political education schools, and this bred a new generation of leaders to take the party into the next two decades.[34]

Some things fell apart in exile. After Luthuli's death in 1967, Tambo took over. He was a maths and science teacher from Pondoland in the Eastern Cape, but lived in exile in London's Muswell Hill, having left South Africa in 1960.[35] Tambo established an ANC office in London at a time when there were turf wars between exiles in Africa and in Europe.[36]

The failed Wankie Campaign also led to discord in MK. In the Tanzanian camps, soldiers had become impatient, and desertion and misconduct surfaced. It was in response to this that the campaign was organised.[37] MK's elite Luthuli Detachment, led by Chris Hani, was sent to Rhodesia where they fought alongside Joshua Nkomo's Zimbabwe People's Revolutionary Army against Rhodesian and South African forces. They were supposed to cross to South Africa after that, but the mission was ill-planned and many perished. Despite this failure, the ANC still hails those who took part as heroes.

Hani was unhappy, though, about the way the campaign was handled by the leadership, and this unleashed massive factional battles in the ANC. Hani drew up a memorandum outlining his grievances along with those of other comrades, which was discussed at the ANC's conference in Morogoro, Tanzania, in 1969.[38] Here the ANC attempted to reorganise and revitalise its structures. It set up a Revolutionary Council to coordinate the struggle in South Africa, and it opened its membership to white people, a position heavily canvassed by the SACP.[39]

A new generation of activists: 1970–1990

The 1970s ushered in a period of strikes for wage increases and student boycotts by the South African Students' Organisation, led by Steve Biko, who also founded the Black Consciousness Movement. The latter was banned in 1973.[40] The 1976 student protests in Soweto—brutally suppressed by police—changed the course of South Africa's history, but the role of ANC-aligned organisations in these events is still contested.[41]

The protests did create a new generation of ANC activists, while MK sabotage operations increased in the aftermath.[42] Reminiscing about these events forty years on, government spokesperson Phumla Williams, who was a 16-year-old pupil at the time, said her activism was caused by the protests. 'I came to realise that African children's education was designed to be inferior to the other races in South Africa, and that the conditions under which I was being schooled were unlikely to change unless I took action.' She left South Africa to join the ANC in Swaziland two years later.[43]

Following Steve Biko's death in police custody in 1977, another security clampdown led to the banning of eighteen more organisations and two newspapers. To fill this void, a number of community organisations sprang up, most significantly the

United Democratic Front (UDF) in 1983. It represented the ANC in South Africa and initially focussed on opposing the introduction of the tricameral parliamentary system, which separated white, Coloured and Indian representatives and excluded black people altogether. Labour unions pulled together in 1985 to form the Congress of South African Trade Unions (Cosatu), which fought for workers' rights and democracy and aligned with the UDF to form the Mass Democratic Movement.[44]

Following a spate of protests and violence, in 1985 the government offered to release Mandela if he rejected violence as a political weapon, but the ANC and Mandela refused. Mandela later held secret talks with government representatives about the possibility of negotiations, often without consulting fellow leaders out of fear they would be opposed to it.[45]

A state of emergency was also declared in 1985, following the violence, and it lasted the rest of the decade. Tens of thousands of people were detained without trial in this time, political meetings were banned, and extra-judicial assassinations took place.[46] Many also died from what was termed 'black-on-black' violence, which the ANC believed was covertly fuelled by apartheid government support for their political rivals, the Inkatha Freedom Party (IFP).[47] The IFP has denied this.

By the time President F. W. de Klerk took over in 1989, the country had reached breaking point and reforms were the only option. He released the Rivonia Trialists, and on 2 February 1990 announced the unbanning of the ANC, PAC and SACP and the release of Mandela. The ANC suspended its armed struggle that same year, but some leaders, like Chris Hani, were resentful because they felt there was no internal consultation.[48]

Soon after his release, Mandela became ANC president after Tambo fell ill.[49] In South Africa and internationally, the lawyer from the rural Transkei became the face of racial reconciliation and forgiveness. Political parties from across the spectrum still use his name in their campaigns, although his legacy has become more complex since his death in 2013. Some younger black South Africans accuse him of having sold out to white capitalists and prefer to revere his former wife, Winnie Madikizela-Mandela.

The politics behind this is complicated, but it speaks to the reverence South Africans have for the underdog, and to high levels of disenchantment more than two decades into democracy. For most of her later life, Madikizela-Mandela was demonised for her radicalism and her alleged role in the murder of 15-year-old activist Stompie Seipei, but she was also a symbol of the many ordinary people who were at home, holding the fort and suffering the injustices of apartheid while others were in exile or prison.

'Madikizela-Mandela was part of the complex politics that dominated the South African landscape as the apartheid regime cracked down on activists. She was deeply enmeshed in smuggling guns and other contraband in and out of the country, and had been imprisoned, detained and banished on numerous occasions,' Sisonke Msimang, who was born in exile to struggle parents, wrote in *The Washington Post* shortly after Madikizela-Mandela's death in 2018. '[L]ike many other leaders and members of the African National Congress (ANC) party, Madikizela-Mandela was in the difficult position of having to lead a revolution while dealing with intense personal trauma.' On the outside, she 'did much to keep [Mandela's] name and story alive' while he was in prison.[50] 'We were the foot soldiers,' Madikizela-Mandela later wrote, while Mandela enjoyed the relative comfort of being safely in jail.[51]

Back from exile: the early 1990s

After Mandela's release, political violence remained a big obstacle to negotiations, killing almost 10,000 people between 1991 and 1994. Much of it was fuelled by the government.[52] Eventually, late in 1991, multi-party talks started at the Convention for a Democratic South Africa, but on 17 June 1992 a raid by hostel dwellers aligned with the IFP killed thirty-nine in the Boipatong township about 90 kilometres south-west of the negotiations centre, causing the ANC to withdraw from the talks. An angry Mandela told a crowd: 'I am convinced we are no longer dealing with human beings, but animals.'[53]

Just as negotiations got back on track, Chris Hani was assassinated, bringing the country back to the brink of a crisis. It took skilful leadership and much negotiation to eventually produce an interim constitution to guide South Africa to its first democratic elections in 1994.[54]

Governing in the New South Africa, 1994–2007

South Africa's first democratic election on 27 April 1994 was also the first the liberation movement, by this point seventy-two years old, ever contested. Campaign slogans such as 'Sekunjalo ke nako' ('Now is the time') and 'A better life for all', and promises of jobs, houses and equal rights, convinced 62.6 per cent of the voters, who patiently waited in long, snaking queues that became emblematic of that day, to place the party in charge of the government of national unity, in which the National Party and the IFP also had representatives. The ANC gained power in seven out of the nine provinces, with the Western Cape going to the National Party and KwaZulu-Natal to the IFP amidst bitter claims from the ANC about violence and alleged irregularities.[55]

Mandela's presidency focussed on a peaceful transition from apartheid to democracy and reconciliation. The Springbok rugby jersey he wore during the Rugby World Cup in South Africa in 1995 was an important symbol of this. Rugby was—and is— more than a sport in a country where politics dictated segregation in every aspect of life, and the springbok had become one of the symbols of apartheid. With this gesture, Mandela reached out to those white people who might have felt distrustful of the goodwill of the new government.

Outside of these grand gestures, the ANC was less well-equipped for the more mundane elements of governing the country, even though it proclaimed itself 'ready to govern' before 1994. Delivering its list of promises made in the Reconstruction and Development Programme (RDP) was rather different to organising protests and surviving underground. The RDP set ambitious targets but was weak on the how-to.[56]

Even worse, the apartheid government had left the country bankrupt, and the ANC had not taken this into account in their planning. There was no money for a 'socialist experiment', said Mac Maharaj, who served on the Transitional Executive Committee that ran the country just before the elections.[57]

Even if there was institutional memory to draw on, it was deficient, and the bureaucrats were uncooperative. 'Most white South Africans thought—and many still think—that, apartheid aside, South Africa had been efficiently run by the white regime and that now, like the rest of Africa, it was going to the dogs under a black regime. The reverse is the case,' the late veteran journalist Allister Sparks wrote.[58] The 'ossified bureaucracy' of mostly white, Afrikaner males was not willing to help develop policies in line with the new dispensation.[59]

Two years into government, the Growth, Employment and Redistribution programme represented a change from a redistribution-first to a growth-first RDP.[60] In a U-turn from the ANC's initial left-wing socialist position in favour of nationalisation, it emphasised the free market. This neoliberal change in direction—engineered by then deputy president Thabo Mbeki, who took care of economic policy while Mandela worked at nation-building—was well-remembered by his leftist critics in the ANC when they voted him out of power just over a decade later.

Mbeki was elected ANC deputy president in 1991 (he outpaced Ramaphosa, who was also a favourite at the time) and president in 1997.[61] He became the country's president in 1999 after Mandela retired, having served only one term (the Constitution allows a maximum of two). To date, this is the only seamless transition the post-1994 ANC has seen. Mbeki and Jacob Zuma were both forced to resign before the end of their terms.

Much of the governing ANC's fiercest opposition has come not from other parties, but from its leftist alliance partners. Cosatu continued its strategy of striking to achieve political ends; some of its most significant recent actions have been against the imposition of e-tolls on Gauteng's highways by its own allies in the ANC. Unhappy with the ANC's neoliberal leanings, it resolved in 2003 to go it alone by 2015 should the ANC not make a turn to the left.[62] This never happened, however, because by that time Cosatu had started falling apart under the strain of involvement in ANC infighting. The police massacre of thirty-four striking miners in the dusty North West province settlement of Marikana, and the formation of new unions as an alternative to Cosatu, who were accused of becoming too comfortable with power, weakened them significantly. Many of their leaders, a number of whom were co-opted into government, preferred to keep the beast close because of the material benefits this presented. These benefits also accrue to the ANC, especially during election times when Cosatu has ready-made structures in place to campaign for its ally.

Mbeki's presidency: 1999–2007

Mbeki was well-received by the establishment when he became president. The ANC's share of the vote increased with him at the helm—to 66.35 per cent in 1999 and again to an all-time high of 69.69 per cent in 2004. The National Party, which was in sharp decline, merged with the ANC in 2001. The party that had been in power for close to half a century was no more.

Mbeki's tenure was not uncontroversial. He had been president for barely a year when he questioned the conventional medical wisdom, widely accepted at the time, that HIV was the direct cause of AIDS. His view was informed by dissident scientists—many of them published on the Internet—and he faced strong opposition from Cosatu and AIDS activists. Mbeki's views on AIDS, however, had strong support from within the ANC—from former firebrand ANC Youth League leader Peter Mokaba, who himself died of AIDS in 2002, amongst others.[63]

There was also the issue of Zimbabwe. Mbeki's 'quiet diplomacy' towards his neighbour—meaning he never criticised then president Robert Mugabe in public—seemed to fall short at a time when that country faced crisis and its citizens poured across the border looking for money and safety.

Diplomacy was Mbeki's focus. He spent much of his presidency trying to bring South Africa back into the fold internationally and within the continent after years of isolation during apartheid.[64] Many hailed him for his 'African Renaissance', which envisaged a post-liberation revival of African politics, economics and culture, but at home his absence was viewed negatively.

Mbeki, whose nickname amongst those who worked for him was 'chief', was also impatient with dissent. In a system where the governing party called the shots regarding deployment, many therefore kept their mouths shut in order to retain their jobs.

If Mandela was the reconciler, Mbeki's presidency was about transforming the ANC into a modern party that governs well. Dealing with corruption was a problem, as pointed out by the party's secretary general Kgalema Motlanthe in his 2002 report to the ANC conference in Stellenbosch. He wrote: 'almost every government project is conceived because it offers opportunities for certain people to make money. A great deal of the ANC's problems are occasioned by this'.[65]

The fight against corruption itself became political. Mbeki's term was marred by the government's multi-billion rand Arms Deal, and those resisting what they considered to be selective prosecution arising from this deal and other contracts eventually rallied around Jacob Zuma and pushed Mbeki out.[66] Some of them later went on to regroup behind Cyril Ramaphosa after they had fallen out with Zuma.

The acquisition of the $4.8 billion Strategic Defence Package took place under Mandela's presidency, but it was finalised in 1999 under Mbeki. Former ANC MP Andrew Feinstein considers it to be the 'point at which the ANC lost its moral compass', after a lot of public money changed hands in kickbacks for a deal some reckoned South Africa didn't need.[67] The complexity of the issue means that the ANC has never mustered enough political will to deal with this comprehensively. After years of campaigning by anti-corruption activists Zuma did appoint a Commission of Inquiry in 2011, but it was considered to have been a whitewash after it exonerated top politicians.

On an ideological level, Mbeki's market-friendly economic policies were what drove Cosatu and the SACP to unite behind Zuma, hoping he was their man on the left. Campaigning for Zuma, Cosatu general secretary Zwelinzima Vavi famously said that he was an unstoppable tsunami, little knowing what damage the man would later do to the country.[68] Vavi himself later fell out of favour and campaigned against Zuma.

There was also the issue of Mbeki's centralist leadership style, which demonstrated little deference to the party. If this was an attempt on his part to pull together a disparate party of trade unionists, capitalists, liberals and communists, it had the opposite effect. Things came to a head after he sacked Zuma as his deputy president in 2005 after the court found Zuma and his former financial adviser, Schabir Shaik, had a corrupt relationship. Some weeks after, the party's National General Council, consisting of about 4,000 ANC representatives from across the country, revolted, refusing to have Zuma step aside as the party's deputy president.

Those who supported Mbeki remarked on the change in the party's character. Frank Chikane, Mbeki's director-general, recalled that there was 'behaviour that was totally alien to the ANC I had known for many years. That language used was uncomradely, people were behaving like enemies rather than comrades-in-arms, and there was a readiness to lie or to support positions which were clearly illogical or ideologically irrational'.[69]

Zuma and Mbeki chose to confront the crisis poker-faced. 'We wish to assert that there is one ANC, and therefore reject the notion that individuals should be required to choose sides, on the basis of the absolutely false assertion that we lead two contending factions within the movement,' they said in a statement to the National Executive Committee three months later.[70]

In 2006 Zuma was charged with (and later acquitted of) the rape of the HIV-positive adult daughter of a struggle friend. The polygamous Zuma, who also has a number of children with women he is not married to, is well-known for his sexual exploits, but still his supporters blamed it on a 'honey trap' set by the Mbeki side.

The four-day ANC conference where Mbeki was ousted, in Polokwane in the northern Limpopo province, started on 16 December 2007. In South Africa this is known as Reconciliation Day, but what happened at the gathering was anything but reconciliation. The behaviour that had so shocked Chikane at the National General Council two years before was amplified. Zuma's supporters used the defiant old struggle song that he had revived and made his trademark tune, 'Awuleth' Umshini Wami' ('Bring My Machine Gun'), whenever party leaders aligned to Mbeki took to the stage.

Mbeki lost, with 1,505 votes against Zuma's 2,329, in a result that surprised and shocked many of his campaigners, who were blind to the impending defeat. All those aligned to Mbeki were also voted out.

The ANC's following programme to renew and unite itself was little more than cosmetic, because its firing of Mbeki—in a late-night decision taken by its eighty-six top leaders, on the basis of a court ruling that there was political meddling in Zuma's corruption case—led to a split in the party. In 2008, some of the most disgruntled Mbeki-ites formed the Congress of the People in what was the most significant split since the formation of the PAC in 1959. Four years later, a fallout with Zuma led ANC Youth League leader Julius Malema, formerly one of his biggest supporters, to found the Economic Freedom Fighters (EFF), now the second largest opposition party.

Tendering his resignation on television, Mbeki told the nation: 'I have been a loyal member of the African National Congress for 52 years. I remain a member of the ANC and therefore respect its decisions. It is for this reason that I've taken the decision to resign as president of the republic.'[71]

ANC deputy president Kgalema Motlanthe, highly regarded by both factions because he rarely voices controversial opinions, was appointed as a placeholder president. Meanwhile, Malema led a process early in 2009 that saw the National Prosecuting Authority drop the corruption charges against Zuma, shortly before the elections on 22 April. Nine years later, a court ruled that the prosecuting authority's decision to drop the corruption charges was irrational, and that they should be reinstated.

Loss of innocence: the Zuma years

With Zuma as leader, the ANC's vote decreased for the first time. Its 16 per cent surge in KwaZulu-Natal was enough, however, to disguise the party's losses in the other eight provinces.[72]

At a huge election rally in the Eastern Cape metro of East London, not far from Mbeki's childhood home, Zuma promised 'decent work' and massive social welfare, just as the global recession hit South Africa. Not much came of these promises. Still, his first 100 days were good, with stock markets rising and South Africans generally pleased by his listening approach. Initially, relations with the opposition in parliament also improved. Zuma appointed a National Planning Commission tasked with drawing up a National Development Plan, adopted as ANC policy in 2012. The leftists, however, objected to the looser labour market regulations aimed at alleviating youth unemployment.

On the down side, Zuma's expansion of the cabinet to a weighty thirty-four (later thirty-five) members—ostensibly to accommodate Cosatu and SACP leaders—drew criticism. Service delivery protests—which started increasing towards the end of Mbeki's term—picked up even more, as did violent incidents of xenophobia.

Corruption and maladministration became more brazen as policy floundered. It emerged early in his presidency that Zuma was using millions of rands in state money for improvements to his Nkandla homestead in rural KwaZulu-Natal. These extended well beyond the security improvements he was entitled to, and the costs were higher than those for any other president before him. ANC MPs, however, rallied around him when the opposition attacked him.

In April 2013, something happened that scandalised the scandal-weary population even further. A private jet with wedding guests landed at the Waterkloof Air Force Base. It belonged to an Indian business family, the Guptas, and Zuma's name was dropped to authorise the very unusual use of a military base for a private plane. Billed the 'wedding of the century' by Gupta employees, it was outrageously lavish and cost millions, with South African taxpayers picking up the bill.[73] The final slap in the face for South Africans was the Guptas' apparent insistence on a whites-only waiting staff.[74]

Zuma's friendship with the Gupta brothers, a family of businesspeople who came to South Africa from India in 1993 and strategically befriended politicians, also started drawing criticism from within the ANC. Speaking for the ANC Youth League at the launch of the ANC's 2011 local government elections manifesto in Rustenburg, Malema said: 'When families are exploiting the resources of this country and are enriching themselves in the name of freedom, when those in political office abuse their power to benefit friends, the youth must rise in defence of the ANC.' The crowd that came out for Zuma at the event barely filled half of the stadium built for the Soccer World Cup the year before.[75]

The ANC's centenary celebrations in Bloemfontein (also referred to as Mangaung, the name of the metro) in January 2012 were a mixed bag for Zuma. There were groups of dissenters in the crowd making the football hand signal for substitution at him. Still, a number of leaders from across the continent came for the party, and Mbeki even showed up for the first time since he was booted out of the presidency.

The ANC's centenary year was also its low point in government. The police massacre of thirty-four protesting miners in Marikana, at a mine run by London-based Lonmin, was one of the most brutal acts of state violence since the end of apartheid in 1994. Malema stepped swiftly into the political void of its aftermath to capitalise on the miners' anger.

Ramaphosa, a non-executive director of Lonmin at the time, was criticised for his role in the killings after an email surfaced in which he called for 'concomitant action' to be taken against the miners. He clarified by saying this meant arrest, not execution.[76] The incident didn't stand in the way of his being elected ANC deputy president four months later.

It was around this time that Zuma's allies in the trade unions also started turning against him, realising he wasn't the leftist saviour they wanted. Vavi told a Cosatu congress a month after the Marikana incident that Zuma's ANC was an organisation 'wracked by factionalism, patronage and corruption'. Those challenging abuses in the party 'find their lives increasingly in danger,' he added. Vavi was removed from his position the following year, after he was accused of sexually harassing a colleague. This would likely not have happened had he still enjoyed political protection from the top, and he claimed the charges were politically motivated.[77]

Traditionalists and former exiles in the ANC also expressed disappointment in Zuma, but he resembled Teflon—nothing stuck. He was comfortably re-elected at the ANC's national conference in Bloemfontein in December 2012, with Motlanthe, his deputy and challenger, biting the dust.

By 2014 the ANC's share of the vote fell, as corruption allegations against its leaders stacked up. However, with a campaign slogan of 'Together we can move South Africa forward', the ANC still got 62.15 per cent of votes. Some votes went to the first-timer EFF (6.35 per cent), and the Democratic Alliance (DA), which gained more than five percentage points, reaching 22.23 per cent of the vote.

Ramaphosa wrapped up his remaining business interests and replaced Motlanthe as the country's deputy president. He kept a relatively low profile—some say he was spineless—and only started speaking out against the abuses of Zuma's government in the months running up to the party's national conference in December 2017.

By the 2016 local government elections, the ANC had lost three of its seven metros to opposition coalitions (the DA was already in control in Cape Town), although it regained Port Elizabeth two years later after one of the parties pulled out of the ruling coalition. The loss was a humiliating blow to the ANC, especially because the country's biggest and most successful metros, like Johannesburg, were now out of its control. It was in danger of being relegated to the status of a rural party. It mustered only 53.91 per cent of the total vote, although local election results tend to favour opposition parties.

ANC leaders in these large metropolitan areas, most notably Gauteng province, blamed Zuma for their ills and started calling for him to go. Still, Zuma survived—with the help of the majority of ANC MPs, pulling together as a party and perhaps also fearing for their jobs—five attempts in parliament to remove him from power.

The tide of Zuma's fortunes as the 'Teflon president' only started turning when a large stash of emails sent by the Gupta brothers and their business associates was leaked to investigative journalists at the *Daily Maverick* and amaBhungane in 2017. Many of those who were previously prepared to support Zuma for the sake of protecting the ANC now had second thoughts. The evidence was brazen, and it became increasingly difficult for Zuma and the Guptas to laugh off the corruption reports as conspiracy theories.

If Zuma had wanted to run for a third term as ANC president—nothing in the ANC constitution stopped him, and there was talk that he was contemplating doing so—the leaked emails possibly convinced him otherwise. He stepped aside and publicly endorsed former African Union Commission chairperson, Nkosazana Dlamini Zuma. She was married to him for sixteen years as his second wife, divorcing him in 1998; they have had four children together.

Dlamini Zuma's campaign focussed strongly on gender issues— she would have been the first woman president of the ANC and South Africa—as well as on 'economic freedom', emphasising the fact that most black South Africans are still poor. A surprise last-minute reversal by Mpumalanga ANC chairperson and premier, David Mabuza, whom she had thought was on side but commanded his supporters to vote for Ramaphosa hours before the party started its elections, meant that Dlamini Zuma lost by 179 votes. Mabuza, now in the powerful position of kingmaker, became Ramaphosa's deputy. This means that a man who has overseen much maladministration and patronage politics in his province is in line to become South Africa's next president.[78]

4

THE POLITICAL OPPOSITION

The unbanning of the African National Congress on 2 February 1990 provided the launch pad for the movement to become the country's dominant party. Its fight for democracy over the best part of a century had given it unique legitimacy. In the eyes of many black Africans it has continued to retain this status. But with power came arrogance and the abuse of office. In recent years, the ANC has come to see itself as indispensable to stability. Jacob Zuma went further, arguing that it was divinely ordained to rule. During a rally at Mthatha on 5 February 2011, the president was quoted as saying:

> When you vote for the ANC, you are also choosing to go to heaven. When you don't vote for the ANC you should know that you are choosing that man who carries a fork ... who cooks people. When you are carrying an ANC membership card, you are blessed. When you get up there, there are different cards used but when you have an ANC card, you will be let through to go to heaven.
>
> When [Jesus] fetches us we will find [those in the beyond] wearing black, green and gold. The holy ones belong to the ANC.[1]

The party suggested this was only a metaphor, but Zuma had no such doubts, repeating the claim whenever he felt like it. There is a well-established tradition in Africa of anti-colonial movements presenting themselves as the natural parties of government once they assume office. Parties across the continent portrayed themselves as the embodiment of their people's hopes and aspirations. Once in government they tend to treat all opposition as suspect—supporting these opponents is seen as an act of treachery, undermining the happy unity of the nation. The National Party, which ruled South Africa from 1948 to 1994, had a similar view. Although the country has been a functioning (if limited) democracy for more than a century, it has had very few changes in government. Since 1948 there have been only two parties of government: the National Party and then, after 1994, the ANC. Even today, South Africa is hardly a model of effective, democratic government offering real choices to its citizens.

The Democratic Alliance

The opposition party that has most dented the ANC's electoral dominance has been the Democratic Alliance, although the Economic Freedom Fighters have put up vocal resistance both in parliament and in the townships. The Democratic Alliance is essentially a liberal party, with formal links to the Liberal International, of which it is a member. The party's basic philosophy is spelled out in its statement of objectives, titled *Our Vision*:

> Our dream for South Africa is of an open opportunity society in which every person is free, secure and equal, where everyone has the opportunity to improve the quality of his life and pursue her dreams, and in which every language and culture has equal respect and recognition.[2]

The vision was given substance by three simple objectives:

1. Individual freedom under the rule of law—an open society;

2. Opportunity with responsibility—an opportunity society; and
3. Full equality for all.[3]

It is worth comparing these statements with the aims and objectives of the ANC. These are the following:

> The ANC's key objective is the creation of a united, non-racial, non-sexist and democratic society. This means the liberation of Africans in particular and black people in general from political and economic bondage. It means uplifting the quality of life of all South Africans, especially the poor. The struggle to achieve this objective is called the National Democratic Revolution.[4]

This is then elaborated as encompassing the Freedom Charter of 1955, which is described as the party's 'basic policy document'.[5]

The statements are diametrically opposed. The Democratic Alliance offers freedom and opportunity regardless of race or creed. The ANC's vision is focussed on the African majority and on the needs of the poor. Without needing to provide a textual analysis comparing the policies of each party line by line, the trend is clear.

The ANC is a nationalist party of the kind that can be found across much of Africa. It led the fight against white rule and had to appeal to the widest constituency. Since the end of apartheid, it has projected itself as a party of the centre-left, offering welfare benefits to those in need. Indeed, following the 2011 budget, the economist Mike Schussler described South Africa as the 'biggest welfare state in the world'. The government was unapologetic, with the social development minister at the time, Edna Molewa, defending the welfare system, observing: 'It is difficult for the government to close its eyes and [not] look at people when they are suffering and do not have anything to eat.'[6] Approximately a third of the country's citizens are in receipt of some form of social welfare payment from the government.[7] The child support grant made up the highest share, with over 9 million beneficiaries. Old age grants are the second highest category.

Whether this is the right direction for South Africa to take is a matter of debate, but the Democratic Alliance had a very different view in its early years. Presenting what it described as an 'alternative' budget, the party said:

> At its current acceleration rate, the social security net is becoming increasingly unaffordable and crowding out other priorities. The DA believes that a caring society must demonstrate its support for its vulnerable members, including the aged, the disabled, the young and the unemployed. The problem with the social security net is not that it is generous, but rather that it supports too many recipients.

> The social security system places a safety net below vulnerable members of society who cannot enter the formal economy. The aim of any kind of social spending must always be to empower as many citizens as possible to help themselves over the long run. Within the ANC's model of the Developmental State, social security creates a system of hand-outs. This is turn breeds dependency on the state and a culture of patronage, and it is destroying potential for using the social security system for more long term benefit.[8]

The implications were clear: fewer benefit recipients and an end to a system of patronage and hand-outs. This is the classic formula proposed internationally by parties of the centre-right. However, in an effort to expand its supporter base to include more black voters, the DA later embraced social grants, and its position now doesn't differ much in principle from that of the ANC.

In recent years, with Mmusi Maimane taking over the leadership of the party, the emphasis on equality and opportunity has been diluted, but it has not been eliminated. In a country in which more than a quarter of citizens are out of work and poverty is endemic, telling people to get on with their lives and enjoy the benefits of an 'opportunity society' is not an easy platform from which to win votes.

THE POLITICAL OPPOSITION

The challenge of the Democratic Alliance

The Democratic Alliance has gradually grown in strength and influence but is poorly understood outside of the country, which is why it deserves examining in some detail. In 2006, it took the city of Cape Town by forming a complex multi-party coalition that ousted the ANC. This was followed in 2009 with control of the Western Cape—the first time the ANC had lost a province to the opposition. In the Western Cape, the Democratic Alliance won 51.46 per cent of the vote, pushing the ANC into second place with just 31.55 per cent support.[9] The party's leader, Helen Zille, was jubilant. 'The results are very good for South Africa,' she told the BBC. 'They are very good for democracy ... The Democratic Alliance has grown by more than 30 per cent nationally and we have doubled our vote in the Western Cape, where we've won the province which is wonderful.'[10]

The loss was a rude shock for the ANC, who were unused to electoral rejection. It dented their preferred vision of their party, which they felt was destined to rule. The ANC and its allies went on the offensive. They attacked Zille for her choice of cabinet, which was—apart from herself—entirely composed of men. The trade union movement declared that the Western Cape was to be run by a 'pale male' executive.[11] Zille, never one to be caught on the back foot, responded in kind. She told *The Sowetan* that she would not take lessons on sexism from the ANC or its allies. She was quoted as saying: 'Zuma is a self-confessed womaniser with deeply sexist views, who put all his wives at risk by having unprotected sex with an HIV-positive woman.'[12]

The remark, although true (Zuma had admitted as much during his rape trial) touched the rawest of ANC nerves. Zuma had just won the presidency and was in the first flush of popularity. The Youth League accused her of appointing only men so that she might 'sleep around' with her 'boyfriends and concubines'.

Umkhonto we Sizwe's Military Veterans' Association threatened to render the Western Cape 'ungovernable' by sending troops there if Zille continued insulting the newly-elected president.[13] Zille herself complained that her remarks had been taken out of context, and that she was only responding to the sexual slurs made against her.

When she got to see President Zuma later that month, Zille used the opportunity to try to lay the matter to rest. 'During a conversation with President Zuma ... I asked him to regard the Western Cape as an opportunity, and not as a threat,' she said. 'I told him that we would always act in good faith and in the interests of all our people when we propose alternative approaches to solve some of our country's most pressing problems. I said that we need the space to implement them.'[14]

The incident, although trivial in itself, highlighted something more profound: just how novel the situation was for both parties. For the ANC, the feeling that electoral support was ebbing away, no matter how slightly, was distinctly unsettling. For the Democratic Alliance, it offered the first opportunity to show what the party was really made of, through governance of a province. The DA's status as the official opposition was strengthened during the May 2014 election. The ANC won by an overwhelming majority, taking 62.1 per cent of the vote, but this was down from 65.9 per cent in the 2009 election. The Democratic Alliance increased its share of the vote from 16.7 per cent to 22.2 per cent. Although this was not quite as good as it had hoped, it still represented close to a quarter of the electorate. In the 2016 local elections, the DA took three major conurbations: the party could no longer be brushed aside. It was only in the 2019 general election that the DA had a setback, stalling under Maimane (see Chapter Thirteen).

Table 1: Democratic Alliance election results since the end of apartheid

Year	Votes	Percentage of total votes cast	Seats	Leader	Result
1994	338,426	1.73%	7	Zach de Beer	ANC victory
1999	1,527,337	9.56%	38	Tony Leon	ANC victory; DA becomes official opposition
2004	1,931,201	12.37%	50	Tony Leon	ANC victory; DA retains official opposition status
2006	3,888,780	14.8%	Local elections	Tony Leon	ANC victory; DA is the largest party in Cape Town and forms a multi-party alliance to control the city
2009	2,945,829	16.66%	67	Helen Zille	ANC victory; DA retains official opposition status and wins Western Cape province
2011	6,393,889	23.94%	Local elections	Helen Zille	ANC victory; DA retains official opposition status, retains Western Cape and wins support in black-only wards
2014	4,091,584	22.23%	89	Helen Zille	ANC victory; DA retains official opposition status with increased share of seats
2016	9,463,498	24.57%	Local elections	Mmusi Maimane	ANC victory; DA retains Cape Town and Western Cape and takes major conurbations: Nelson Mandela Bay, City of Tshwane and City of Johannesburg
2019	3,621,188	20.77%	84	Mmusi Maimane	ANC victory; DA retains official opposition status with decreased share of seats

Party history

The origins of the Democratic Alliance are to be found in the turmoil that beset South Africa following the Second World War—the period that was so formative for the ANC, the Communist Party and their allies in the trade unions. In 1959, twelve MPs broke away from Jan Smuts's United Party over its refusal to oppose the apartheid legislation being introduced by the National Party government.[15] The rebels formed the Progressive Party. They elected Dr Jan Steytler, the son of a Boer War veteran, who had studied medicine at Guy's Hospital in London, as their leader. It was a position he was to hold until his retirement in December 1970.[16]

The Progressive Party resisted apartheid through parliament. It called for an entrenched constitution in which the powers of the provinces would be protected. It also stood for an economy based on unfettered capitalism.[17] The party received financial support from big business (including the mining giant Anglo American), but it had little success at the polls. After the general election of 1961, it was virtually wiped out. Only Helen Suzman was able to retain her seat.[18] The lone parliamentary voice speaking up for South Africa's oppressed, Suzman became internationally famous for her outspoken criticism of apartheid. She was an outstanding orator, holding her own as an English-speaking woman of Jewish descent in a parliament dominated by male Afrikaners.[19]

Suzman retained her seat, and for thirteen years was the sole principled MP opposing racial discrimination. She fought detention without trial; pass laws; influx control; job reservation on the grounds of colour; racially separated amenities; forced removals; capital punishment; the banning of the Communist Party; and gender discrimination, especially against black women. It was often a lonely position, but it stood her, and her successors, in good stead.

In 1974, six more Progressive Party members won seats in parliament. Soon thereafter, fellow anti-apartheid activist Harry Schwarz and others left the United Party to form the Reform Party, which in turn merged with the Progressives to form the Progressive Reform Party in 1977.[20] That year, the party was further strengthened by other defections from the United Party. Under the leadership of Colin Eglin, the Progressive Reform Party became the official opposition. In 1988, Zach de Beer took over as party leader and after careful negotiations succeeded in successfully merging three small parties to form the Democratic Party on 8 April 1989.[21] The National Party called for an election in September that year. Under a combined leadership, the Democratic Party won thirty-six seats in parliament.

These were the dying days of white rule. The National Party had fractured, with groups of MPs leaving to form the Conservative Party. Then, in February 1990, President F. W. de Klerk unbanned the ANC and other parties, and the whole edifice of apartheid came tumbling down.[22] In 1994, South Africa held its first truly democratic election. The ANC won a resounding victory, leaving the Democratic Party with just 1.7 per cent of the national vote.[23]

It seemed that the need for a liberal party was about to be extinguished. If the Democratic Party was to survive it would have to reinvent itself. Yet despite this unpromising beginning, the party gradually carved a place for itself, taking a growing share of votes in national elections.[24]

Tony Leon

Under the leadership of Tony Leon, and with only a handful of MPs, the party attempted to establish a new role. It fought for the legitimacy of the opposition, transparency in government and the importance of holding members of government to account. Gradually the strategy began to pay dividends. The 1995 municipal elections showed a swing back to the Democratic Party. This continued during the 1999 national elections, when the party won over 9.56 per cent of the national vote and returned thirty-eight members to parliament.[25] The Democratic Party had become the largest opposition party once more. Leon attacked Thabo Mbeki's government for its centralisation of power and its installation of ANC loyalists in key positions in the media, business, public and private sectors, as well as in sport, culture and the offices of the Public Protector. The ANC was transforming itself from a governing party into a ruling party, attempting to dominate the public sphere. Tony Leon argued that democracy could only be strengthened and protected by building a strong opposition able to limit and curb the one-party tendencies of the ANC.[26]

Attacks on the government, while essential for an effective opposition, would not in themselves bring the Democratic Party to power. Leon knew that he could not wait for the gradual erosion of ANC support. A new strategy was called for. The National Party was in terminal decline, and Leon saw an opportunity to construct a wider alliance. For a party whose roots lay in fighting apartheid, making a bid to National Party MPs and supporters was both risky and painful. He decided that it was the only way his party could make progress, but it meant a move to the right. As one observer put it:

> The DP (Democratic Party) transformed itself, under the leadership of Tony Leon, from a liberal, English-dominated voice for freedom to a more conservative party offering vocal, aggressive opposition to the ANC. This enabled it to win much of the Afrikaner vote from the NNP (New National Party).[27]

In 2000, the Democratic Party reached an agreement with Dr Louis Luyt, of the small Federal Alliance. Talks also commenced with the New National Party, and this led to the final change in party name with the formation of the Democratic Alliance.[28] The deal drew fierce criticism from some party loyalists, including the doughty Helen Suzman, who told Leon in no uncertain terms that he had made a 'huge mistake' and would 'come to rue doing business with these people'.[29] It was, as Leon himself was later to describe it, a 'marriage made in hell'.[30] Despite this, it was effective. The party won a number of municipalities, including the jewel in the Democratic Alliance's crown: the city of Cape Town.

The newly refigured party had considerable difficulties; the relationship between old Progressive Party stalwarts and former National Party members was distinctly uneasy. Tensions between the factions escalated. A rupture finally came in October 2001 over a decision by Leon to suspend the controversial mayor of Cape Town, Peter Marais, from the party on several grounds, including sexual harassment.[31] In response, the New National Party leader, Marthinus van Schalkwyk, left the Democratic Alliance and found fresh allies in an even more improbable partnership with the ANC.[32] They seemed unlikely bedfellows, but the relationship between the ANC and former National Party members endured.

In the 2004 general election, the Democratic Alliance began to build momentum. It gained 12.37 per cent of the vote and a total of fifty seats in the National Assembly.[33] In absolute terms, the party expanded its support by over 400,000 votes. In the 2006 local government elections, this support continued to grow.[34] The Democratic Alliance increased its share of the vote to 16.3 per cent—a 4 per cent rise. The party increased its representatives in all six of the metropolitan councils, most notably in the Cape Town area, where its share of the vote rose from 27.1 per cent in 2004 to 41.9 per cent. This put the Democratic Alliance ahead of the ANC in the city.

The Zille years

On 15 March 2006, Helen Zille, previously a Democratic Alliance MP and the party's national spokesperson, was elected mayor of Cape Town. A former journalist, she had broken the story of Steve Biko's death and was a rare example of a white South African politician who had learned isiXhosa as an adult. The race to lead Cape Town was fiercely contested, but she won the position by forging an unwieldy seven-party coalition. Zille became mayor with a slim three-vote majority. This included an ANC councillor, who voted for her secretly. It was a fragile hold on power in the city, but Zille gradually cemented her position. In August 2010, after protracted negotiations, the Democratic Alliance managed to persuade the Independent Democrats—a Cape party with a predominantly Coloured base, led by Patricia de Lille—to join them.[35]

Tony Leon announced on 26 November 2006 that he would step down as the leader of the Democratic Alliance, and Zille was elected as his successor at the party's 2007 Congress.[36] The 2009 general election saw a further rise in Democratic Alliance support, with the party winning control of the Western Cape province. It maintained its position as the largest opposition party, and appeared to be gradually eroding support for the ANC in the latter's heartlands.[37]

The May 2011 local elections were something of a turning point. Zille's campaign attempted to move voters away from racial stereotypes. Her key phrase, repeated throughout the election campaign, was 'making the issues the issue'.[38] The election saw the Democratic Alliance's vote rise by 7.7 per cent, while the ANC's share of the vote fell by 2.7 per cent. Had the ANC not routed the Zulu-based Inkatha Freedom Party in KwaZulu-Natal, their losses would have been even more dramatic. As it was, the Democratic Alliance strengthened its support in most of the municipalities it contested in 2006, growing by 17.8 per cent in the Western Cape, the region it already dominated.

The Democratic Alliance made much of its record of service in the towns and rural areas that it administered. While ANC local government is notoriously corrupt, the DA won plaudits for its clean administrations. In its 2009 assessment, the international credit rating agency Global Credit Ratings awarded the city of Cape Town one of its highest long-term debt ratings: AA-.[39] The most comprehensive indication of the Democratic Alliance's ability to provide effective services in the Western Cape came from the government itself. An official report published in October 2010 showed that the province was the best service provider in almost every category.[40] It is a record that the DA has retained.

The ANC reacted nervously to the Democratic Alliance's electoral and administrative success. The party's general secretary, Gwede Mantashe, admitted that the ANC had major problems with its local councillors, and could learn something from the opposition.[41] This sentiment was echoed by others inside the ANC, with an anonymous party stalwart bemoaning the quality of ANC local politicians: 'It's not as if the ANC has a truckload of decent councillors that it can just pick from and install.'[42]

Faced with the May 2014 general election, Zille contemplated how to respond to ANC attacks which claimed that the DA was led by whites, for whites. She searched for an appropriate black leader. Lindiwe Mazibuko, party spokesperson and then parliamentary leader from 2011 to 2014, was seen by many as a possible future leader. After a disagreement with Zille, however, Mazibuko left politics altogether, later claiming that Zille was trying to pull her down and was doing the same to Maimane. Zille denied this, saying that she supported Mazibuko 'at every level' but thought she had run for caucus leader too early (Mazibuko was thirty-one at the time).[43]

In late 2013, Zille commenced discussions with someone she did deem fit to be party leader—Mamphela Ramphele, a senior black politician whom she knew well. Ramphele was formerly the partner of the black consciousness leader Steve Biko, and had gone on to carve out a distinguished career of her own. She had risen to become vice chancellor of the University of Cape Town, and seemed a viable candidate to lead the Democratic Alliance into the 2014 election. But it soon became clear that she had another agenda: she wanted to establish her own party, Agang SA, and was prepared to consider an alliance with Zille to fight the election on that condition only. After complex, lengthy and finally unsuccessful negotiations, the planned alliance failed. Each party stood on its own. While the Democratic Alliance took 22.2 per cent of the vote, Agang was wiped out, taking just 0.28 per cent of the vote.[44]

Maimane leads

The result left Zille as the head of the opposition, but did not answer the question of how to find a suitable black leader. This was finally resolved in May 2015 when Mmusi Maimane, previously the party's spokesman and candidate for Gauteng provincial premier, was elected to lead the party. Maimane was an eloquent and charismatic speaker, with an ability to woo crowds that he had learnt as a preacher. He succeeded in blunting criticisms that the party was really a home for whites and other ethnic minorities.[45] Maimane's identity and lifestyle encapsulates the DA's attempt to broaden its appeal. As a black African, he represents a growing proportion of the party's membership; as a black man who married a white woman, he proves that reconciliation between the ethnic groups is possible.

Maimane made a point of this in his keynote speech to the party's April 2018 Congress. 'I am a proud black South African,' he said. 'I am a proud Sowetan. I am a devout Christian. And I am the proud son of Xhosa and Tswana parents.' Maimane spoke about being moulded by his experiences as a black man: 'I said if you don't see that I'm black, then you don't see me. But the flipside of this is also true. If all you see is that I am black, then you equally don't see me.' He went on to say that his ethnicity did not define everything about him: 'At the end of my life I will be judged on whether I was a good husband, a loving father, a loyal son, a patriotic South African, someone who contributed to society. None of those questions will be defined by my race.'[46]

It was well-argued and eloquent, but leading a liberal party that questions the role of the state, when so many people are reliant on it, is no easy task. While the Democratic Alliance has been trying to shed its image as a white-dominated party, the ANC has moved in the opposite direction. It once represented all of South Africa's ethnic groups; today it is almost exclusively black African.[47] There are few other ethnicities represented in its key leadership positions or visible at ANC rallies, although under Cyril Ramaphosa's lead some in the party are attempting to portray it as a home for people from all races.

Would Maimane be able to win support for his vision of a non-racial country in which meritocracy rather than race was the key criterion for advancement? The results have been mixed. Maimane took the party into the 2016 local elections, and although he only increased its share of the vote by about 2 per cent, he succeeded in winning a string of major conurbations. The Democratic Alliance became the largest party in Tshwane (which contains the capital, Pretoria), Nelson Mandela Bay (containing Port Elizabeth) and Johannesburg.[48] In all of these areas, Maimane's party had to find allies to retain control. President Zuma and the ANC were left with some important metropolitan areas, including Durban, Bloemfontein and Kimberley. The ANC continued to control central government, but it was a severe setback for the party.

The question for Maimane was whether his party could deliver well-run and law-abiding administrations across such a wide range of locations, while at the same time holding together fragile alliances. Perhaps the toughest municipality for the Democratic Alliance was Nelson Mandela Bay, which was notorious for corruption. An ANC task team sent in to clean up Port Elizabeth had failed; one of its key members fled from the city fearing for his life.[49]

Athol Trollip, a white but isiXhosa-speaking mayor, set his sights on rebuilding the area's reputation. Outlining his plans for his first 100 days in office with promises of jobs and a clean administration, Trollip said:

> Political instability in this metro has rendered this city moribund and unresponsive ... It is time to lock the revolving doors of corruption, cadre deployment and cronyism and bring about a new model of administration by this multiparty government, that will eschew the blight of such practices and that ushers in a model of good government ...[50]

Delivering this has proved immensely difficult, with several small parties removing support for the Trollip-led alliance. Although the administration at first survived several challenges, it collapsed in August 2018.[51]

Nor has Nelson Mandela Bay been the only thorny question for Maimane. His party had to face other motions of no confidence in their coalition administrations in Tshwane and Johannesburg. The mayor of Johannesburg, Herman Mashaba, has been attempting to clean up some of the gross corruption that he uncovered when taking over the city. But despite investigating some 4,000 dubious contracts and identifying what the mayor said were serious crimes, he has accused the authorities of failing to prosecute those that have been identified.[52]

In Cape Town, the party's bastion of support, disputes with its mayor, Patricia de Lille, led to legal action, and to de Lille finally walking out of the party.[53] Maimane was also drawn into a bitter internal wrangle with his predecessor. Helen Zille posted a poorly judged tweet suggesting that the legacy of colonialism was not entirely negative. This was factually accurate, as anyone benefitting from western medicine, driving a car or even reading the message on their mobile phone would have known, but it caused a storm of protest in a country where colonialism (and later apartheid) inflicted much humiliation and pain. Maimane attempted to remove Zille from her position as provincial leader, but Zille fought back and Maimane was forced to accept a compromise. She kept her position while apologising—through clenched teeth—for what she had said: 'I realise the wounds of history that my tweet and subsequent defence of it has opened. In particular, I recognise that my actions were insensitive to South Africans who suffered under colonial oppression. For this, I am genuinely sorry.'[54] Zille remained a premier in the Western Cape, but was stripped of any leadership role in the party.

Under Maimane the party has had to face a crucial question: should it remain true to its free market, liberal roots, or move towards the social democratic interventionism of the ANC? Its head of policy, Gwen Ngwenya, supported by others in the party leadership, proposed that it should dump the racially defined policy of Black Economic Empowerment (BEE), claiming that it had not worked for the country. In a 152-page document titled 'Vula: The "Open" Economy, Open for Business', Ngwenya suggested that the party should replace BEE—or the later version of the same policy, Broad-Based Black Economic Empowerment (B-BBEE)—with an Environmental, Social and Governance (ESG) index that removes race from the scorecard. The document went on to argue that quotas currently in place should be dropped, since B-BBEE had created 'insiders and outsiders'. The 'insiders' were predominantly African men who had hoovered up directorships and places on company boards, leaving most of the population, of all racial groups, excluded from key positions. 'DA empowerment policy would seek to be comprehensive by recognising a wide range of voluntary environmental, social and governance disclosures and interventions, of which ownership schemes and diversification could be a part, but with no minimum requirements,' stated the paper.[55]

Maimane decided that the policy was unsaleable to the electorate. Rejecting Ngwenya's suggestions, he moved the party closer to the policies the ANC has pursued since 1994. This has meant downplaying the Democratic Alliance's traditional commitment to values of equality and merit and focussing instead on supporting the ANC's long-held plans to back 'previously disadvantaged' groups: black Africans and, to a lesser extent, Coloureds, Indians and women. This has—inevitably—caused tensions. Ngwenya resigned in disgust, accusing the leadership of failing to support her or her initiatives. In her resignation letter she quoted Maimane's own words, arguing that she was doing no more than working towards his own objectives. She quoted her leader as saying: 'we need a wholesale change in empowerment policies, to move away from race-based policies that enable elite enrichment, towards policies that fundamentally break down the system of deprivation that still traps millions of South Africans in poverty'.[56] True or not, when facing the 2019 election, Maimane found the relevant policy changes too difficult to stomach.

The growth of the Democratic Alliance is, to a considerable degree, a reflection of the failure of the ANC in government. The public's disgust at the gross corruption in local and national administration is reflected in the contempt in which Jacob Zuma is held by large sections of society. The commentator Gareth van Onselen, who has previously worked for the DA, wrote: 'For every brick pulled from the ANC's weakened and crumbling wall, one is added to the DA's fortress, strengthening and extending its size.'[57] With Zuma now forced from office, and Cyril Ramaphosa promising a clean administration, the ANC is a considerably harder target for the DA to attack.

Inkatha Freedom Party

With only 2.4 per cent of the vote in the 2014 election, the IFP is a small party with a big history. When its founder and leader Mangosuthu Buthelezi celebrated his ninetieth birthday on 27 August 2018, there was a mixed reaction. He's variously been praised as 'the anvil on which apartheid ultimately faltered', and vilified as former president F. W. de Klerk's dog.[58] From the young leaders of the opposition Economic Freedom Fighters, there was an admiring tweet saying Buthelezi 'should have shared a peace prize with Mandela' because he put 'black unity' first. South Africans who grew up in the 1980s in communities terrorised by Buthelezi's Inkatha disagreed with this quite vocally.[59] Both the IFP and the EFF are rooted in nationalism.

Buthelezi, who was leader of the apartheid-era KwaZulu homeland at the time, launched the Inkatha Cultural Liberation Movement in 1975. It later became a political party called the Inkatha Freedom Party, with its headquarters in the homeland. Buthelezi formed the party with fellow former ANC members, but also included both the traditional Zulu leadership and members of the new urban middle class who were opposed to the existence of a KwaZulu homeland. Ironically, though, the traditional leaders who supported Buthelezi were dependent on the apartheid state for their privileged status.[60] Membership was extended from Zulus-only to all black South Africans in the 1980s.

Buthelezi fell out with the ANC in exile in 1979, after a London meeting where he differed from the party's stance on sanctions and their armed struggle strategy against the apartheid government, which he said stood in the way of a peaceful change. Buthelezi presented a real threat to the ANC, unlike the other homeland leaders, whom the party regarded as mere puppets.[61]

Hostilities between Inkatha and the ANC grew as Buthelezi tried to forcibly suppress student and community opposition to homelands. There were open clashes with the United Democratic Front—which represented the ANC-in-exile in South Africa— and its affiliates. These played out around Inkatha strongholds in Natal and Gauteng townships. Later, in the Truth and Reconciliation Commission, it was alleged that Buthelezi worked secretly with the apartheid regime's police, security police and state-sponsored assassination squads.[62]

Initially the IFP refused to negotiate with the apartheid government, insisting that political prisoners should be released first, but later, during transition talks at the Convention for a Democratic South Africa, it aligned itself with the white, right wing Conservative Party. It sat most of the negotiation process out, however, and almost landed the country in a crisis when it decided at the last minute to take part in the 1994 elections after all. A special sticker was placed on the ballot papers to facilitate the IFP's participation, but this brought its own problems as the stickers were omitted on some ballot papers. Subsequently, there were also serious questions about how elections were run in the party's strongholds.[63]

The party got just over a tenth of all votes in 1994, but steadily declined in the years after. Former president Jacob Zuma attracted many IFP voters to the ANC with his strong focus on Zulu nationalism.[64]

IFP MPs have made waves in parliament—for instance, the maverick Mario Oriani-Ambrosini, who pushed for the legalisation of cannabis for medical use before losing his fight with cancer.[65] Another, Liezl van der Merwe, has consistently and heroically voiced concerns over the shambles in the social welfare payments system, despite initial mockery from other MPs.[66] Despite the IFP's ageing leadership at the top, it has also produced young, bright MPs like Mkhuleko Hlengwa, who was elected in 2014 at the age of 27.[67] At the time of writing, Buthelezi has recently announced his intention to step down.[68]

Congress of the People

Thabo Mbeki's sacking as president enraged his loyalists in the ANC, who served 'divorce papers' to the party in October 2008 and founded the Congress of the People—abbreviated, with no apparent irony, to Cope. The party had strong beginnings, getting 7.42 per cent in its first election in 2009 on the back of national outrage about Mbeki's dismissal, but infighting and bad organisation in the party reduced the vote to less than 1 per cent in 2014.

Cope's formation represented the first mass schism in the ANC since the Pan Africanist Congress of Azania was formed in 1959. The founders of Cope—including former ANC chairman Mosiuoa 'Terror' Lekota, who is still the party's leader—pledged loyalty to the Constitution because they said that those who remained in the ANC under Jacob Zuma had violated it. Cope was named after the 1955 Congress of the People gathering in Soweto, where the Freedom Charter was drawn up. The mass gathering at which the party was founded took place three days before the United States elected its first black president, Barack Obama, which gave the founders the feeling that anything was possible.

Lyndall Shope-Mafole, Cope leader in the Gauteng Legislature at the time, described the significance of the new party as follows:

> The ability of Cope to lay claim to struggle credentials and as a genuine representative of the people in post-apartheid South Africa, has ushered in a new era which allows ordinary citizens to reclaim

patriotism. The era where a patriot could only be defined by years served in exile, the under-ground or prison, or being a member of a particular party, is now happily behind us. By calling on South Africans to rally together in support of our Constitution and constitutional democracy, Cope has ushered in a new era of patriotism open to South Africans of all persuasions.[69]

Political journalist and commentator Allister Sparks predicted that Cope would 'cut [the ANC] down to size and in doing so change our entire political landscape, opening the way for a new era of coalition politics and the prospect of periodic regime change through the ballot box in the not too distant future'.[70] Even though the party floundered, it signalled an important shift in the South African political landscape. It set the tone for the emergence of other challengers to the ANC's hegemony, such as former ANC Youth League leader Julius Malema's Economic Freedom Fighters. It also ushered in the start of greater cooperation between opposition parties, which became a political force for the first time.

Cope was broken up by bitter infighting amongst leaders, and there was also talk that ANC moles and spies had infiltrated the party.[71] Its decline spurred academic and businesswoman Mamphela Ramphele to found a new party, Agang, in 2013, aimed at drawing support from the black middle and upper classes, as well as white voters who were looking for a viable opposition to the ANC without as much historical baggage as the DA. Ramphele abandoned Agang the next year after a brief flirtation with the DA. It mustered a disappointing 0.28 per cent of the vote.

In the months running up to the 2019 elections, Lekota reinvented himself as a supporter of white farmers. A farm owner himself, he teamed up with the white, right wing pressure group AfriForum in the land debate to oppose amendments to the Constitution that would provide for expropriation without compensation.[72]

Economic Freedom Fighters

The Economic Freedom Fighters only received 6.35 per cent of the vote in its first elections in 2014, but the party has caused political disruptions disproportionate to its size. It is led by Julius Malema, who formed it after he was expelled from the ANC Youth League in 2012. The main issue behind his expulsion was his public criticism of Zuma, a man who, three years before, had praised him as a 'leader in the making'. At a gathering in Malema's home town of Seshego, Zuma said: 'The ANC recognises talent and leadership and we give people an opportunity. Julius has illustrated that he is indeed a good leader and that he understands the people.'[73] These words turned out to be prophetic as well as ironic.

Malema was publicly humiliated by his expulsion. His supporters caused mayhem during his disciplinary hearing by the ANC, throwing bricks and bottles at police and journalists and burning ANC flags and t-shirts with Zuma's face on them. Barbed wire barricades were put up around the ANC's headquarters, Luthuli House in the Johannesburg Central Business District, each time the hearing sat. During that time, Malema also led a defiant march from Johannesburg to the Union Buildings in Pretoria 60 kilometres away, where the Presidency is located, to make his grievances clear to Zuma. The march included a stop at the Johannesburg Stock Exchange in Sandton, where Malema delivered a memorandum expressing a wish for 'economic freedom'.[74]

In the end, it was Cyril Ramaphosa—then deputy president—who turned down Malema's appeal against his expulsion. The decision provoked mixed responses in members of the ANC Youth League, meeting with jubilation from some and anger from others. Newspaper headlines at the time declared it was the end of Malema.[75] It was really only the beginning.

After a brief hiatus, during which Malema publicly mentioned that he was considering attending political school in China (many ANC politicians went to China for training), he re-emerged as a political force, declaring that he would start a party: the Economic Freedom Fighters (EFF). The EFF was formally launched on a scorching day in October 2013, but had already become a phenomenon in the months before that, and its trade-mark red beret had become a coveted fashion item. Supporters trekked to an open piece of ground in Marikana, the same site where, one year earlier, thirty-four striking miners were shot by police. The massacre had become symbolic of the collusion between government and big business against ordinary people, and Malema, in his fight for 'economic freedom' for all, positioned himself alongside these underdogs.

Malema, who was thirty-three at the time, told a sea of supporters gathered on the dusty site and on the *koppie* (small hill) around which many striking miners had been shot dead by police: 'A different baby is born today, a giant, a child that walks immediately, a baby that fights for your living wage. You must be afraid of that child.'[76] He outlined what he called the party's 'non-negotiable' visions and goals, which later became its 'seven cardinal pillars'. These are as follows:

1. Expropriation of land without compensation
2. Nationalisation of mines and banks
3. Free education, healthcare, and houses
4. An increase in state and government capacity
5. Massive protected industrial development
6. Massive investment in the development of the African economy
7. Open, accountable, corruption-free government and society

The party also has a strong focus on race issues, which is highly African nationalist in character. Malema denies that the party dislikes white people when asked about it straight up, and it even has a handful of white supporters. 'White South Africans, you have nothing to worry about us, you must worry about yourselves,' Malema said at the party's launch. 'If you're not prepared to share, then you are your own enemy, but for those who are willing to share, we will kiss each other, black man, white wife.'[77]

Malema has tested the boundaries of hate speech on numerous occasions. First, in 2011 as ANC Youth League leader, he was found guilty of hate speech when he sang an old struggle song with the lyrics 'Kill the Boer', a reference to the apartheid system. He then went on, somewhat teasingly, to change the lyrics to 'Kiss the Boer'. By 2019, the conversation about race politics and white privilege had moved on to such an extent that when Malema was hauled before the South African Human Rights Commission for saying he would 'not yet' advocate the killing of white people for land, and for making racist comments about Indian people, the commission, in a contentious ruling, judged that this was not hate speech because it was said in a specific context. 'This did not prompt any harm,' the commission ruled.[78]

By the time Malema launched the EFF in Marikana, he had declared himself a public enemy of Zuma. The place had become a no-go zone for the president because of the government's slowness to condemn the police actions there, but Malema received a hero's welcome. Malema further taunted Zuma by adopting the title 'commander-in-chief', which was normally reserved for the president as head of the armed forces. It was Malema's way of signalling to Zuma that he had disregarded him as president completely, and that he was more of a 'people's president' than the populist Zuma, which would possibly have irked the old man even more.

Malema's militaristic approach to his party is also reflected in his leadership style, which doesn't tolerate dissent or overt competition. A number of founding members of the EFF left in 2014 after a fallout over leadership positions. Some of them went on to support Zuma, including Andile Mngxitama, who started Black First Land First (BLF)—a party which is even more radical than Malema's with regard to race and land, and whose members have become defenders of sorts for Zuma. The party received fewer than 20,000 votes in the 2019 elections.

The EFF has applied the ANC's formula to its gatherings. Rallies are a spectacle of show and dance with large crowd numbers, complete with VIP seating areas and noisy bikers, but they are less slick and have a more gritty and authentic feel than those of the ANC, possibly because the EFF budgets are smaller. In the early years, before the 2014 elections, the EFF would often complain that it had trouble booking public stadiums or halls for events because the administration was controlled by the ANC. The party had to be creative, and there were instances when it would just appropriate an open piece of ground for a public gathering.

The EFF has also come to be associated with more serious land grabs, inspired by those of neighbouring Zimbabwe's former president Robert Mugabe.[79] Party leaders have re-appropriated seemingly unused private land to settle poor people. One such space is called Juju Valley, on a few hectares of private land bordering Malema's home town of Seshego, in the Limpopo province's capital city. The landowner, who has emigrated, agreed with party leaders there that they could erect shacks on half of his land. Legalising this agreement has, however, proved tricky, and the municipality has been unable and unwilling to provide services like water, sanitation and electricity.[80] Not all of the party's land grabs have been this polite, with some ending violently.[81]

The economy is the main tenet of the EFF's policy. Malema had announced the slogan 'economic freedom in our lifetime' when he was still ANC Youth League leader in 2010, echoing an older party slogan from the 1940s. It was catchy and was retained by the ANC Youth League and later the ANC, even when Malema took this slogan with him to the EFF. Malema's call for the nationalisation of mines and land was meant to be an alternative to the ANC's Black Economic Empowerment policy, which many young people feel has failed them. The EFF's policies have also pushed the ANC to adopt the rhetoric of radical economic transformation, and to support a motion calling for an amendment to the Constitution which would allow land expropriation without compensation. Remnants of the 'radical economic transformation' slogan still live on in the Zuma faction of the ANC. Originally it was a clarion call to transfer ownership of the economy into black hands faster, but this sentiment has unfortunately also come to be associated with those involved in corruption and state capture.

Malema, like many of the young people who grew up post-1994, has questioned the negotiated transition from apartheid led by former president Nelson Mandela. He has also tapped into a growing disgruntlement with politicians and political parties in general. The party's style has been to be present not only in parliament but also on the streets, picketing and illegally occupying unused land. They operate by participating in the system while at the same time distancing themselves from its failures.[82] Winnie Madikizela-Mandela, considered by many to be a radical firebrand and the antithesis of Mandela's reconciliatory philosophies, was close to Malema from the beginning of his political life. Although she never joined the EFF formally, Madikizela-Mandela maintained close ties with the party until her death in 2018.

Even though the EFF has styled itself as 'corruption-busting', there have been questions about the ethics of the party's leaders themselves. In his ANC Youth League days, Malema was caught dodging millions of rands in taxes (he subsequently apologised).[83] In October 2018, a report found that senior members of the EFF had helped themselves to substantial funds from a small bank used by poor people for their savings and pensions. The party's deputy president, Floyd Shivambu, was accused of benefiting to the tune of R10 million via his brother, Brian. Shivambu denied receiving the money.[84] There have also been reports that the party is funded by cigarette smugglers, with pictures on social media showing Malema posing with them.

The EFF's parliamentary style has proven to be disruptive, and MPs have pushed boundaries in an institution which was formerly polite, and—with the overall calibre of ANC MPs declining since the first democratic parliament in 1994—becoming increasingly boring. They started with the dress code, insisting that their male MPs wear red overalls and red berets to parliament and that their female MPs wear maids' uniforms, in keeping with what they professed their working-class supporters to be wearing. When there was talk of tightening parliamentary rules to forbid this, Malema threatened to attend parliament naked.[85]

EFF MPs are loud and generally disdainful of parliamentary etiquette. They have disrupted and embarrassed Zuma many times—first with demands that he 'pay back the money' spent by the government on expensive improvements to his personal rural home at Nkandla (Zuma claimed it was for security purposes, but an enquiry by the Public Protector found that some of it was not), and later by taunting him for his closeness to the Guptas, a family of businessmen who siphoned money from state institutions. They have been removed from parliament many times by members of the parliamentary security services. More seriously, they have also at times been on the receiving end of previously unheard-of police brutality within the parliamentary chamber itself. Parliamentary security has been stepped up to such an extent that the precincts are surrounded by fences and concrete barriers on red letter days such as the annual opening of parliament. Videos and memes of the party's parliamentary interactions frequently trend on social media in South Africa and across the rest of the continent, where Malema's youthful resistance to authority—unusual in many African cultures—has been an inspiration to some.

United Democratic Movement

Bantu Holomisa's UDM is small, but it has had consistent support; this has enabled Holomisa to play the role of opposition unifier, especially in the period of Jacob Zuma's presidency. The UDM has never had more than 3.4 per cent of the vote, and in 2014 it barely had 1 per cent, with much of its support concentrated in the Eastern Cape.

Holomisa came to be the leader of the former Transkei homeland's military government through a lunch hour coup in 1987, which he justified with the claim that the deposed prime minister, Stella Sigcau, was corrupt. After the unbanning of the ANC, he became a National Executive Committee member, having been elected with the most votes. However, he was expelled in 1996 for 'bringing the party into disrepute' with a remark to the Truth and Reconciliation Commission that Sigcau, then minister of public enterprises, accepted bribes, even though the party insisted she was cleared of wrongdoing.[86]

He founded the UDM on 27 September 1997 with former National Party Chief Negotiator Roelf Meyer, whom he had met during the multi-party transition negotiations in the years before. The launch took place at the World Trade Centre in Kempton Park, where these talks had been held. Meyer, however, resigned from politics three years later.

However, the UDM has been one of the most enduring small parties, positioning itself as a moral party which is 'the political home of all South Africans, united in the spirit of South Africanism by our common passion for the country, mobilising the creative power inherent in our rich diversity'.[87] Holomisa has remained the leader since he founded the party, and he has applied an approach to opposition that is constructive, in contrast to the adversarial approach adopted by the DA.[88]

The party's biggest moment came after the August 2016 local government elections. Holomisa was upbeat as the results trickled in and the ANC's dismal performance in the metros became apparent. 'It is clear now that the opposition parties are being given a mandate by the people of South Africa saying "it's your turn",' he said. In one of its biggest blows, the ANC lost the Nelson Mandela Bay Metro, encompassing the seaside city of Port Elizabeth, in its Eastern Cape heartland. 'We should try to depoliticise [the metro] and talk issues of governance, and make sure that, if there is a coalition there, we use it as a showpiece to the rest of the country,' Holomisa added.[89]

The UDM became part of the governing coalition in that metro, but two years later politics and personalities clashed, and a fallout between the DA and the UDM collapsed their coalition. In a deal with the ANC, the UDM got the mayoral position and the ANC was returned to power in the metro.

African Christian Democratic Party

At the height of its popularity in 2004, the ACDP commanded 1.6 per cent of the vote, but in 2014 it received just 0.57 per cent. Kenneth Meshoe, a former teacher and reverend, has been president of the party since its formation.[90] Even though it appeals largely to conservative Christians, the party has said that it is not restricted to 'Bible-believing Christians', asserting that it is also for 'those who have a high regard for moral values'. Its election campaigns have focussed on family values.[91]

Abortion has been one of the party's biggest rallying points after its founding in 1993, 100 days before the first democratic elections in 1994. Its objection to abortion on demand and gay rights, as well as to the secular nature of the Constitution, meant it was the only party in Parliament to vote against the adoption of the Constitution in 1996, but with only two seats, its opposition could not veto it.[92]

Late in 2017, an ACDP MP had a Private Members' Bill passed giving fathers the right to take paternity leave. A subsequent attempt to pass a bill that would make it more difficult for women to have an abortion was, however, rejected. Previously, the party had sought unsuccessfully to restrict women's access to abortion by proposing an amendment to the Constitution to include the rights of the unborn child.[93]

Pan Africanist Congress and other Black Consciousness parties

The PAC is a party with big ideas, but it has struggled in pragmatic terms. In 2014, the party got one seat in the National Assembly with 0.21 per cent of the vote, down from 1.3 per cent in 1994.

The PAC was born in 1959 after an Africanist grouping broke away from the ANC because they objected to the adoption of the Freedom Charter in 1955, especially the preamble that stated 'South Africa belongs to all who live in it, black and white'. They also objected to the role played by the South African Communist Party, which had white members, in drawing up the Charter. PAC leaders argued that this reduced the anti-colonial struggle for land to a 'mere civil rights movement'.[94]

The PAC played an important role in the struggle against apartheid, organising an anti-pass campaign on 21 March 1960 which ended violently when the police shot sixty-nine people dead in Sharpeville. The PAC was banned, and, in similar fashion to the ANC, it launched a struggle against the apartheid government with its armed wing, Poqo. It was beset by organisational problems in exile, but survived until its unbanning, together with other liberation organisations like the ANC, in 1990.[95]

The party has nurtured some of South Africa's greatest minds, such as former Deputy Chief Justice Dikgang Moseneke, and influenced thinking within the ANC, where it still has many admirers. However, infighting and embarrassments, rather than great ideas, have dominated the PAC in recent years. The funeral of Zondeni Sobukwe, wife of PAC founder Robert Sobukwe, in August 2018 was a particular low point. It collapsed in chaos as infighting between the party's factions and unhappiness about ANC government figures leading the official funeral programme, as is the custom, led to the collapse of proceedings. Deputy President David Mabuza had to leave shortly after arrival because some mourners became violent. They demanded that Narius Moloto, leader of one of the PAC's two factions, leave too.[96]

Leadership infighting as far back as 2007 led to one of the party's younger MPs, Themba Godi, crossing the floor to form the African People's Convention, 'to be the alternative voice ... that will never betray the revolution'.[97] He occupied the party's sole parliamentary seat.

The Azanian People's Organisation (Azapo) was born out of the Black Consciousness Movement in 1978, following the banning of organisations such as the South African Students' Organisation and the Black People's Convention. Azapo boycotted the 1994 elections but took part in subsequent ones. It has only ever held one seat in Parliament, and failed to win any in 2014.[98]

Freedom Front Plus

The Freedom Front Plus—or the Vryheidsfront Plus, its official name in Afrikaans—is a right wing party of white, predominantly Afrikaans-speaking people, which received 0.9 per cent of the vote in 2014. It is currently led by MP Pieter Groenewald, and governs in coalitions in Johannesburg, Pretoria and other municipalities.

The Freedom Front was founded by an apartheid Chief of the South African National Defence Force, General Constand Viljoen, in 1994 as a more conservative alternative to the National Party, in support of a *volkstaat*, or self-determination for white people. In its first election in 1994, the party received 2.2 per cent of the vote, predominantly in the rural areas of the Orange Free State and the former Transvaal, where many white farmers were concentrated. It has almost 100 per cent support in the privately-owned white enclave town of Orania, in the Northern Cape.

The party added the 'Plus' to its name after it merged with three other right wing parties to contest the 2004 election. The party is still calling for an Afrikaner volkstaat, claiming that the 'right to self-determination' is recognised 'internationally', as well as under Article 235 of the South African Constitution.[99] Most recently the party has aimed to 'internationalise' its objections to the government's intentions to expropriate land without compensation, a policy white farmers feel would hit them the hardest. In August 2018, the party wrote to the United Nations' human rights commission in Geneva to ask them to put pressure on the South African government, claiming that the policy would be a violation of Article 17 of the UN's Universal Declaration of Human Rights, which protects private ownership of property.[100]

5

CORRUPTION

THE LEGACY OF APARTHEID

From apartheid corruption to the Arms Deal

Corruption didn't start the day Nelson Mandela was inaugurated as president, but it also didn't stop there, despite Mandela's commitment to cleaning up the government. Apartheid corruption spilled over into the new South Africa, encompassing the new black elite. Much of this apartheid corruption has never been properly exposed or prosecuted, because doing so would have touched too many powerful global interest groups, including oil traders, lobbyists, arms dealers, bankers, political parties, foreign leaders and intelligence agencies, as well as the local defence force, during the sensitive transition period in the early 1990s. There have been calls to revisit this corruption, more so in the past decade as state capture allegations against former president Jacob Zuma surfaced, and particularly after the establishment of an enquiry to investigate this state capture.

The apartheid-era hangover was huge. Mandela's new administration was a patchwork of former white-administered provinces and black homelands, each with its own networks of entrenched civil servant interests and corrupt networks. Within the ranks of the liberation movement itself, there was a mixture of crooks, opportunists, and those who relied on money from all kinds of donors to survive. Many of these activists got jobs in government, either as politicians or civil servants, and brought their networks with them. At the same time, the private sector remained dominated by the white business interests which had thrived during apartheid.[1]

Writer and activist Hennie van Vuuren has conducted one of the most extensive investigations to date into apartheid-era corruption. In the fifteen years before the end of apartheid in 1994, the apartheid economy had built 'a massive infrastructure to bust international sanctions', helped by 'friends across the globe who smelt profit', he wrote in his book *Apartheid, Guns and Money: A Tale of Profit*. 'A highly secretive machinery was created to corrupt politicians, launder public and private funds, and break international sanctions. This effectively criminalised key institutions within the public and private sector. And it relied extensively on the support of right-wing business, political and intelligence networks across the globe.' There was also double-crossing. Many countries secretly aided and abetted apartheid while officially supporting sanctions against South Africa, or openly funding liberation movements.[2]

Corruption in South Africa even predated apartheid. From the time of the first European settlements in the Cape in the seventeenth century, there was wheeling and dealing, and money changing hands. The settlers looked after the interests not of a government, but of the Dutch East India Company, one of the wealthiest corporations at the time due to the spice trade. Fast forward two centuries, and much of the struggle for power between the British Empire and the Boers was about controlling the gold-rich territories. With the rise of Afrikaner nationalism and the coming into power of the National Party (NP) in 1948, apartheid became state policy and black South Africans were stripped of whatever political power they still had. When South Africa became a republic in 1961, independent from the British Commonwealth, English capital had to support apartheid in order to accommodate the interests of new white Afrikaner corporations with strong ties to the NP government.[3]

The apartheid government had allies in many places, despite a common belief that it was an isolated regime. Van Vuuren found that forty-seven countries in Europe, the Americas, the rest of Africa and Asia collaborated with the regime by ensuring that arms, loans and oil continued to flow into South Africa at premium prices.[4] This contravened a 1977 UN Security Council arms embargo, which was put in place four years after the UN General Assembly declared apartheid a crime against humanity. The sanctions became the longest lasting in modern international politics.

The Big Five on the UN Security Council—the Soviet Union, China, France, the United States and the United Kingdom— were supposed to police the embargo, but instead they were complicit in assisting the South African state-owned company Armscor, set up for this purpose, to illegally purchase weapons. Armscor reproduced or improved these weapons locally, tested them in battle in Angola, and marketed them to other countries as a source of foreign revenue. The 'deep state'—intelligence agencies, arms companies and middlemen in these countries— helped them to do so. France permitted a thirty-strong Armscor delegation to direct sanctions-busting activities from South Africa's Paris embassy, while China, through state-owned company Norinco, secretly supplied the apartheid military via Zaire (now the Democratic Republic of Congo).[5] Due to the BRICS grouping, Russia and China are two of South Africa's biggest latter-day allies.

Banks were also complicit. Kredietbank Luxembourg, for example, helped Armscor establish a global money laundering network of secret bank accounts and shell companies to sidestep sanctions. Executives supported the white supremacist ideology, but these operations also yielded good profits. There was a vast network of over 800 such bank accounts, and 100 secret companies, between Panama and Liberia.[6] The loans provided to the apartheid state by some major European banks left the new government heavily in debt in 1994. The majority of South Africans neither consented to nor benefited from these loans.[7] Even after the end of apartheid, the sanctions-busting activities of international actors were kept secret, because they could face embarrassment and prosecution.[8]

The deep state networks that helped bust apartheid sanctions continued operating under Mandela's new government, and corrupted democratic politics. New elite pacts, based on criminality and corruption, were made.[9] The arms companies and middlemen that sold weapons systems to the apartheid regime in the 1980s went on to allegedly bribe ANC politicians for the multi-billion rand Arms Deal, concluded in 1999.[10]

The Arms Deal, officially known as the Strategic Defence Package, was meant to modernise the South African National Defence Force. Military hardware like naval craft, submarines, fighter aircraft, helicopters and other equipment were purchased from foreign arms dealers. Bid winners were required to invest in South Africa by building factories to create jobs.[11] Divisions in the ANC began to take place in 2001. It was then that senior ANC MP Andrew Feinstein started to question the deal; when the government moved to curtail a probe into it, he resigned. Feinstein later moved to London, where he campaigned to raise awareness around the global arms trade.

It was the first major corruption scandal in post-apartheid South Africa. Former president Jacob Zuma was one of the key figures in this deal. He is still due to be tried on sixteen corruption charges, founded on accusations that he took bribes from French arms maker Thales over a contract worth $5 billion during his time first as provincial economy minister and then as deputy ANC president. The bribes totalled over R4 million, in 783 payments handled by his financial advisor, Schabir Shaik. Shaik was convicted and jailed in 2005, but Zuma successfully evaded conviction until 2017, when his star waned and corruption charges were reinstated.

Zuma's fight to stay out of jail has defined politics in South Africa for over a decade and a half, and it is still ongoing. Feinstein alleged that some of the kickbacks from the deal were also used to fund the ANC's 1999 general election campaign, which might explain elements of the cover-up. The party was, for instance, never called to testify at the much-criticised Arms Procurement Commission of Inquiry that later probed but cleared the deal, despite damning allegations.[12]

Armscor destroyed many of its records at the end of apartheid, but Van Vuuren argues that a proper airing of Armscor's activities at the end of apartheid could have made it more difficult 'for the corrupt European corporations, middlemen and South African politicians to benefit from the post-apartheid arms deal'.[13] Shipping magnate Tony Georgiadis personified the way in which apartheid-era corruption spilled over into the new government. Georgiadis's company was linked to nearly fifty sanctions-busting oil shipments to South Africa. He later paid $40 million to facilitate the Arms Deal. In 2010, he formed part of Zuma's business delegation to the United Kingdom.

A probe of apartheid-era graft is becoming increasingly difficult, because of the destruction of documents and the attrition of possible witnesses. The political environment has become toxic and muddled, too. Those most vocal in calling for an investigation of apartheid-era crimes are often doing so to detract from their own allegedly corrupt dealings. They are the same figures who have rallied around Zuma in the name of 'radical economic transformation', and these threats to investigate apartheid-era corruption are often used merely to smear and threaten detractors.

State capture

Black economic empowerment and radical economic transformation in many instances became a cloak for graft, and for another large-scale corruption scandal which gripped the country. It was referred to as 'State Capture', a euphemism 'to describe a situation in which the narratives, the direction and the value system of a society, including patterns of accumulation, are under the control of an elite group'.[14] It was first defined in a World Bank report in 2001, but came to be applied in South Africa to the way in which three brothers—Ajay, Atul and Rajesh 'Tony' Gupta—bought their way into controlling politics and presidential appointments in South Africa. It was akin to a soft coup, and involved a number of international companies.[15]

The rhetoric of radical economic transformation—originating with ANC Youth League leader Julius Malema and taken up by Zuma and his supporters in the ANC—found fertile ground in a country where the rich are mostly white and the poor are mostly black. It argues that South Africa's constitutional settlement has been an obstacle to radical economic transformation, and that entrenched institutions should therefore be bypassed. The focus has been on development driven by the state, as an enabler of wealth and a generator of contracts. The reality has been, however, that this provided opportunities for the entrenchment of patronage networks, with a strong dependency on the decision-makers at the top of the pyramid. The Gupta brothers, who came to South Africa from India in 1993, became the state's external brokers.[16]

The first time the media and public took notice of the family was when their business, Sahara Computers, employed Duduzile Zuma, Zuma's daughter, in 2008. By 2010, talks between the ANC and the Guptas about an ANC-sympathetic newspaper were taking place.[17] *The New Age*, and later the television station Africa News Network 7, turned out to be a mouthpiece for the party's Zuma camp; it stayed afloat with sponsorship money from, amongst others, parastatals and sympathetic provincial governments. Both outlets closed in 2018 amidst rumours of money troubles.

In that same year, the Guptas and Zuma's son, Duduzane, acquired part of steel conglomerate ArcelorMittal's multibillion-rand empowerment deal. This raised questions over whether the Guptas should benefit from a scheme intended to empower black people who were disadvantaged by apartheid. Family spokesperson Gary Naidoo said: 'The Guptas' participation in the Ayigobi consortium is not premised on them being black in the definitional sense. It must be noted that the BEE [Black Economic Empowerment] legislation does not prohibit non-blacks from participating in BEE companies or consortiums.'[18]

Cosatu leader Zwelinzima Vavi, who had supported Zuma's rise to power a few years before, was critical, describing the deal as outrageous. 'We are heading rapidly in the direction of a full-blown predator state, in which a powerful, corrupt and demagogic elite of political hyenas increasingly controls the state as a vehicle for accumulation,' he said. Similarly, Malema questioned BEE, which he said was effectively enriching 'the children of those in power and the friends of those who are in power'.[19]

Allegations that Zuma's family members and future wives had received jobs and benefits continued to grow (Duduzane occupied a senior position in the Gupta business). Meanwhile, the Guptas saw a number of favourable deals coming their way. State-owned enterprises were milked. Eskom coal contracts went to a Gupta company under dubious circumstances, and they were awarded a R54 billion contract—bigger than the Arms Deal—for locomotives at state-owned Transnet. The locomotives turned out to be the wrong size to operate on South African rails, and the promised offsets of local capacity-building were later rubbished by investigators, in an outcome similar to that of the Arms Deal.[20]

When the National Treasury stood in the way of further irregular deals and irresponsible spending by state-owned enterprises, as well as the acquisition of nuclear power stations which many felt the country could not afford, an onslaught was launched against South Africa's purse. A false intelligence report emerged in 2015 which pointed to individuals who were afterwards removed in a short period of time, stripping the treasury of much of its institutional memory. 'Project Spider Web' bizarrely asserted that the 'white establishment' and the private sector had a 'huge influence' over the treasury through a plan called 'Project Grapevine', hatched in the dying days of apartheid. The plan was supposed to have been drawn up by national intelligence and funded by established big-business families like the Oppenheimers and the Ruperts.[21]

Neither the report's claims nor its source was probed, but it did result in the firing of the finance minister. Nhlanhla Nene was replaced by Des van Rooyen, an unknown backbencher, in December 2015, but senior leaders in the ANC stepped in and forced Zuma, within a day or two, to reverse his decision and appoint Pravin Gordhan, a previous finance minister. Mcebisi Jonas, who was deputy finance minister at the time, later claimed he was offered R600 million to become finance minister in a meeting that involved one of the Gupta brothers and Duduzane Zuma.[22] Gordhan was subsequently hounded out of office after the police and intelligence ministers announced they were investigating Gordhan's role in a 'rogue spy unit'. By the end of March 2016, Jonas was also gone.

According to a 2017 report on state capture, the Guptas became 'key strategic brokers of the networks that connected the constitutional and shadow states'. They turned the political capital of access to the president to their advantage to secure deals in his name, in return for a percentage of the contract.[23] Zuma's close association with the family lost him many former allies in the ANC, and tampering with the treasury seriously dented his power.

Public Protector Thuli Madonsela's damning report on state capture by the Gupta family forced Zuma to appoint a Commission of Inquiry, chaired by deputy chief justice Raymond Zondo, to investigate these allegations. Very cleverly, Zuma formulated the terms and conditions in such a way that the commission could also look at allegations beyond the Guptas. It started hearings in 2017.

Zuma's supporters rejoiced when, thirty-four days into its hearings, the commission heard testimony about state capture which, for a change, didn't involve the much-maligned Gupta family, but rather a security company owned by a white South African, Gavin Watson, who used his 1980s struggle ties with the ANC to score tenders for everything from prison fencing and catering to youth and repatriation centres. His company, formerly known as Bosasa and now as African Global Operations, allegedly paid off everyone, from prison warders to MPs and ministers to Zuma himself. They also supported the ANC with large donations, a process which was—until recently—allowed by law to be conducted out of the public eye.

Former president Thabo Mbeki has attempted to explain corruption under the ANC government, saying when there is liberation following a dictatorship, 'people who have been oppressed and disadvantaged economically argue that they lost a great deal in the past. Hence they believe they are entitled to "make up for it"'.[24] His former spokesperson in the ANC, Smuts Ngonyama (now an ambassador), famously said of his alleged questionable business dealings in 2007, 'I did not struggle to be poor.' Former intelligence officer and writer Barry Gilder wrote: 'Those of us who came out of struggle or deprivation into the private sector, assailed by the same temptations, seemed to have no choice but to play economic and lifestyle catch-up through the only advantage we had—our social, political and struggle networks.'[25]

The party has tended to pull together over this matter. A former ANC MP said he was told 'we mustn't treat this comrade like that' when the parliamentary committee he chaired asked questions about seemingly corrupt prison bosses.[26] MPs similarly pulled together to protect Zuma, even when evidence of wrongdoing started to stack up. The party is identified with the masses, which inoculates it against public criticism.[27] However, corruption had become so endemic to the ANC that many had began to think that, for the party to cleanse itself, it had to commit suicide.

Party funding

Party political funding has been unregulated and kept secret for seven decades, although efforts are being made to regulate it with the Political Party Funding Bill, which at the time of writing is still in the offing. This has prevented the public from truly knowing how these relationships operated. The governing ANC, for example, has accepted cash 'from mega-corporations, rogue businesspeople and murderous politicians alike'.[28] Chancellor House, its funding vehicle until recently, was a trust that did business with the government as a 'politically preferred' partner to companies, such as Japanese giant Hitachi, that were looking for black empowerment partners in the country. Chancellor House was liquidated years after media reports about it first emerged in 2006.[29] The ANC's funding vehicles have displayed similarities to those of the old NP—unsurprisingly perhaps, because the ANC has employed as fundraisers a few of the NP leaders it inherited when it merged with the former apartheid party in 2004.

The ANC's Progressive Business Forum (PBF), for instance, follows a similar model to that of the NP's secret front, Projek Republiek, which had a membership model that required annual contributions by donors—often donors who did business with the government.[30] The PBF has a measure of openness about its affairs. Journalists have access to its fundraising gala dinners, and it even has a website.[31] Cell phone companies, banks, South African Breweries and smaller government contractors have supported it. Although it is not illegal, corruption watchers are concerned about the practice of businesspeople paying—in tiers—to get access to ANC government leaders and officials, and even the president. Former president Jacob Zuma's pronouncements at the forum's dinners that the ANC was 'a good investment' also raised concerns.[32]

The public doesn't know much about opposition party funding either. It is only by chance that questionable funders and practices are exposed. The Democratic Alliance, for example, has in the past received money from the Gupta family—former party leader Helen Zille even dined on curry at their compound, describing it as 'the best meal I have ever had in my life'—as well as convicted fraudster Jürgen Harksen, while EFF leaders have allegedly received benefits from cigarette smugglers and benefited from the executive looting of the VBS Mutual Bank.[33] Opposition parties have, however, expressed concern about declaring their funders for fear of negative bias when applying for government business.

Apartheid tricks?

There is a quote that is often attributed to a speech delivered by Nelson Mandela at labour federation Cosatu's Fifth National

Congress in 1994, which is as follows: 'If the ANC does to you what the apartheid government did to you, then you must do to the ANC what you did to the apartheid government.'[34] Jay Naidoo, a former general secretary of Cosatu, remembering Mandela's words, drew parallels between the increasing securitisation of the ANC-led state under Jacob Zuma and the apartheid years. 'Having lived through the brutal repression of the Apartheid state, I developed more than a healthy mistrust of securocrats of any political colour, including the current crop that seem intent on taking away a number of our Constitutional rights,' he wrote in 2012, just before the ANC elected Zuma for a second term.[35]

The Secrecy Bill, which Zuma's government appeared intent on passing, and which would have made it an offence to leak or publish classified documents, epitomised this. 'Freedom of expression is not a neoliberal principle. It is the embodiment of the democracy we fought for,' said Naidoo.[36] Attempts to curtail it would be akin to the actions of the apartheid government. The bill was part of a rising trend of paranoia and secrecy in the state under Zuma's presidency, and was meant to cloak whatever he chose to disguise from public scrutiny.

After Zuma took over in 2009, the South African Police Service became a police force, as it had been before 1994, with military ranks, and police officers were unofficially licensed to 'shoot to kill' by politicians. The country's spooks became increasingly subordinate to political agendas, and everything that the government didn't want to account for was made secret in the interest of 'national security'. Apartheid-era security laws were on occasion dusted off for this purpose. So was the 1980 National Key Points Act, which threatened those who published pictures showing the state-funded renovations of Zuma's controversial Nkandla home with legal action. The law was subsequently replaced. Another strange legal instrument surfaced after police shot thirty-four striking miners dead at Marikana in 2012—the biggest state-sponsored killing under the democratic government. The state, bizarrely, went on to charge 270 miners with the murder of their colleagues, citing 'common purpose'. This instrument had its origins in English law and was used by the apartheid government to charge activists for the death of their peers at the hands of the police.[37]

Will Ramaphosa make ground on graft?

Corruption convictions plunged to a low while concern about state capture was at its highest. From 2015 to 2019, almost 2,000 cases of suspected corruption were reported to the police, but only 135 convictions were secured. White collar and organised crime went largely unpunished. Just over a quarter of the 2,000 cases reported to Hawks, the directorate for priority crime investigation, resulted in convictions.[38]

Tackling the scourge of corruption is important not only for restoring faith in the ANC government and for freeing up money to deliver government services, but also for investment. The United States, the United Kingdom, Germany, Switzerland and the Netherlands, representing 75 per cent of total foreign investment in South Africa, expressed their concern to Ramaphosa's investment envoys that inconsistent application of government policies and non-enforcement of the rule of law could cause investment to suffer.[39] Making South Africa more attractive to foreign investors has been one of the key items on Ramaphosa's agenda since he stepped up to become president in February 2018.

It took him a long time to get going, partly because he is a cautious operator, but also because his hold on power in the ANC is somewhat tenuous. The party has been split almost down the middle between those who support him and those who support Zuma, many of whom fear prosecution's themselves. His caution was evident when, in a reshuffle of the cabinet soon after he became president, he retained some ministers who were implicated in wrongdoing but held important positions in the ANC. However, he did manage to clean up the economic cluster of ministers.

Despite reports pointing to corruption in state-owned enterprises and recommending prosecution, in the first year of Ramaphosa's presidency there were no high-profile arrests. It also took close to a year to get the new prosecutions head, Shamila Batohi, instated following Zuma's appointments of either lackeys or incompetents who brought the institution to its knees. A presidential Commission of Inquiry was appointed to look into this. 'We are hoping the appointee ... will not be captured,' Ramaphosa told South African diplomats. 'We want them to be as slippery from the hand of capturers as possible, because they have an important role to play.' He admitted that corruption was so endemic that South Africa had come close to being a 'failing state'.[40]

Ramaphosa's battle against corruption was made more difficult when he himself was accused of taking money from Bosasa for his own presidential campaign. He has been doing his best to contain the fallout, but an important test for his fight against graft will be whether he subjects himself to the same scrutiny that South Africans want to see applied to all of those who have been implicated in corruption.

Table 2: Ten big corruption scandals in South Africa's recent history

Date	Case	Importance
Mid-1970s	Information Scandal/ Muldergate	R64 million was shifted from the defence budget to undertake a propaganda war that involved buying a local newspaper and influencing

		international news agencies to report favourably on the government.
1995	Sarafina	R14 million was paid to a playwright for a play on HIV/AIDS, which turned out to be a flop. The losing bidder could have done the job for a mere R600,000. The Public Protector found that procurement rules were broken. Nkosazana Dlamini Zuma, then the health minister, was found to have lied to Parliament, but was let off the hook by the ANC.
1999	Arms Deal	The defence department spent R30 billion on military equipment it didn't need. British and French arms dealers were found to have paid kickbacks to South African politicians, while the offsets they promised never materialised.
2006	Travelgate	Seventy-nine MPs were accused of defrauding Parliament of millions in money allocated for official travel, with fourteen pleading guilty. Parliament eventually had to write off an outstanding R12 million owed to it.
2016	Nkandla	Former president Jacob Zuma was ordered to repay almost R8 million after it was found that some of the more than R240 million worth of upgrades at his Nkandla home should not have been paid from the public purse.

2009–2017	State Capture	Evidence suggests that former president Jacob Zuma was in cahoots with the Gupta family of businessmen, illegally redirecting billions of rands worth of state resources into private pockets. The family also took over some executive functions, such as the appointment of cabinet ministers.
2016	Grant payment scandal	The Department of Social Development was ordered to appoint another company to pay out social grants after irregularities were picked up, but dragged its feet to such an extent that it endangered the timely payout of grants to millions of people.
2017	Steinhoff	Described as the biggest case of corporate fraud in South African business history, the global household goods and furniture company Steinhoff (also referred to as 'the Ikea of Africa') collapsed after large-scale accounting fraud wiped 85 per cent off its share value, which amounted to billions of rands.
2018	VBS Bank looting	In what a report called 'one of the most unsophisticated bank heists', R2 billion was stolen by the VBS Bank's directors and senior executives and some well-connected politicians, causing the bank to collapse. Fifty individuals politically connected to the ANC and the EFF allegedly benefited, while many lost the meagre savings and pensions they had entrusted to the bank.

CORRUPTION

2005–2019	Bosasa	Bosasa received more than R10 billion in prison and security contracts before going into liquidation after being exposed by a disgruntled former employee, who also disclosed that the company spent between R4 million and R6 million a month paying bribes to politicians and officials. The company also sponsored ANC election campaigns.

6

THE ECONOMY

EXPLAINING THE FAILURE TO THRIVE

From insignificant colony to global mining hub

From the beginning of colonialism in the seventeenth century until late in the nineteenth century, the world regarded South Africa as not much more than an outpost on the way to somewhere more useful. For many years, Britain considered the Cape as a colony that produced some agricultural goods at the cost of troublesome and expensive conflicts—little else. This changed, dramatically, with the minerals revolution of the late nineteenth century, which saw the discovery of gold and diamonds. There then followed at least four other phases: basic industrialisation after the First World War, secondary industrialisation after the Second World War, growth and then stagnation under apartheid, and finally the quarter of a century of largely unsuccessful development under the ANC.

As explained in Chapter Two, the discovery of diamonds and gold in the 1870s and 1880s transformed South Africa. Investments and migrants flooded into the country, upsetting the uneasy balance that the Afrikaners had established with their black neighbours in the republics. The white population of the British colonies and Boer republics in 1865 stood at 265,000. By 1900 that figure had quadrupled to 1,100,000 with the influx of miners and other settlers.[1] Greed and imperial ambition led to the Anglo-Boer War (1899–1902), which devastated the country and left control in white hands. Britain provided £3 million for reconstruction, while Chinese miners were briefly introduced to get the mines on their feet. Once the Union of South Africa was brought into being in 1910, former Boer War generals were running the government. This was the situation the troops were met with when they returned home following the First World War. The interwar period was one of rapid growth in manufacturing, despite the setbacks experienced during the global depression of the 1920s.[2]

At the same time, many white farmers found it impossible to succeed in agriculture following the devastation of the Boer War, droughts and animal diseases, and flocked to the towns and cities. By the 1920s the urban areas were awash with impoverished people of all races, competing for scarce jobs. Racist 'civilized labour' policies were introduced to reserve the best work for whites, entrenching white privilege. Wage differentials between races, already substantial, widened still further.

Despite these measures, white poverty was not eradicated. In 1932 a Commission identified as many as 300,000 'poor whites' out of a total white population of 1.5 million.[3] Most of the poor were Afrikaners, and steps were taken to build Afrikaner businesses to compete with those of English-speaking whites. Some were group enterprises, designed to further the Afrikaner cause. These included the insurance company Sanlam, the Volkskas bank and the funeral company AVBOB. The government also recognised that it was necessary to create jobs by encouraging the expansion of secondary industry. This policy was accompanied by strong state support for, and ownership of, various industries. The railways were taken into state ownership, and this was followed in 1923 by the establishment of a range of state-owned enterprises. The Electricity Supply Commission (Eskom) was established in 1923, and the Iron and Steel Corporation (Iscor) in 1928.[4] In the ten years from 1938/9 to 1948/9 the Afrikaner share of commerce soared from 8 per cent to 25 per cent of the economy.[5] Their share of manufacturing doubled, from 3 per cent to 6 per cent. Only mining remained a truly English-speaking preserve. By the time the National Party won political power in 1948, Afrikaners were as much a nation of shopkeepers as of farmers.

By the Second World War, South Africa had a substantial industrial and manufacturing sector to add to its mines and agriculture. Many of the English left to fight in the war, leaving vacancies which were filled by Afrikaners and black Africans who were drawn into the towns. The economy—freed from international competition—prospered.

This was a period of expanding opportunities and rising wages. 'Manufacturers responded vigorously to the opportunities created by wartime shortages of imported products, and to new demand made by South Africa's war effort.'[6] The volume of output doubled. With the war over, growth continued. The 1950s and 1960s were periods of rapid diversification away from the mining sector, but at the same time the gold mines of the Orange Free State were developed, adding to the strength of the economy. The new mines created surplus capital which could be invested outside of mining.[7] This went into industries allied to mining, but also into import substitution. African Explosives and Chemical Industries (AE&CI), established in 1924, was a case in point:

> In the 1950s AE&CI began to extend its output from explosives for mining to a wide range of products required by other sectors, including nitrogenous fertilizers, plastic material such as polyethylene and PVC, synthetic fibres (nylon) and many industrial chemicals. By the

end of the 1960s it was one of the largest industrial concerns in the country ... and had a total labour force of 15,000.[8]

The government also used tariffs and import restrictions to build the manufacturing sector. The same was true of the motor industry, which required a gradually increasing quantity of 'local content' for cars. By 1969 this programme set the local content level at 66 per cent, to be reached by 1976. As a result, employment in private manufacturing more than doubled, from 440,000 in 1948 to 1,160,000 in 1971.[9] The decade was a period of sustained growth: the economy grew at an average annual rate of close to 4 per cent throughout the 1970s.[10]

The strategy was an economic success, but it had two fatal flaws. Firstly, the economic programmes were predicated on apartheid, and were therefore vulnerable to political upheaval. Initially they served the immediate interests of business well, by keeping the pay of Africans at a bare subsistence minimum. The power of black unions allied to the ANC had been broken in the 1960s, and strikes and protests had been suppressed. By 1973, wages were so low that the black population was close to breaking point. Adam Raphael, the *Guardian*'s South Africa correspondent, published a story that shocked British opinion. Headlined 'British Firms Pay Africans Starvation Rate', it named the companies involved.[11] Its publication coincided with an upsurge in strikes, particularly in the Durban area, which—over time—precipitated the rebirth of the trade union movement. This was followed in 1976 by the Soweto student uprising. Many children were killed, and, although suppressed, the uprising marked the revival of public resistance to apartheid. With the union movement growing and civic societies and local movements on the rise, black people found a voice and an influence they had lacked since the early 1960s. Protests rocked the country; while this would ultimately help to bring apartheid to its knees, it also brought uncertainty. 'The lengthy and substantial confrontation was to set a precedent for political struggle over the next eighteen years, and it had an immediate effect on confidence in the economy.'[12] This resulted in a deterioration of economic conditions and declining growth.

International campaigns exposed the realities of apartheid. Over time, South Africa's access to the international capital markets on which its sophisticated economy relied was restricted. In July 1985, Chase Manhattan Bank provoked a crisis of confidence when it stopped rolling over loans to South African borrowers. 'We felt the risk attached to political unrest and economic instability became too high for our investors,' the bank explained. 'We decided to withdraw.'[13] Other banks followed, leaving South Africa seriously compromised: two-thirds of the country's $24 billion foreign debts were in short-term loans. In August 1986, the US Congress enacted a Comprehensive Anti-Apartheid Act, instituting a comprehensive programme of sanctions.[14] The writing was on the wall.

Secondly, and perhaps less obviously, apartheid prevented the development of a mass market. Most South Africans were too poor to purchase the goods they made. Without a mass market (and the accompanying economies of scale), manufacturing was incapable of competing with cheap imports from the Far East. The economic historian Charles Feinstein concludes that by the 1970s the high-water mark of industrialisation had been reached:

> Little further scope remained for light industries to displace imports, while comparable displacement of more complex intermediate and capital goods was severely constrained by several factors, including the small scale of South Africa's domestic market, the lack of necessary skills and technological capabilities, and the inability to raise protection of these industries sufficiently to displace imports without doing great damage to other domestic industries. The desperate poverty of the black urban population also effectively closed off another possibility touted by some: 'inward industrialization'.[15]

This view was echoed by a Harvard University study which compared Malaysian growth with South African decline. While the Malaysians have managed to expand and develop their manufacturing, South Africa has actually suffered de-industrialisation. It was a sorry tale indeed.[16]

Growth—which had appeared so promising in the post-war period—simply petered out. From the position of a world leader, South Africa sank to the bottom of the global growth league. Table 3 reveals the declining growth in gross domestic product per capita at constant prices—in other words, the increasing value of the economy per person, taking inflation into account.[17]

Table 3: Growth in GDP per capita at constant prices

	1913–50	*1950–73*	*1973–94*
South Africa	1.3%	2.2%	−0.6%
The rest of Africa	0.6%	2.0%	0.8%
Asia, not Japan	0.0%	3.5%	4.3%
World	0.5%	4.0%	2.0%

South Africans were becoming poorer year by year, at a time when the rest of the world was achieving positive growth. Even other African countries—long derided by South Africans as competitors—were beginning to perform more effectively. Capital began flowing out of the country, searching for more lucrative and secure markets. As the end of apartheid began to look inevitable, many in the business and political elite scrambled to deposit their funds abroad. The security services facilitated this process, engaging in corruption of their own.

The ANC takes charge

The economy that the ANC inherited in 1994 had both strengths and weaknesses. On one hand, South Africa had by far the largest, most developed and sophisticated economy in Africa. Visitors touching down in Johannesburg regularly commented that they could have arrived in an American or European city. Complex motorways moved commuters seamlessly from plush suburbs to the city centre, while modern factories churned out a vast array of products. Electricity pylons spanned the landscape, while immaculate rows of maize stretched as far as the eye could see. The mines were world class, producing minerals that the global economy relied upon. There was a relatively strong currency. This stood at R3.50 to the US dollar in 1994 (it had fallen to R13.84 to the dollar by January 2019). The state-owned enterprises functioned well, and there was a diversified manufacturing sector.

Yet on the edges of towns and in the 'homelands' (far from the eyes of most visitors), black families scraped a living together in conditions of dire poverty. Deprived of electricity, sanitation, clean water and modern homes, they were a world away from the majority of their white counterparts. South Africa was among the most unequal countries in the world.

The implicit 'deal' that the ANC had struck during the lengthy negotiations with the National Party government was simple, but never openly stated. The black population would—finally—be given full democratic rights. In return, the white population, having lost its political monopoly, would retain its wealth. The majority were left with the polity, while the minority controlled the economy. In part, this was the result of what happened when the Portuguese left Mozambique and Angola. Their abrupt departure for their homeland had seen the colonisers conduct a scorched-earth policy: lift wells of incomplete buildings were filled with cement; even lightbulbs were removed from their sockets. The ANC was determined not to replicate this by provoking a white flight. The skills and capital of the white population were considered too valuable to the success of the economy. Without them, there would be insufficient resources to address the plight of the impoverished masses. It was a tough bargain, which was implicitly concluded.

The urgency of this deal was driven by the outflow of capital. South Africa had been haemorrhaging capital at the rate of $2 billion a year by the time President F. W. de Klerk came to power in 1989.[18] Some of this was the result of rampant larceny and corruption, as government and business elites squirrelled away as much money as they could possibly hide abroad before majority rule came about. Their fear was that the ANC might seize or nationalise assets of individuals or companies. Some R50 billion was reportedly spent on secret accounts to evade an arms embargo imposed by the UN.[19] If this outflow was to be staunched, international and local investors had to be reassured.

Derek Keys—de Klerk's finance minister—briefed the ANC team once negotiations to end apartheid got under way. Keys provided Trevor Manuel, the head of the ANC's economic team, with an unsparing assessment of the situation. Manuel in turn briefed Mandela. 'And I got frightened,' Mandela later recalled. '[I]t appears to me that if we allow the situation to continue ... the economy is going to be so destroyed that when a democratic government comes into power, it will not be able to solve it.'[20] The deadlock in the negotiations was broken and a deal was reached. This was further cemented when Mandela—by this time president-in-waiting—attended the World Economic Forum in Davos in 1992. Although the ANC had long called for radical economic measures, including nationalisation, these were abandoned in the face of concerted pressure from the international business community. As Mandela then argued: 'The business community worldwide is not going to have any truck with a government that wants to nationalize; it's a reality. Do you want to fly in the face of this reality? You can't do it.'[21] Radical reform was put on hold; in its place, the ANC instituted Black Economic Empowerment.

THE ECONOMY

Radical reforms replaced by 'empowerment'

There can be little argument that the status quo in 1994 was completely unacceptable. Black men and women occupied fewer than 3 per cent of management positions, while owning less than 1 per cent of the shares on the Johannesburg Stock Exchange.[22] A programme of 'Black Economic Empowerment' (BEE) was initiated. It was designed to address this issue by requiring all businesses (except the very smallest) to comply with a complex system of black participation. This ranged from ownership and management to training and procurement policies. Points were awarded depending on whether these targets had been met in relation to 'previously disadvantaged groups'. This, of course, required that South Africa preserve its notorious system of racial classification, since without it there would be no way of deciding whether a target was being achieved. The population continues to be grouped into African, white, Coloured and Asian.

The result of Black Economic Empowerment was unsurprising and predictable. It did indeed expand black ownership and management. There was a rush to do deals with approved black candidates. As the social scientist Roger Southall concluded:

> by 2002 BEE companies' ownership of the petroleum industry had increased to 14 per cent from 5.5 per cent two years earlier; the major mining firms have all struck alliances with emergent black companies; and over the last couple of years, in one of the largest BEE deals so far, Standard Bank has announced its sale of 10 per cent of its shares to black partners (40 per cent of these going to a consortium led by tycoons Saki Macozoma and Cyril Ramaphosa), while the purchase of 50.1 per cent of the shares of ABSA Bank by Barclays (UK) would directly involve the Batho Bonke consortium led by Tokyo Sexwale and, indirectly, the Ubunthu-Batho consortium, led by Patrice Motsepe.[23]

With so few black businessmen and women available as partners, there was a rush to strike deals with 'appropriate' and politically connected partners. Some black leaders associated with the ANC became very rich indeed. Among them was none other than current president, Ramaphosa:

> Cyril Ramaphosa, former ANC General-Secretary, is executive chairman of the Shanduka Group (previously Millennium Consolidated Investments), which is largely funded by Old Mutual. Although he recently lost control of (what was left of) Johnnic, he has strong connections with First National Bank and Investec as well as Anglo-American/De Beers, and serves on the boards of SABMiller, Macsteel, Alexander Forbes (pensions) and Standard Bank.[24]

Ramaphosa benefited enormously, becoming one of Africa's richest businessmen.

A narrow black elite emerged, which was soon living in suburbs previously reserved for whites. Their ties with fellow black citizens became remote. This naturally failed to satisfy most of those classified as 'previously disadvantaged', and the ANC set about altering its policies. In 2007, in an attempt to broaden the appeal of Black Economic Empowerment, the government initiated 'Broad-Based Black Economic Empowerment'. These polices have been tweaked several times since their implementation. Despite some successes, their critics continue to maintain that the policies have failed to do more than slightly enlarge the black middle class that emerged post-apartheid. The majority of African people were left impoverished and with little prospect of climbing aboard this departing train. In 2010, *The Economist* concluded that:

> Largely as a result of the emergence of this new BEE elite, post-apartheid South Africa is still one of the most unequal countries in the world. Although poverty has been alleviated by providing welfare benefits to more than one in four of South Africa's 49m inhabitants, the gulf between rich and poor has widened. The richest 4% of

South Africans—a quarter of whom are black—now earn more than $80,000 a year, 100 times what most of their compatriots live on.[25]

The then president Jacob Zuma acknowledged that BEE had resulted mainly in 'a few individuals benefiting a lot'. He might have added that this included many among his own family. Even if the ANC's policies had achieved a measure of redistribution, there was the question of what they had done for the economy. Here the outcome was more contested, since some of the black men and women who were put into positions of authority did not have adequate skills or expertise to contribute. Their progress was often the result of their political rather than their business acumen. Some of those who took up their new roles were soon floundering. A class of consultants emerged offering bespoke advice to new black appointees (and were dubbed 'whisperers'). Moeletsi Mbeki, analyst and brother of the former president Thabo Mbeki, claimed that BEE had struck a 'fatal blow against the emergence of black entrepreneurship by creating a small class of unproductive but wealthy black crony capitalists'.[26]

Another consequence of the black empowerment policy of the ANC was that young white South Africans were deprived of the right to win senior positions in many sectors of society. Many white professionals, as well as Indians and Coloureds, decided that they had little future at home and set off for Sydney, New York and London. A range of talented, well-educated young people has been lost to the country.

Failing to thrive

Perhaps the most worrying element of the ANC's quarter of a century in power has been the lack of economic growth. While there was a brief period (2004–2007) when growth per person was at or above 3 per cent a year, this was the exception rather than the rule.

TAble 4 shows the growth per capita in South Africa since 1994:[27]

Table 4: growth per capita in South Africa, 1994–2017

Year	GDP per capita
1994	0.9
1995	1.0
1996	2.3
1997	0.9
1998	−1.1
1999	0.8
2000	2.6
2001	1.3
2002	2.3
2003	1.6
2004	3.3
2005	4.0
2006	4.4
2007	4.3
2008	2.1
2009	−2.6
2010	1.8
2011	1.9
2012	0.8
2013	1.0
2014	0.3
2015	−0.1
2016	−1.0
2017	0.1

There are many reasons for this lack of success, but it is partly because the ruling party failed to stick with and implement the policies that it came up with. The Reconstruction and

Development Programme (which was part of the ANC's platform in the 1994 election) was ditched in favour of Growth, Employment and Redistribution (GEAR) in 1996 and then replaced in 2005 by the Accelerated and Shared Growth Initiative for South Africa (ASGISA) and finally in 2013 by the National Development Plan (NDP). None has been implemented effectively. Policy changed as presidents came and went, but this resulted only in increased uncertainty.

The cost of this failure to thrive has been paid for by the poorest in society, who have faced increasing levels of unemployment. Officially one in four people in the economically active population have no work; if this definition is widened to include those who have given up looking, the total is over one person in three.[28] These figures are grim indeed. Young people—particularly young black men and women—face a future in which there is little prospect of the kind of well-paid, interesting work that they hope for. The social issues, crime and violent conflicts that have bedevilled the country can, on the whole, be traced back to this single source. There are only limited prospects for future improvement.

In 2007 Miriam Altman, Executive Director of the government's Human Sciences Research Council, published extensive research in which she showed that only if South Africa managed to break out of its low growth and achieved 6 per cent growth until 2024 would unemployment be halved.[29] Even then, a third of the population would live in poverty. 'I was shocked because I thought if you halved unemployment, you would halve poverty,' she commented. The report found that even if unemployment were halved to 13 per cent, 35 per cent of the population might still live below the poverty line. 'Poverty is something that we are likely to see in South Africa for many generations,' said Altman. 'We have to stop thinking about social grants as a short-term solution, even if unemployment fell dramatically.' Sadly, the target of 6 per cent growth has proved illusory. Since 2007 it has never been met. Indeed, since 2014 growth has not even hit 2 per cent.[30] South Africans are failing to escape from the low growth, high unemployment scenario Altman discussed in 2007. The economy has not even performed as well as her worst case low growth scenario predicted.

South Africa's unemployment problem is essentially an ANC problem: a result of past policies and practices. Professor Vimal Ranchhod of the University of Stellenbosch summed up the issue: 'Investors are wary of risks. This includes threats to property rights, social and political instability, and perceived levels of corruption. If people are not willing to invest in a country, it is almost impossible to generate new jobs.'[31]

State capture

Violence and crime have also dissuaded investors. So too has rampant corruption, which has so bedevilled the country that sections of the elite associated with the ANC and President Zuma in particular are said to have engaged in what has been termed 'state capture'.[32] This became so pervasive because, in the view of the former ANC finance minister Pravin Gordhan, the party had lost sight of the ethos that inspired its fight against apartheid. 'State Capture and corruption are consequences of the unleashing of the worst-human instincts—self-enrichment, neglect of the higher mission, placing one's self-interest before the community's interests.' It was, in Gordhan's view, an ethos that pervaded the Zuma presidency. He had witnessed events in which members of the government were 'misled, lied to, manipulated and abused'.[33] Government corruption is currently the subject of an official investigation—the Zondo commission.[34]

The term 'State Capture' was officially used by Thuli Madonsela, the Public Protector—a position established under the Constitution to review the behaviour of government. Her lengthy report found that the president and his associates had engaged in a raft of improper and possibly corrupt practices. So severe were these practices that they amounted to controlling state institutions, including the appointment and dismissal of cabinet ministers. The combined effect of these illicit activities was summed up in a report by some of the country's top academics, published in May 2017. 'While corruption is widespread at all levels of development, state capture is a far greater, systemic threat. It is akin to a silent coup and must, therefore, be understood as a political project that is given a cover of legitimacy by the vision of radical economic transformation.'[35] A number of foreign companies were associated with state capture, including KPMG and McKinsey as well as the British public relations company Bell Pottinger, which collapsed after its role was revealed.[36]

An associated issue is the mismanagement of the parastatal sector by political placemen and placewomen who have been 'deployed' by the ANC to run it. This encompasses organisations like Eskom, which controls the critical electricity supply sector. Financial services company Standard and Poor's has warned that Eskom risks defaulting on its debts.[37] In an attempt to grapple with the issue, President Ramaphosa has ordered that Eskom be split into three state-owned entities dealing with generation, transmission and distribution.[38] Speaking during his State of the Nation speech, the president said that this would be done without burdening the government with unmanageable debt. However, this will be difficult to achieve given that Eskom is deep in a financial and operational crisis, with a debt burden of R419bn which it is unable to service from the revenue it earns. It is also struggling to maintain its power supply, with repeated breakdowns of its aging plant and neglected maintenance.

The state-run airline, South African Airways, which has not generated a profit since 2011, is regularly cited by ratings agencies as a drain on the government purse and has already received state guarantees totalling nearly R20 billion ($1.6 billion).[39] So severe is its financial situation that finance minister Tito Mboweni called for radical measures in November 2018. The airline is 'lossmaking,' he declared: 'it's unlikely to sort out the situation, in my view we should close it down.'[40] Similarly, Gordhan estimated that a plan to build Russian nuclear power stations capable of generating 9.6GW of electricity, which President Zuma attempted to promote, was so costly that it would have bankrupted the country.[41] The R1 trillion ($71 billion) estimated cost of the nuclear deal was, said Gordhan, equal to South Africa's entire annual expenditure budget and completely beyond the country's financial capacity. The reluctance of two finance ministers to sign off on the mega-deal—Gordhan and Nhlanhla Nene—played a role in getting them fired.

Perhaps the most worrying issue is that South Africa has plucked all of its low-hanging fruit. The minerals sector has been thoroughly prospected: there is unlikely to be a major new discovery. Indeed, the existing mines are mostly aging and employment is falling. The primary industries have all been developed, whether they are breweries or textile firms. Commercial agriculture is at peak production: there is no new land to open up. While the country still benefits from all of these industries, plus a vibrant tourist sector, there are limited opportunities for new developments. To break into new areas would require a highly skilled, self-motivated workforce that could innovate and discover entirely new spheres of production or industry. South Africa does have young men and women who could do this, but they do not exist in the numbers that are so prevalent across Asia, as well as parts of Europe or the USA. South Africans have spent the last quarter of a century bickering over how to divide up the existing economy; they have failed to grow it.

One of the key factors inhibiting the South African economy has been the low growth rate of small- and medium-sized businesses, despite many attempts by government and non-governmental organisations to remedy this. It is growth in this sector that has provided employment in similar economies. As the World Bank pointed out, the share of small-scale firms in South Africa is estimated to be between 45 and 50 per cent of GDP, while they contribute more than 60 per cent in other low-income countries and 70 per cent in middle-income countries.[42] It is perhaps this failure to sufficiently develop these smaller enterprises, and the reliance on large-scale businesses, that explains the other phenomenon underlined by the World Bank: the fact that income and wealth inequality in South Africa is not just the worst in the world, but has increased since the ANC took power. Perhaps the only ameliorating factor has been the growth in social security payments, which have been a major source of income for the poor—particularly in rural areas. As the World Bank observes: 'In rural areas, income from grants was by far the largest contributor to reducing the poverty gap. Sixty nine percent of the decline in rural poverty gap can be explained by income from grants alone.'[43]

In the end, responsibility for the 'failure to thrive' must be laid at the door of the ANC. Its constant attacks on whites and on the businesses that they run have undermined confidence. The party's use of Marxist rhetoric and its talk of expropriation of land without compensation has done nothing to give investors (local and international) much confidence. The decade-long lack of clarity over mining that resulted from attempts to introduce a new mining charter has had the same effect. As a result, companies have simply refused to make investment decisions. This is the conclusion of the University of Johannesburg's Centre for Competition, Regulation and Economic Development:

> South African companies are accumulating reserves and not investing in the economy while acquisition-led growth has increased concentration and led to anticompetitive behaviour ... Cash reserves in the

JSE's largest 50 companies had increased from R242bn to R1.4-trillion ($95 billion) between 2005 and 2016, said Thando Vilakazi, senior economist at the centre.[44]

Prospects for growth

There are some signs that the ANC under Cyril Ramaphosa has begun to root out these issues to encourage the country's growth. He has slowly levered key Zuma associates out of positions of power and influence. These include the Commissioner of the South African Revenue Service and the National Director of Public Prosecutions. There has been a clamour for the president to act more swiftly and more radically, but his tenuous hold on the ANC leadership makes this difficult. President Ramaphosa claims that his reforms, along with an appeal to companies to invest in the country, are paying dividends. In October 2018, he announced that an investments summit had received pledges of more than $100 billion over the next five years.[45] How much of this actually materialises remains to be seen. Although the president says that there has been a 'new dawn' for South Africa, he also admits that the country has been through what he described as a 'very dark period of our recent history'.[46] The cost of populist economic decisions, together with the rampant corruption tolerated by the government, is being borne by the poorest—whether they are the urban unemployed or the impoverished citizens stranded in rural areas.

Looking ahead, the prospects are improving. According to Goldman Sachs, it is anticipated that the economy will grow by 1.7 per cent in 2019.[47] This would be a considerable improvement on the 0.8 per cent achieved in 2018, but old problems remain. The World Bank's prognosis for South Africa highlights these issues.[48] Its Economic Update, published in April 2018, shows that, far from improving, inequalities in wealth have increased in recent years. Perhaps the most optimistic finding was that this is less associated with race than it was previously (although race is still a critical factor). The World Bank points out that at present the country is trapped (or 'constrained', as it puts it more politely), by what the Bank calls South Africa's 'low growth potential'. 'Slow private investment growth and weak integration into global value chains prevent the country from reaping the new economic opportunities emerging around the globe, and from catching up with living standards in peer economies,' observes the Bank.[49]

To achieve economic growth will require three things—a skilled workforce (which the country's education system is failing to provide in sufficient numbers) the certainty that will encourage domestic and international investments (which is currently undermined by the ANC's talk of seizure of land without compensation and its equivocation over mining rights) and an attack on the endemic corruption.

As the World Bank points out: 'To reduce such uncertainty—which remains detrimental to private investment and innovation—requires consensus on sustainable interventions to effectively and equitably redistribute assets.'[50] One of the few potentially positive developments has been the discovery (after years of exploration) of a major offshore oil and gas deposit. The find was announced by the French company Total at the 'Brulpadda' (Bullfrog) well, 175 kilometres off the coast, which is said to hold 1 billion barrels of oil.[51] The discovery 'is potentially a major boost for the economy,' minerals minister Gwede Mantashe said. 'We welcome it as we continue to seek investment.' While no doubt a boost for South Africa, the experience of other African oil-extracting countries is salutary: it can produce major distortions of the economy and increase corruption. The handling of oil revenues when production begins in around eight years' time will be a challenge.

In the end, it is political uncertainty and lack of consensus, combined with a failed educational system and corruption, that has left South Africa trapped in a vicious cycle of low growth, low wages and high unemployment. This has—inevitably—led to violent protests and high rates of crime. Escaping from this downward spiral will be no easy task. Simply servicing the country's debts costs the government R500 million ($35 million) *a day*.[52] Cyril Ramaphosa needs to return the country to the positive direction of travel and the political consensus that was so prevalent during the early years following the end of apartheid. What is required is the renewal of the Rainbow Nation over which Mandela presided, with hope, optimism and a willingness for South Africans to share and learn from each other. This is as essential to the country's economic wellbeing as it is to its political health.

7

LAND AND AGRICULTURE

THE THORNIEST TOPICS

You don't have to travel very far south of Johannesburg to come across fields of maize (or corn, as it's called in the United States). Immaculate rows stretch as far as the eye can see. Not many kilometres from Durban, the hills give way to a sea of green, carpeted with sugar cane. Drive out of Cape Town and the suburbs soon merge into vineyards, each tended and cared for as carefully as any on the slopes of Bordeaux. This is South African agriculture at its best.

Its contribution to the economy is considerable. The country exports everything from oranges, wine, table grapes and apples to nuts, maize, wool, and mohair. Together, these made up 12 per cent of South Africa's total export earnings in 2016, with a value of $9.2 billion.[1] Agriculture provides employment for around 800,000 people—not an inconsiderable figure in a country where one in three adults is unemployed.[2] No one doubts that its farms and farmers play a vital role, feeding people and sending products around the world. Yet the sector is now caught up in the most vitriolic controversy about equity and heritage. To put it simply, the allegation is that the best land was stolen and the wealth that the farms now generate has been illegitimately appropriated by the white minority.

It is not difficult to see why. For every lush vineyard around Stellenbosch there are desolate acres of land in the Eastern Cape. The landscape around the village of Qunu, in which Nelson Mandela grew up, is very different. There is little farming to be seen, beyond a handful of goats or cattle, and small plots of vegetables or maize. Like much of the territory that was once designated as black reserves or 'homelands', people live mainly on the remittances sent from relatives in the cities, social security grants, or meagre pensions. One in three South Africans live in the former homelands—a total of 17 million people.[3] Agriculture supplements their income, but it is mostly for subsistence. Fruit and vegetables are sold by the side of the road or in markets, but this makes little dent on the total agricultural output of the country.

This disparity between black and white farmers didn't just happen: it was the direct result of government policy. In the nineteenth century, Africans proved themselves to be first rate farmers and quite capable of supplying the emerging market in the towns and on the mines. It was the restrictions placed upon them and the dispossession of land that produced the current situation. Today there is intense poverty in these rural areas, as well as in many of the shanty towns or 'informal settlements' that ring the cities. It is poverty and a burning sense of injustice that have fuelled demands for land redistribution.

There are few issues more difficult or more pressing for South Africa than land. More difficult because it involves competing historic and contemporary claims; more pressing because attempts to resolve the land question have so far failed.

LAND AND AGRICULTURE

The politics of land

Land redistribution has been driven by Julius Malema's Economic Freedom Fighters. 'It's a completely new generation running out of patience,' declared Malema. He claims the populist rhetoric of his party and its pressure on the ANC have changed the political climate. 'The EFF said to our people—the most practical way to get the land is to occupy the unoccupied land to put pressure on the state, and it has worked,' he explained. 'Now the state and the owners of the land are beginning to say "maybe we should do something".'[4] The EFF policy is clear: all land should be expropriated without compensation and transferred to the state, which will then grant twenty-five-year licences to farmers.[5] The party, which won only 8 per cent of the votes in the 2016 local elections, hopes to make a major breakthrough in the 2019 general election by tapping into the frustration of young and unemployed South Africans. Experts warn that if the EFF's demands are to be addressed there will have to be a complete transformation of the patterns of land holding.[6] Professor Ben Cousins, of the University of the Western Cape, said:

> I think that the agricultural industry does not fully appreciate the significance of the scale issue. At least 60% of commercial farmland will have to be distributed, otherwise the destructive forms of populism, as embodied in the EFF, will take hold amongst the unemployed youth of the country.

The ANC has been struggling to find an appropriate response to the EFF's populism. In December 2017, the party resolved at its national elective conference to adopt the policy of expropriating land without compensation.[7] Then, in February 2018, they decided to support an EFF motion to expropriate without compensation in Parliament. At first it looked as if this would be followed by steps to amend the Constitution, but this was dropped. Instead, the ANC said it would use provisions in Section

25 of the current Constitution to pursue the policy. In August 2018, President Ramaphosa laid this out in a televised address:

> On land reform, the ANC applauds our people, from all walks of life—including the rural poor, farm labourers, the unemployed, the landless, urban residents, farmers and traditional leaders—for expressing their views on this critical matter. Our people have been expressing their views on the land question openly and without any fear or favour. They have been putting forward solutions on how the land question can be resolved. This is the constitutional democracy that we fought for.

> The ANC reaffirms its position that the Constitution is a mandate for radical transformation both of society and the economy. A proper reading of the Constitution on the property clause enables the state to effect expropriation of land with just and equitable compensation and also expropriation without compensation in the public interest. It has become patently clear that our people want the Constitution to be more explicit about expropriation of land without compensation, as demonstrated in the public hearings.[8]

The ANC is not alone in resisting attempts to change the Constitution. Its powerful trade union ally Cosatu has also rejected this option, and says it is willing to tackle populist rhetoric, particularly after the EFF called on 'progressive' union members to leave the union movement.[9] 'We will fight race hustlers like the EFF and their race-baiting tendencies, the same way we fight arrogant and entitled white supremacists,' Cosatu declared.

The ANC's decision represented, of course, only the bare bones of a policy, but it was enough to spook the markets. The rand fell in value by sixteen cents in an hour.[10] Unsurprisingly, the value of land has dropped by nearly a third.[11] In an attempt to reassure local and international investors, the president gave a lengthy interview to the *Financial Times*. 'This is no land grab; nor is it an assault on the private ownership of property,' he told the London paper. 'The ANC has been clear that its land reform programme should not undermine future investment in the economy or damage agricultural production and food security. The proposals will not erode property rights, but will instead ensure that the rights of all South Africans, and not just those who currently own land, are strengthened.' He went on to assure readers that his government was not going down the path trodden by Zimbabwe. 'South Africa has learnt from the experiences of other countries, both from what has worked and what has not, and will not make the same mistakes that others have made.'[12]

Like most performances by President Ramaphosa it was assured and well-judged, but exactly how he will balance the concerns of the poor with the need to avoid damaging the farming sector is hard to see.

The scale of the problem

There is no doubt that land and farms are not equitably distributed among the country's population groups. In his *Financial Times* interview, the president gave these figures for agricultural land ownership by race: '72% of farms and agricultural holdings are owned by whites, 15% by coloured citizens, 5% by Indians, and 4% by Africans.'

While no one doubts that land is not equally shared, these figures have been challenged. At the end of apartheid in 1994, it was often said that 87 per cent of all land was owned by whites.[13] This assumed that the giant nature reserves were 'white'. Their scale is huge: the Kruger National Park alone is the size of Wales. It also excluded the black 'homelands' or African reserves, which were not considered part of South Africa by the apartheid government. If these, and other parts of the country owned by the state, are included in the calculation then the picture looks very different. One analysis suggests that 42.7 per cent of all land is controlled by the state—a huge figure, which would appear to allow the government to remedy much of the inequality without expropriation.[14]

Another obvious point is that not all land is of equal value. Anyone who has flown over the country will see vast portions of west and central South Africa that are semi-desert. Giant farms dominate this landscape, rearing no more than a few head of sheep per hectare, or else acting as game farms. Transferring a few dozen of these farms from white to African ownership would make a considerable difference to the percentages of land held by each respective racial group. There are few advocates for such a solution.

In reality these are quibbles—even if they are important. There is a burning sense of injustice that goes back for generations. The black African population was dispossessed of the land of its forefathers, and not in the dim and distant past. In 1913 the Land Act was passed, which forbade Africans from owning, or even renting, land outside of the designated reserves that made up 13 per cent of the country. It was only the latest episode in a long history of dispossession, but it made an indelible mark. Who can forget Sol Plaatje's famous lament, with which he opens his political tract *Native Life in South Africa*? 'Awaking on Friday morning, June 20, 1913, the South African native found himself, not actually a slave, but a pariah in the land of his birth.'[15] Dispossession continued throughout the intervening years, and was intensified under apartheid. The path-breaking Surplus People Project of the 1980s found that in the twenty-three years up to 1983 a total of 3.5 million people had been forcibly removed from 'white' areas.[16]

One question that has come up is whether land removed by colonial conquest prior to 1913 should be included in the restitution process. Again, there is no easy answer. Some farms have been in white hands for almost as long as colonisation itself. Simon van der Stel was granted the estate of Groot Constantia, on the outskirts of Cape Town, in 1685. Ironically, van der Stel would have been considered 'coloured' under apartheid: he was descended from Monica van Goa, a former slave of Indian descent.[17] Can it be argued that claims for land should go back more than three centuries? Land conquest was also not restricted to whites. Some two thousand years ago the Bantu peoples arrived in southern Africa, forcing its first peoples, the Khoi-san, out of the vast majority of the country. In the period 1815–40, the Zulu nation drove vast numbers of Africans from their traditional lands, and killed something like a million people in brutal wars of conquest known as the *Mfecane*. Should land restitution attempt to correct these injustices? These are legitimate issues, and finding a means of redressing past wrongs is very complex indeed.

Since it came to power, the ANC has gone a long way towards resolving the claims brought before it. A Restitution of Land Rights Act was passed in 1994, and since then the Commission on the Restitution of Land Rights has been processing and investigating restitution claims. It has done this either by restoring land or by making payments described as 'equitable redress'. Since it came into being, the Commission has approved 76,023 of the 79,696 claims that were filed with it.[18] It has made payments of R22.9 billion. Just 3,673 claims are still being investigated. This task is coming to an end, although the process has slowed to a crawl. Just thirty-three land claims were settled in the year 2009–10, with a 'huge budget deficit' blamed for the lack of progress.[19] The ANC set a target for the entire land reform programme (restitution, tenure reform, redistribution) to transfer 30 per cent of white-owned land within five years.[20] When it became clear that this could not be achieved, the target date was extended to 2014.

While the state has been attempting to redistribute land, there has been another, more subtle process going on. Frans Cronje, of the liberal South African Institute of Race Relations, pointed out as early as 2011 that Africans, Coloureds and Indians have been buying into the agricultural sector, and this has changed the balance of land holdings:

> Africans probably now own close to 20% if one adds in an estimated 2-million hectares purchased on the open market and 6-million transferred by the state through various land reform and restitution processes. The state owns possibly 25% of the country. That slice was previously part of the white 87%. It should now be subtracted from the white share and added to the black share, which pushes the latter up to about 45%. Add in coloured and Indian ownership, which some people estimate at a high 10%, and the total black slice rises to about 55%.[21]

So many attempted reforms have failed

The attempt to redistribute land has been a sorry saga of failure. The ANC has itself admitted that most efforts have not succeeded. There is evidence that the majority of Africans do not really want land itself at all; instead, land is seen as a means of escaping poverty. Given the choice of taking land or cash, 92 per cent opted for financial compensation.[22] This sad fact was revealed by the minister of rural development and land reform, Gugile Nkwinti. It is not difficult to see why this is the case—or why so many farms that have been redistributed end up being abandoned, or sold back to the white farmer from whom they were initially purchased.

Most of the land redistribution schemes have required that a farm, which once provided a decent living to one white farmer, is handed over to a group of Africans. They are required to manage it as a group or collective. Few have the skills to manage such a complex task; even if they do they seldom have the cash required to run a modern agricultural enterprise. Since none owns the farm individually, they find it difficult to raise a loan from a bank to provide the capital for seed, fertiliser and equipment. Without the relevant skills, capital or expensive equipment, such redistribution is a recipe for failure. A study by the government's Human Sciences Research Council in 2003 provided heart-breaking examples from across the country of how and why the schemes failed.[23]

Edward Lahiff, who has written extensively on the subject, provides an eloquent insight into the obstacles these schemes face. He points out that these new farmers get little, if any, support once they receive their land. 'Recent studies show that land reform beneficiaries experience numerous problems accessing services such as credit, training, extension advice, transport and ploughing services, and veterinary services, as well as input and produce markets.'[24]

Even if these problems can be overcome, there is the question of getting the crop or the livestock to market. South African supermarkets are as demanding as any in the world in terms of the packaging, standards and quality assurance of the products they buy. Any first-time farmer selling to them faces immense difficulties. Attempting to export products around the world, given the mountain of paperwork and regulations, can prove impossible. Even if these obstacles are somehow surmounted, the income from the farm must support not just one family, but the dozen or more families who are its new owners. Is it any wonder that so many attempts at land redistribution have failed?

Worse still, according to Lahiff, the new farmers are required to abide by preconceived plans drawn up by the government, which have little to do with their real needs. Effectively dumped on a once-productive farm, black prospective farmers have little chance of making a go of it. Visiting areas of KwaZulu-Natal, one is struck by the number of farms that now stand idle, with weeds growing rampant where there were once tall rows of maize. Stalls for cattle are empty, while a few chickens peck the earth outside shacks and unemployed young men stand around, hoping for something to turn up. Little wonder that many of the new black farmers resorted to selling the land back to its previous white owners. According to Nkwinti, this happened to nearly a third of all farms. He said that in 2011 the government had bought about 6,000,000 hectares, of which nearly 2,000,000 hectares had been resold.[25]

There is evidence that much of the land that has been transferred now lies idle or abandoned. In 2007 the state broadcaster, the SABC, reported that seventy commercial farms in Limpopo province, which the government bought for rural communities, had collapsed. The farms, which cost the government more than R100 million to purchase, were rendered unproductive, according to the province's member of the national assembly for agriculture, Dikeledi Magadzi.[26] Magadzi said:

> We can't leave the state assets, the state money being under-utilised. When we are saying we need to halve poverty we need to create jobs, to me that is unacceptable ... What is of essence is that the national assets and the national money cannot lie fallow like we see.

The failure to produce vibrant, productive farms was put down to, among other factors, infighting and lack of good financial management.

As early as 2009, the South African *Sunday Times* began warning of the impact of reforms on agricultural output, publishing a lengthy expose entitled 'Farms collapse as land reform fails'. 'South Africa's food security is threatened by its chaotic rural land reform programme,' reported Bongani Mthethwa. 'Thousands of once-productive farms, mainly in KwaZulu-Natal, Limpopo, Mpumalanga and the Eastern Cape, lie abandoned and are causing serious shortages of staple foods. The country now imports more food than it exports and local production of grain, fruit and vegetables can no longer keep pace with the growing population.'[27]

The journalist described a two-week visit to farms around the country, during which he discovered that:

- Twenty top crop and dairy farms in the Eastern Cape, bought for R11.6 million and returned to a Kokstad community, are now informal settlements;
- A once-thriving potato farm in the KwaZulu-Natal midlands is now a makeshift soccer field;
- 10,000 people given back 8,000 hectares of prime fruit and macadamia farms in Limpopo are crippled by a R5 million debt;
- A former multimillion-rand tea estate in Magoebaskloof in Limpopo has become an overgrown forest;
- More than five tons of a macadamia nut crop on a reclaimed Limpopo farm was so poor that it was dumped into the Levubu river; and
- A R22 million irrigation system built by the government to supply water to new farmers in KwaZulu-Natal lies unused.

The article went on to quote the acting chief land claims commissioner Andrew Mphela, who claimed that it was too early to measure performance or to talk of failure. He said that, contrary to 'popular rhetoric and biased reporting from certain quarters', projects had not collapsed, but instead experienced 'challenges'. While some of the claims in the article appear exaggerated, the idea that these problems are simply 'challenges' to be overcome is difficult to sustain. Nkwinti has acknowledged publicly that past attempts at reform have been unsuccessful.[28] 'We cannot afford to go on like this,' he said. He went on to warn that if land is not used by those to whom it has been given, it will be reallocated to farmers who could run the farms productively. It was a case of 'use it or lose it'.

Land in the rural 'reserves'

A third of the population, some 17 million people, lives in the former 'homelands'—the ten areas of land designated by the apartheid government in the 1950s as separate 'ethnic' zones where black people were meant to live, enclosed by but politically separate from the rest of South Africa. Most of this group are subsistence farmers working tiny plots on communal land. They do not own the land they farm: there is no 'individual title' to the land. Rather, it is held in trust by the traditional rulers or chiefs. Exactly what rights the chiefs have and how it is exercised is a matter of fierce debate.

Academics suggest that, in reality, individuals and families do have rights to the same residential and agricultural land.[29] They negotiate access, with other families, to common property resources such as grazing, forests and water. But unlike other South Africans, they do not have absolute, private rights, which can be enforced by law, to a surveyed parcel of land to which they hold exclusive title deeds. In addition, many chiefs have used their status to exercise ruthless power. Little wonder that the former South African president Kgalema Motlanthe accused many traditional rulers of acting like 'tin-pot dictators' towards people living in their villages.[30]

Far from reining in the power of chiefs, the ANC has enhanced their status since coming to power. It is not difficult to see why: the chiefs exercise considerable influence over 'their' people, and the ANC regards them as a useful vehicle for mobilising the rural vote during elections. A series of laws has been enacted which enhance these powers. This includes the Communal Land Rights Act (subsequently struck down by the Supreme Court), which was introduced just before the general elections in 2004. This gave traditional leaders and councils wide-ranging powers, including control over the occupation, use and administration of communal land. The chiefs have also asserted their rights over minerals in the territories they control. Some, like the Bafokeng chieftaincy, secured enormous mineral royalties—ostensibly on behalf of the entire community.[31]

President Zuma went out of his way to encourage traditional rulers to assert their rights:

President Jacob Zuma told the House of Traditional Leaders on 27 February 2014 to line up their lawyers and prepare to lodge claims for land restitution. King Goodwill Zwelithini kaBhekhuzulu announced in July 2014 that he would make a large land claim ostensibly on behalf of the Zulu nation. King Zwelithini's claim will be managed by the Ingonyama Trust Board (ITB), which was the outcome of a deal between the National Party and the Inkatha Freedom Party during the dying days of apartheid. The ITB already holds close to 3 million hectares of land in KwaZulu-Natal. Through its proposed new land claim, the Trust intends to acquire much more land in KwaZulu-Natal, as well as in the Eastern Cape, Free State and Mpumalanga. In addition to King Zwelithini, traditional leaders of the Hlubi (KwaZulu-Natal) as well as the Rharhabe and Thembu (both Eastern Cape) have also stated their intentions to lodge restitution claims.[32]

As the ANC grapples with land, it has to decide whether it will challenge the power of men like King Zwelithini (unlikely), or simply delegate responsibility for rural people to the traditional rulers. There is a danger that people who live in the 'reserves' will be formally or informally treated as subjects rather than citizens.

Many rural communities are desperately poor. This is confirmed by official studies. One report that took a comprehensive look at the Eastern Cape came to this stark conclusion: 'More than a decade into our successful democracy, the Eastern Cape Province remains trapped in structural poverty that shows in all aspects of its demographic, health and socioeconomic profile ...

Poverty in the Eastern Cape Province is a national disaster.'[33] The ability to provide support to these communities is undermined by the poor state of local government, which is frequently at its least effective in rural areas. The worst-performing municipalities are almost all found in the former 'homelands'.[34]

Conclusion

In the end, the land question is just too difficult a problem to tackle with any simple set of measures, and evading disruption of the agricultural sector, a priority for the Ramaphosa government, is likely impossible. As Theo de Jager—deputy president of AgriSA, the commercial farmer's lobby group—complained to London newspaper *The Independent*, 'The basic problem is that the government has never treated land reform and agriculture as two sides of the same coin.'[35] It is clearly vital that the country continues to provide plentiful supplies of cheap food while at the same time dealing effectively with the problem of past injustice.

To try to resolve these complex issues, the Ramaphosa government went to the public in an extensive consultation. Thousands of submissions were made, and packed public meetings heard the views of local people. So much information was collected that the committee gathering the information had to appeal for an extension of its mandate.[36] The government is attempting to forge a new consensus. A task team led by former ANC secretary general Gwede Mantashe and senior Communist Party member Jeremy Cronin is drafting an amendment to a forthcoming expropriation law which also sets out clearly which land will be expropriated without compensation.[37]

The task team has begun by identifying land and property which is eligible for expropriation—unutilised land, commercial property held unproductively and purely for speculative purposes, underutilised property owned by the state, and, finally, land farmed by labour tenants with an absentee titleholder. By identifying these four types of land, the ANC is attempting to create certainty about which land will be targeted. Cronin is quoted by HuffPost as saying that the Bill of Rights and the property clause in the Constitution are not obstacles to effective land reform, either agrarian or urban. 'Expropriation with or without compensation is only one and probably not the major means to achieving just, equitable, sustainable and absolutely necessary land reform.' He added that South Africa 'needs to have a rational, constitutionally compliant and patriotic discussion on how to address the land question as part of a new dawn for all South Africans'.[38]

What this chapter indicates is not just the complexities and sensitivities surrounding land, but the almost insuperable problems of reform. Embedded within the pattern of landholding in South Africa are the injustices of past centuries. To the immense frustration of the ANC, this issue has highlighted only too clearly the limitations of the party's powers in government and its inability to tackle an issue that it has been determined to confront for generations. The party has so far been incapable of answering the Freedom Charter's call for all land to be 're-divided amongst those who work it to banish famine and land hunger', while at the same time feeding the people and maintaining a viable agricultural export sector.[39]

8

EDUCATION

THE WEAKEST LINK

You will see them across South Africa: little knots of children, happily chatting as they make their way home. Yet for many parents, buying the smart school uniforms they wear is an enormous sacrifice. For most poor families, schooling is free, but keeping up with the other demands means scrimping and saving, year after year. Families who endure this hardship do so in the hopes that their children will get a better education than they did; that this will be the pathway to a good job and a secure future. Yet generations of children are being betrayed. The education they receive, at such a cost to their families, is often appalling. The assessment of *The Economist* was brutal: 'South Africa has one of the world's worst education systems.'[1] Indeed, South Africa's schooling is arguably less satisfactory today than it was under apartheid, when 'Bantu education' was designed to keep black men and women in the worst jobs, with the fewest prospects.

As the educationalist and politician Dr Mamphela Ramphele put it, if those who fought and died for freedom in the Soweto uprising of 1976 were to return today, how would anyone explain that the education system is 'worse today than the "gutter educa-tion" the country had under the apartheid government'?[2] Nor is Ramphele alone. Rabelani Dagada, a lecturer at the Business School of the University of the Witwatersrand, said in 2013: 'After 20 years of democracy, the education levels have plunged. It's worse than the so-called Bantu Education.'[3]

In some ways, the comparison is not fair. During apartheid many children from poor families did not go to school at all; today there is compulsory universal education. The best schools of the past are being compared with average schools today. Nonetheless, the record is still a shameful indictment of the ANC's tenure in office. To many it is quite inexplicable, since it is exactly the opposite of what the ANC promised and what the ANC leaders wished for their people. So how did this tragic state of affairs come about?

The path to failure

The ANC's own history is of men and women who excelled at their studies. Sol Plaatje, the first ANC secretary general, was educated by missionaries in a remote village near Kimberley. Yet such was the excellence of the teaching of Ernst and Maria Westphal, and so eager was the young Sol to learn, that he became one of the most eloquent writers of his generation.[4] Plaatje translated Shakespeare into Setswana, and his diary of the siege of Mafeking during the Boer war is unsurpassed. Nor was he alone: editors, scholars and religious leaders supported the ANC. Many early lawyers were found in its ranks, a tradition continued by Oliver Tambo and Nelson Mandela. It is this his-tory that makes the current state of affairs so painful.

To understand why it came about, one needs to consider what education meant under apartheid. The Bantu Education Act of 1953 was one of the cornerstones of the National Party's policies.

Its provisions required the racial segregation of all educational institutions, from kindergartens to universities. Its aim for African pupils was spelled out by the architect of apartheid, Hendrik Verwoerd: 'There is no place for [the Bantu] in the European community above the level of certain forms of labour ... What is the use of teaching the Bantu child mathematics when it cannot use it in practice?'[5] Similar racially discriminatory legislation was introduced for the Coloured and Indian populations. For their children, education was not designed to enlighten and stimulate, but to subjugate and contain.

Hardly surprising, then, that the education section of the ANC's Freedom Charter of 1955 should open with the ringing declaration that 'the doors of learning and culture shall be opened'. It went on to repeat the pledge contained in the 1955 Universal Declaration of Human Rights:

- Education shall be free, compulsory, universal and equal for all children;
- Higher education and technical training shall be opened to all by means of state allowances and scholarships awarded on the basis of merit;
- Adult illiteracy shall be ended by a mass state education plan;
- Teachers shall have all the rights of other citizens;
- The colour bar in cultural life, in sport and in education shall be abolished.[6]

The Soweto uprising of 1976 was, in large part, brought about by the pent-up fury of school pupils on the outskirts of Johannesburg at the education they were receiving. It was the imposition of Afrikaans as the medium of instruction in particular subjects (a language many Johannesburg teachers didn't understand, or only spoke poorly) that was the final straw. From 16 June, for three long days, the children took on the police. Armed with automatic weapons, the police fired on the pupils.

On the first day alone, perhaps as many as 200 were killed: there is no definitive death toll.

The education that was being offered as apartheid drew to a close was highly unequal, although less so than in 1976. There was a substantial increase in spending on black education following the Soweto uprising. Nonetheless, there was still gross inequality. This was the state expenditure per child in 1993: R1,659 for Africans, R2,902 for Coloureds, R3,702 for Indians and R4,372 for whites.[7] While white children were generally taught in modern buildings in relatively small classes, many African pupils were being instructed in makeshift schools, with crowded classes and inadequate books and other resources. In rural areas and on farms, multiple classes of African children often had to share classrooms without desks, writing on slates.

To make matters worse, the teachers in many African schools were less trained and poorly rewarded. White teachers came through fully accredited universities and colleges of education, with degrees which allowed them to leave the teaching profession, if they wished to, at a later date. Africans saw teaching as one of the few ways a clever and ambitious child might escape poverty, but their education did not provide them with transferrable degrees. As one author concluded: 'Under apartheid, the black population's higher education options were effectively limited to "teaching or preaching".'[8] Sadly, this continues to be the case. 'Education remains one of the least selective faculties to gain admission to across all universities,' wrote Melanie Smuts, who worked in some of the poorest schools. 'This is partly because of teacher-shortages, partly because teachers earn less than other graduate professionals, partly due to the structures of education faculties themselves and the way that bursary schemes operate.'[9] Before the end of apartheid these conditions were even worse. Angered by their inadequate conditions and frustrated by their inability to provide their classes with an adequate education, teachers joined a range of trade unions.

The South African Democratic Teachers' Union (SADTU), founded in 1990, had a membership of 30,000 at its inception, many of whom had been members of previous unions. Allied to the ANC, it was predominantly an African organisation. Soon it became one of the party's most influential supporting organisations, since its members had the educational and organisational abilities many others lacked. By 2014, the union had a membership of around a quarter of a million. Its members were active in the ANC, forming 10 per cent of the party's 'inner core'.[10]

One of SADTU's demands to the ANC was that the party should address the issue of the school inspectorate once it was in power. African teachers loathed the inspectors, many of whom were white, Afrikaner men, who wielded apparently limitless power over the teachers. Teachers dreaded their surprise inspections; these visits, sometimes complete with abusive and racist language, were the bane of their lives. This antipathy towards the inspectorate was reflected in the ANC's education policy document, drawn up in 1994. The document observes that: 'The system of teacher appraisal has been largely inspectoral and bureaucratic ... It shared, together with all other aspects of the education bureaucracy, a top-down, closed, hierarchical and authoritarian character.' Teachers, the ANC recognised, were right to complain about their treatment; the document notes that:

One teacher union's criticisms include:

- political bias in the system, including political victimisation of teachers
- unchecked power and abuse of patronage which inspectors wield
- extended probation periods for new teachers
- incompetence
- sexual harassment, and discrimination against women promotion candidates
- 'one-off' visits, secrecy, irrelevant criteria, absence of contextual factors and arbitrariness in appraisal processes

- the difficulty of challenging the inspector's assessment
- the abuse of 'merit awards'[11]

When the ANC came to power it faced the task of reforming education. The party had a huge debt to the teachers, and to SADTU in particular. It was determined to end the powerlessness that they felt. Henceforth, they would receive training at universities (and not teacher training colleges, which left them without full degrees and stuck in the teaching profession), and the system of inspections would be transformed. Teachers would be guaranteed the right to strike and the right to union membership. While the ends were laudable and entirely understandable, the long-term consequences were disastrous.

The new government set about its task with a will. The aim was:

- The creation of a single, non-racial education dispensation wherein there is space for all participants.
- The entire overhaul and democratisation of education management.
- The upgrading and improvement of the education infrastructure.
- The transformation of curricula in order to eradicate the legacy of apartheid in the system.[12]

Outcomes-based education

Some aspects of these reforms were relatively straightforward. Ridding the syllabus of overt racism might take time, but it had to be done. After 1994, history textbooks were revised so that the worst forms of racial bias were removed, but the new government was determined to go much further. The entire orientation of education would be changed by the implementation of what was called 'Curriculum 2005'. Introduced by the then education minister, Kader Asmal, in 1997, this brought in 'Outcomes-based education'. The aims of the reforms were extraordinarily ambitious. As a report to the minister put it: 'Curriculum 2005 is probably the most significant curriculum reform in South African education of the last century. Deliberately intended to simultaneously overturn the legacy of apartheid education and catapult South Africa into the 21st Century, it was an innovation both bold and revolutionary in the magnitude of its conception.'[13]

Guidelines produced by the Department of Education in March 1997, 'Outcomes-Based Education in South Africa', declared that the new system was nothing less than a 'paradigm shift'. In the introduction to Curriculum 2005, the government stated that the system 'aims not only to increase the general knowledge of the learners, but to develop their skills, critical thinking, attitudes and understanding'. Furthermore, the Department of Education declared that 'Outcomes-based education is [a] learner-centred, results oriented design, based on the belief that all individuals can learn' and that it 'provides a richly textured learning opportunity for the learner and an enabling facilitative role for the educator since the onus for lifelong learning development rests with the learner primarily in achieving the stated outcomes'.[14]

What was Outcomes-based education, and why was it so central to these reforms? The policy was drawn from experiences abroad and from education practices in New Zealand and Australia in particular.[15] It was based on Freirean practices of adult education, which was based on the work of Paulo Freire and held that students must construct knowledge from knowledge they already possess.[16] South African trade unionists abroad had picked the concept up during the 1980s and 1990s and brought it home with them. In a nutshell, Outcomes-based education was not designed to pass on knowledge and information. Rather, it aimed to encourage the pupil to learn for his or herself: to collect, analyse and organise their resources in order to understand how to solve a problem. The teacher was expected to be a facilitator of learning, rather than the repository of knowledge, in keeping with the general ethos of progressive education. Teachers were required to shape their teaching to the individual requirements of each child, so that they might achieve the required knowledge without its being given to them directly.

What these ambitious aims ignored were the circumstances in which South African children lived. While the system might have worked in schools whose pupils had access to qualified teachers, books, libraries and the internet, for those living in squatter camps (known as 'informal settlements') or in many rural areas, these resources were simply not available. Outcomes-based education was built on quicksand.

It was not just an issue of resources. The problem was exacerbated by the poor education of teachers in impoverished areas and the sizes of the classes they had to teach. The capacity simply didn't exist within the teaching profession. The language of the new system was so opaque that the training was incomprehensible to most teachers; they could not understand what their role was, except that they could not do what they had done before. The one concept that was understood well by the teaching profession was 'learning by doing', but this was now frowned upon. Under the new syllabus, pupils spent more and more time collecting things and constructing contraptions in the classroom instead of learning to read, write and calculate (skills which Curriculum 2005 seemed to take for granted, as if they were absorbed by osmosis). It was essentially content-free education, and the void it left was filled with chaos.

The objective was to break with the previous system of teaching. This had essentially required teachers to pose questions, with the children chanting in unison the approved answer.[17] While most teachers had a clear idea of this 'chalk and talk' form of pedagogy, they struggled with the new system. Their pupils simply did not have the background or resources that the system required. As a senior teacher in a rural secondary school complained: 'OBE is a good policy—but it's not for us.'[18]

Imposed on the advice of foreign consultants, Outcomes-based education was an unmitigated disaster. By 2010, the minister of basic education, Angie Motshekga, had had enough: the system was scrapped. Although she resisted suggestions that the programme had produced a 'dark age' in education, or that a generation had been sacrificed to the ideology, she was scathing about its inadequacies. The minister pointed to what she called 'structural flaws', including a weak and superficial curriculum that was 'unrealistic' and assumed that 'pupils had access to research facilities such as telephones, the Internet, libraries and newspapers'.[19] Most children had few of these resources, and the disastrous programme was radically modified—but not before it undermined the education of many students.

While the system has been abolished, the results that pupils achieve are still disappointing. Motshekga welcomed the 2018 secondary school matriculation pass rate of 78.2 per cent. But—as the opposition Democratic Alliance pointed out—this masks the true state of things.[20] Pupils who are unlikely to pass their exams are often 'culled' from the system and not allowed to sit them. According to the opposition, the true figure is therefore far lower. Slightly more than half of those who embark upon their final two years of secondary education end up sitting the matriculation examinations. This means that the 'adjusted' pass rate is 37.6 per cent. If one considers the number entering primary education but failing to eventually pass their matriculation exams, the number is lower still.

Class and education

Middle-class South Africans—of all races—now do everything in their power to send their children to what used to be called

'Model C' schools, or, if they can afford it, to private schools. The classification of schools dates back to 1991, when schools were required to select one of four 'Models': A, B, C, or D. Model C was a semi-private structure, with decreased funding from the state, and considerably increased autonomy for the schools. By 1993, the overwhelming majority of white public schools became Model C schools. Although this model was abolished by the ANC government, the term is still commonly used to describe formerly whites-only government schools—although all now take pupils of every race. The rich and well-connected fled from the public sector, preferring to send their children to private schools (whose intake doubled to 500,000 by 2013) or to the best Model C schools.[21] The fees of the fully private schools are much higher than those of the Model C schools. This can be seen from two neighbouring Cape Town schools: Bishops, which is fully private, and Westford, which is not. The fees at Bishops were R113,440 a year in 2016, and 98 per cent of pupils qualified with marks that allowed them to enter university. Westford High School charged R31,600 and had a 99 per cent pass rate.[22]

For the children whose parents could not afford this route, the outcome was quite different. The vast majority of African pupils are taught in 24,000 public schools. In 2012, fewer than 3 per cent of African children were not in the public sector (291,903 out of a total of 10,439,583).[23] The schools attended by most of these children are simply terrible. As *The Economist* declared: 'In a league table of education systems drawn up in 2015 by the OECD club of mainly rich countries, South Africa ranks 75th out of 76.' Even comparisons with other African states show the country in a poor light. 'A shocking 27 per cent of pupils who have attended school for six years cannot read, compared with 4 per cent in Tanzania and 19 per cent in Zimbabwe.'[24] Why is the situation so dire? South Africa spends more on education than any other African country: some 6 per cent of GDP, according to the BBC.[25] At the same time, it is important to note that this has been declining: funding per schoolchild has declined by 8 per cent in the last seven years.[26]

This is partly because of the conditions under which teaching takes place: the long walk some children must make to school; their poor nutrition; and the massive class sizes. Many come from impoverished backgrounds. None of this makes education any easier, but these are issues that are also faced in Tanzania and Zimbabwe—both of which have far better results. There was also the problem that once the ANC came to power many of the most talented teachers, who had also been active in movements against apartheid, left to join the administration. Some of those that remained were not teachers of the highest calibre.

Teachers and their union

Perhaps the most intractable issue is the role of the teachers' union. As indicated above, SADTU insisted that the system of monitoring their work should be transformed: 'surprise' inspections would no longer be allowed. Inspectors had to give schools a year's notice before they arrived.[27] The results were predictable. Teachers behaved as they wished. They taught if they felt like it, but had no obligation to attend the classes that had been allocated to them. This extract from an article on a school in the Eastern Cape gives a flavour of what can take place:

> It's hard to see a future for Nontembeko Kwaziwa and the rest of her class—all 153 of them.
>
> The pupils of Meyisi Senior Secondary School in Flagstaff, Eastern Cape, like Grade 10B's Nontembeko, have new buildings, but very few teachers.
>
> This is because of a critical shortage of teachers in the Eastern Cape and the provincial education department's refusal to extend the contracts of temporary teachers. This leaves the school of 800 pupils with just nine permanent and two temporary teachers.

They need at least 11 more.

At 8.20am on a blistering hot Thursday, all of Grade 10B's 153 pupils are crammed into a single classroom. The noise is deafening and there is no sign of a teacher.

The subject on the timetable is isiXhosa, but there is no teacher for this subject a week after schools opened in the province with the nation's lowest matric pass rate, 61.6%.

The clock ticks on. At 8.35am there is still no teacher in sight and some pupils sell sweets or play cards, while others sleep.

Nontembiko (17) looks sad when asked about her future: 'There is no future for us here. If we were rich at home, I would look for a better school.'

Thanks to a staff meeting scheduled for 1.30pm, all classes are cut from 55 minutes to 45 minutes. It turns out it doesn't matter.

At 9am, there is still no teacher. When asked why, a staff member, who speaks on condition of anonymity out of fear of victimisation, says this class doesn't have a maths teacher either.

Again, 45 minutes pass and nobody in Grade 10B has learnt a thing. Geography is next and another 45 minutes go to waste without a teacher. It is only at 10.30am that a history teacher makes an appearance.

Back in 10B, it's now English at 11.45am and the heat is unbearable. Pupils use paper and book covers as makeshift fans.

For 10 minutes, the English teacher pleads with them to settle down, without success.

The classroom is in uproar and the teacher has lost her grip. About 10 pupils are sleeping. Some chew gum, others look the other way. The rest chat, disregarding the teacher completely.

As the teacher tries to continue, more fall asleep. Others shine their shoes.

Asked why he slept in class, Aphiwe Mnaba (18) says: 'I don't see any point in listening to the teacher. I am sitting here at the back and I can't hear a word the teacher says.'

The English teacher leaves at 12.30pm. It was the last lesson for the day.

The teachers say they are doing their best.[28]

In these circumstances, is it any surprise that pupils fail? An extensive investigation commissioned by the education minister and led by the respected educationalist Professor John Volmink took place in 2016.[29] The findings were shocking. They revealed that the union, SADTU, had effectively taken over the Department of Education. The report summarised the commission's conclusions by stating that:

> where authority is weak, inefficient and dilatory, teacher unions move into the available spaces and determine policies, priorities and appointments achieving undue influence over matters which primarily should be the responsibility of the Department. Weak authorities, aggressive Unions, compliant principals and teachers eager to benefit from Union membership and advancement are a combination of factors that defeat the achievement of quality education by attacking the values of professionalism.[30]

The Volmink report itemised the abuses that the union had allowed to proliferate in the country's 24,000 public schools. These included the selection of school principals, frequently in return for bribes, and the sale of teaching posts:

> The Task Team is appalled at the degree to which relations between the Department and the Unions are essentially conflictual, where the real interests of educators and learners are consequently unattended to. If, for example, undue influence is now a dominant way of achieving one's goals, and that using this method as a teacher has become normal practice, then obtaining a desirable position through bribery and corruption is a naturalised and normalised procedure. After all, that is how things are done. The environment has become a corrupt one. The logical conclusion of the analysis in this section is that 'undue influence', a polite name for corruption, appears to be endemic to greater and lesser degrees in the entire educational sys-

tem, in offices, in schools, Unions and everywhere else. Weak authorities, aggressive Unions, compliant principals and teachers eager to benefit from Union membership and advancement are a combination of factors that defeat the achievement of quality education by attacking the values of professionalism.

Owing to the pervasive implications of cadre deployment [the system under which the ANC instructed its members which jobs to fill], the Task team has sought to think through what the impact of this is being on education in South Africa. The more generic term for South Africa's practice of cadre deployment is 'patronage-based political appointments'. Teacher unions, especially SADTU, have developed the capacity to offer their members who display especial loyalty and activism in the Union's interests opportunities for appointment to well-paying and influential posts in public schools and Departmental offices.[31]

Unions control the hiring and disciplining of staff. As a result, teachers behave as they wish. Allegations of sexual abuse by teachers regularly appear in newspapers. In February 2018, for example, it was reported that six teachers in the Eastern Cape, including a school principal, had been accused of sleeping with their pupils.[32] These abuses are a frequent source of HIV infection and pregnancy.

It is hard not to agree with the principal conclusion of the Volmink report—that politicians need to wrest control from SADTU. The report recommends that 'the Department of Basic Education regain control of administering the education system in all Provinces so that clear distinctions are established between the roles and functions of the DBE and the concerns of Teacher Unions'.[33] This conclusion was reinforced by *Financial Mail*, the South African equivalent of *The Economist*. 'If Ramaphosa really wants to transform education,' the magazine wrote, 'he has to do more than hand out iPads; he has to manage the influence of Sadtu, to ensure real accountability for shoddy teaching ... Ramaphosa has to confront Sadtu, and make it clear that they must see themselves as educators first and union members second.'[34]

Universities ablaze

South Africa has many fine universities. They have produced excellent graduates who have practised their professions around the world, including ten Nobel laureates. Four were awarded Peace Prizes for their opposition to racism and their work towards ending apartheid: Albert Luthuli, Nelson Mandela, F. W. de Klerk and Archbishop Desmond Tutu. The other six were recognised for academic excellence: Aaron Klug (chemistry), Max Theiler, Allan Cormack and Sydney Brenner (medicine), and J. M. Coetzee and Nadine Gordimer (literature).

Their achievements should not blind us to the problems that continue to afflict the universities. The legacy of apartheid was a divided and segregated higher education sector. By the beginning of 1985, a total of nineteen higher education institutions had been designated 'for the exclusive use of whites', two 'for the exclusive use of Coloureds', two 'for the exclusive use of Indians', and thirteen 'for the exclusive use of Africans'. The African universities included seven institutions in the Bantustans, or 'homelands'.[35] The exclusively white universities offered a far higher standard of tuition. Since the end of apartheid, these divisions have been eliminated. All universities are open to all students and welcome many from across Africa and around the world. They offer many excellent courses and some are generally well-regarded, but the international standing of the universities has sadly not been maintained. South Africa's highest-ranking university, the University of Cape Town, fell from 107th in the world in 2010–11 to 171st in the year 2018.[36] Other universities have also had their ratings reduced.

One reason is that, as the universities have moved away from the segregation imposed on them by apartheid, they have taken in students who have come through Indian, Coloured and African schools. The students had had less spent on them per pupil, and their education was inferior to that received by most whites. As a result, the universities established graduated entrance requirements in an attempt to include students of promise, even if they did not have the necessary grades. Additional tuition was offered to these students, to assist them in reaching the required standard. What was not changed was the standard of the final exams and other degree requirements.

It would have been challenging to overcome these legacy issues alone, but the universities also faced new problems, suffering a range of increasingly violent protests. A number of factors have prompted this. Many protesters had experienced the challenges faced by young students around the world when first arriving at university, but were poorly equipped to respond to them. In the formerly white universities, black students, who made up the majority of the protesters, felt that they were in alien environments, often far from home.

In 2014, a group of postgraduate politics students at the University of the Witwatersrand (Wits) in Johannesburg produced a document entitled 'WITS Transformation Memo 2014'.[37] They complained of a number of issues, including the slow pace of advancement for black lecturers.[38] In some universities, racial quotas were rigidly enforced. This resulted in some staff finding their careers blocked because they belonged to the 'wrong' ethnic group. This is reported to have taken place at the University of South Africa—the country's largest higher education institution with over 300,000 students, who use distance learning to gain degrees. Some Coloured women on the staff complained they could not advance professionally after being told that their faculty had 'enough "coloured" women, indeed we have "too many"'.[39]

The protesters also called for the 'decolonisation of the curriculum'. They claimed that the political theory they were being taught was neither universal nor neutral, but rather rooted in a 'Western scholarship' that leaves out the 'viewpoint of the colonised'. They called for the inclusion of the works of African thinkers, such as Ali Mazrui, Ben Magubane, Archie Mafeje, Anna Julia Cooper, Kathryn Gines and W. E. B. Du Bois. Their demands do not end there. They called for all 'western' science and mathematics to be scrapped, and for traditional belief systems to replace them.[40]

Their complaints were reported, but it was only when a far more dramatic incident occurred at the University of Cape Town that the protest really took off. In March 2015, a politics student decided to act against the statue of Cecil Rhodes that had sat on the campus for many years. Rhodes, a mining magnate and one of the strongest proponents of British imperialism, had also been a great philanthropist—donating the land on which the university grew. The student, Chumani Maxwele, threw a bucket of human excrement over the statue.[41] A campaign, Rhodes Must Fall, took off, and within a month the university's vice chancellor, Max Price, had decided that the statue should be removed.

This unleashed protests that included threats and abuse of staff, the removal and destruction of other works of art from university residences and disruption of teaching. The protests spread to a number of other campuses, including the University of the Witwatersrand and Rhodes University in Makhanda. The vice chancellor of the University of the Witwatersrand, Adam Habib, wrote:

> The Rhodes statue was simply a trigger point for a broader unhappiness about race, racism, and marginalisation at the University. The universities, particularly the historically white ones, have been immersed in a bubble. They assumed that their intellectual atmosphere and their middle-class constituencies protected them from a

social explosion around race. But this was not to be because there is legitimacy to the criticisms of the students. How can there not be when there are universities 20 years after our democracy that still have more than two thirds of their students white?[42]

Some lecture halls were destroyed as clashes escalated, with further demands that student fees should be reduced or abolished.

The Fees Must Fall campaign began in mid-October 2015 at the University of the Witwatersrand and soon spread across the country. The spark that ignited the campaign was an announcement that fees would increase by 10.5 per cent to keep up with the costs of books, academic salaries and other expenses. Students, some of whom were already faced with the choice between eating and buying books, erupted in fury. There were fierce clashes on campuses between students and security firms, with the police intervening. Some universities closed and others found themselves unable to hold exams, as protesters disrupted the proceedings.

Tragically, the violence finally contributed to the death of one of South Africa's finest black academics. Professor Bongani Mayosi, one of the country's top cardiologists and Dean of the Faculty of Health Sciences at the University of Cape Town, committed suicide. His family believed the aggressive behaviour of the 'Fallist' students were at least partly responsible for his death. As the educationalist Jonathan Jansen explained:

We know Professor Mayosi struggled with depression in recent times. We also know that he suffered greatly when students occupied his offices during the fees protests, humiliating and insulting this gentle man to the extent that he had to take two months of leave to recover. He never did and was admitted to hospital recently as a result of psychological breakdown.[43]

The university is conducting an inquiry into what took place.

In December 2017, President Jacob Zuma announced that university fees would be abolished. Estimates of the cost of the decision range from R12 billion to R40 billion. There are also question marks over who it will benefit, since only a small proportion of South Africa's youth goes to university. Fewer than 5 per cent of the poorest 70 per cent of the population become university students.[44] Should such large sums be concentrated on them? It should also be noted that Zuma's proposals were only aimed at first-year students.[45] It was not clear who would pay for their fees as they progressed. The World Bank criticised the proposal, describing it as fiscally unsustainable and unlikely to supply more skills to the economy. The programme's high cost would likely make the target of doubling enrolments by 2030 'elusive', the Bank warned. 'This would inevitably create frustration among youth who would be barred from entering institutions even though they would be academically eligible and qualify for financial support.'[46]

Improving the education of South Africans—from the very first year they are at school right through to the postgraduate sector—is a priority for the country. Only a well-educated workforce can hope to transform its sluggish economy growth and thereby diminish the unemployment that so blights the population. Ending poverty and ensuring the development of a contented polity is a slow process, but without effective schools and universities this is unlikely to be achieved. What the country really lacks is a functional and productive apprenticeship system with high-grade technical and vocational tertiary education. That is where the emphasis should lie, because it is the lack of these skills that is impeding the formation of a more prosperous, modern economy.

9

JUSTICE AND THE LAW

On 31 March 2017, South Africa's Constitutional Court declared that the country's president had 'failed to uphold, defend and respect the Constitution as the supreme law of the land'.[1] It was a big blow to Jacob Zuma, but a triumph for the justice system and the separation of powers between parliament, the judiciary and the executive, entrenched for just over two decades in the Constitution. The president had failed to do his job by riding roughshod over lawful institutions when his personal homestead was enhanced using government money, and the country's highest court held him accountable. It was a first for South Africa's young democracy, and a particularly high point for Chief Justice Mogoeng Mogoeng, a traditionalist Christian who many thought would be a lapdog when he was appointed by Zuma to the position in September 2011, aged fifty. Mogoeng's detractors were proved wrong.

The country's legal system has been tested many times since 1994, and it has helped shape the country's politics as old apartheid laws were replaced by new laws. South Africa has a mixed legal system based on laws inherited from the Dutch and the

British, as well as on indigenous African law. The Dutch brought Roman-Dutch law when they arrived in the Cape in 1652, and the British added their jurisprudence when they arrived in 1806. English law was most firmly established in the exercise of public power (constitutional and administrative law), the administration of justice (laws of criminal and civil procedure and evidence), and business and industry (company law, bills of exchange, insolvency law). Roman-Dutch law remained for conventional private and criminal matters.[2] The requirement to study Latin for a law degree was dropped in 1994.[3] Laws and judgments are all subject to the prescripts and values of the new, post-apartheid Constitution.

South Africa prides itself on having strong institutions and a judiciary which is independent of meddling by the executive or the legislature, but courts have frequently found themselves in the political crosshairs. The necessity of holding politicians to account has tested the courts severely. In democratic South Africa, presidents from Nelson Mandela to Thabo Mbeki found themselves disagreeing with the courts; ultimately, however, they respected their judgments. But when Zuma found himself charged with offences like rape and corruption, he dismantled important parts of the criminal justice system, while attempting to alter the judiciary as well.

Previously there were strict laws prohibiting photographs in the courtroom, but in 2004 the public broadcaster, the SABC, got permission to transmit court proceedings into public living rooms for the first time. The accomplishment of justice could now be witnessed. The case in question involved Mark Thatcher, son of former British prime minister Margaret Thatcher, contesting the validity of a subpoena forcing him to answer questions about a failed coup in Equatorial Guinea.[4]

The broadcasting of court cases has, unfortunately, turned them into soap operas. For instance, the murder trial of paralympian Oscar Pistorius was streamed live from the courtroom in Pretoria to millions around the world. Some hitherto obscure legal terms became part of popular parlance. In a country whose crime rate is amongst the highest in the world, South Africans have become transfixed by the real-life dramas played out in the courts. The 'celebrity' cases are, however, in the minority. Cases that don't make the news often take years to be heard as the justice system creaks under a backlog and insufficient resources.

Early days

Archaeologists do not agree on the value systems and laws of those who preceded *Homo sapiens* 3 or 4 million years ago. More is known about relatively recent history. San hunter-gatherers and Khoikhoi pastoralists inhabited the territory of modern-day South Africa 20,000 to 30,000 years ago, mostly free from outside interference. The San were organised into small, nomadic groups with little hierarchy, and decision-making was by consensus. The need for law appears to have been minimal.[5] Traditional Khoikhoi society was more hierarchical, with systems of patrilineal descent. Hereditary headmen and their councils adjudicated in criminal matters and civil disputes.[6]

Sometime between the second and fifth centuries CE, Bantu-speaking Africans crossed what is now known as the Limpopo river, the northernmost border of present-day South Africa, from the west and the north west in search of pastures. They brought with them their religions, which included a strong belief in the intercession of ancestors. Traditional African religions were communitarian, and informed by the belief *umuntu ngumuntu ngabantu* ('I am what I am because of who we all are'). The concept of *ubuntu*, translated as 'humanity', is born out of this belief, and has found its way into modern South African law—amongst other examples, it was used in the judgment justifying the scrapping of the death penalty.[7]

Human rights and the Constitution

The treatment meted out to slaves and indigenous people by officials from the Dutch Vereenigde Oostindische Compagnie (United East India Company or VOC) and colonists who arrived from the latter half of the seventeenth century set the tone for apartheid two and a half centuries later. The Cape was dependent on slavery, because the VOC constantly needed more sources of labour. Some slaves were artisans and craftspeople, and were sometimes allowed to do contract work on their own account, while others were manual workers on farms, at the mercy of their owners. The VOC's judicial system dealt brutally with slaves who disobeyed slave laws or provisions of the criminal law. Desertion was the only way out, and many runaway communities hid in the mountains or at the coast. Absconding was, however, punishable by death.[8] Slaves were freed in the Cape in 1828.

When the Union of South Africa was established in 1910 and English and Afrikaans-speaking white South Africans were united, they embraced the Westminster style of government. This did not include a bill of rights, and the parliamentary sovereignty of governments that followed favoured white supremacy.[9]

Neither the 1961 Constitution of the new Republic of South Africa nor the 1983 tricameral Constitution gave all citizens fundamental rights. Black people were increasingly denied civic and political rights in the period leading up to the 1936 segregation laws, or Hertzog Bills.[10] Prime Minister Jan Smuts was a big campaigner for the insertion of human rights into the preamble of the United Nations Charter in 1945, but, ironically, he didn't consider applying this domestically. He was condemned by the international body as a hypocrite.[11]

One of the most important documents in South Africa's human rights history is the 1955 Freedom Charter. It was drafted by an assembly of ordinary people from all races and all walks of life, and was so comprehensive and hard-hitting that it had a very significant influence on the country's modern-day 1996 Constitution.[12] In fact, it is still often cited in conjunction with land rights by those who feel that these were watered down too much in the negotiations that led to the end of apartheid.

The Freedom Charter didn't please everyone within liberation groups. The pan-Africanists did not agree that 'South Africa belongs to all who live in it, black and white'. There have been differences within the ANC about how to approach human rights. While supporting rights was a useful antithesis to apartheid—a blatant violation of human rights—and a good way to garner sympathy from Western governments and the United Nations, there were differences of emphasis. Some took a more liberal view, with a focus on individual rights, while the trade unions were more oriented towards broad social and political transformation.[13]

Shortly after the 1994 elections, the parties had limited time to thrash out a Bill of Rights and Constitution. Most of the bargaining about which rights to include took place behind closed doors, because time was tight. This meant that public scrutiny was deferred, and with hindsight this has had negative long-term consequences. The Constitution is hailed as one of the most progressive in the world, but it has been criticised frequently since its adoption on 16 December 1996.

In 2011, for instance, a senior ANC member and advocate, Ngoako Ramatlhodi, said that the Constitution 'reflects the great compromise, a compromise tilted heavily in favour of the forces against change'.[14] He felt that emptying the legislature and executive of real power, and giving it to judges, was an effort to retain 'white domination under a black government'.[15]

Many in violence-wracked South Africa have called for capital punishment to be brought back after it was outlawed under the right-to-life provision.[16] A former police chief, Riah Phiyega, said that criminals were brazen because 'we have the most beautiful Constitution that allows rights, and rights are not limited'.[17] This sentiment is frequently echoed by the public and crime-fighters alike.

The Constitution has also been unsuccessful in keeping LGBTQ people from being targeted for rape and murder, especially in townships. However, South Africa was one of the first countries to legalise gay marriage in 2006, and in this regard it is amongst the most progressive in the world. The Constitution also entrenched property rights, but some political parties, including the ANC and the EFF, want to see these rights relaxed so that expropriation of land without compensation is allowed.[18]

The courts and politics

Before the Constitution became the supreme law of the land after the 1994 elections, parliament was paramount. Where a statute contradicted common law, the statute took precedence. This allowed the state to legislate for separate amenities, group areas, and even for apartheid in intimate personal relationships.[19] It also enabled government to keep people in solitary confinement, and to impose detention without trial.[20]

Still, there were instances in which the courts confronted the government. The appeal court ruled in 1952 that the law that stripped Coloured voters in the Cape of their voting rights was invalid, because the correct parliamentary process wasn't followed.[21]

Another example was a well-publicised ruling under the Terrorism Act of 1967. The Dean of the Anglican Cathedral in Johannesburg, an English immigrant, was accused of furthering the aims of the banned ANC by inciting violence and distributing money to its supporters. On appeal, the Chief Justice found the evidence in the case lacking, thus paving the way for anti-apartheid civic organisations and trade movements to continue their work.[22]

Many of those who subsequently rose to power in South Africa, as well as those who were appointed to high positions in the judiciary, had a brush with the apartheid justice system. Nelson Mandela, a lawyer by training, is the most famous of these. He was arrested in 1952 after addressing a crowd of 500 people and calling on them to peacefully resist the implementation of objectionable laws such as pass laws during the Defiance Campaign. The ANC's strategy was to clog the justice system. 'We shall not rest until all the gaols are filled,' he told the crowd.[23]

Mandela was found guilty but given a lenient sentence: nine months, suspended, instead of the prescribed ten years. He also survived an attempt to get him struck from the roll as an attorney, because two English-speaking judges, appointed before the National Party came into power in 1948, found that he didn't commit the offence in his professional capacity, and that his motives were to 'serve his fellow non-Europeans'.[24] While the apartheid government used ministerial diktat and security police to try to restrict Mandela, the law did not disown him. Justice Edwin Cameron, emphasising in his personal memoirs the need to stand up for what was right, said this showed that 'even in a wicked legal system, judges committed to justice and fairness may do more good than harm'.[25]

Three years later Mandela was again accused, along with 155 others, in what became the biggest trial in South Africa's history, following a government crackdown after the Congress of the People gathering in 1955. Those arrested went to the Old Fort Prison in Johannesburg, which is now a museum in the precincts of the Constitutional Court. The prisoners came from all races and a variety of professions, and they were all charged with high treason under Roman-Dutch common law, which carried the death penalty.[26]

It turned into a political trial, and was used by the accused and their lawyers to shine a spotlight on the government's oppressive racial policies. In the next four decades, activists used the courts to expose the injustices of apartheid. Leading defence advocate Vernon Berrange said: 'What is on trial here are not just 156 individuals, but the ideas which they and thousands of others in our land have openly espoused and expressed.'[27] After a lengthy and draining trial, all were acquitted for lack of evidence, with Mandela crediting a superior defence team.

Not long after this, Mandela was back in court on charges of sabotage, which again carried the death penalty. He was sentenced to life imprisonment with six of his comrades. Again, the court was used as a political platform, and the speech Mandela delivered during his trial is still frequently quoted. 'I have fought against white domination, and I have fought against black domination,' he said, poignantly concluding that 'it is an ideal for which I am prepared to die.'[28]

The Centre for Applied Legal Studies (CALS) and the Legal Resources Centre were established in the 1970s, and continued using legal cases to fight against political injustices such as forced removals and pass laws. After 1994, these institutions worked on cases that dealt with individual and especially socio-economic rights. Some of the biggest post-apartheid human rights cases fought by CALS helped shape government policies on HIV/ AIDS. These also concerned the free provision of life-saving medication to people who were dying of AIDS—something the government at the time, under the leadership of Thabo Mbeki, resisted.[29] Most recently, organisations like AfriForum, a pressure group that favours white minority rights, and the Organisation Undoing Tax Abuse, which focuses on whistleblowing and tax collection, have been pursuing their activism through court cases.

Opposition political parties have increasingly been turning to the courts to rule on political matters. This 'lawfare' has raised concerns among experts that courts are being over-used, and might end up reaching into the political domain and telling institutions like Parliament what to do. The Constitution has entrenched the separation of powers, a democratic principle that is fiercely guarded by constitutionalists. This means the power of the state is divided between three different but interdependent arms: the executive (cabinet), the legislature (parliament) and the judiciary (courts).

Cathy Powell, a senior law lecturer at the University of Cape Town, told a local radio show that the opposition often turns to the courts because the other two branches of government, the legislature and the executive, 'are not doing their job'. It is a national disaster, she reckoned.[30] South Africa prides itself on its strong institutions, and an over-reliance on courts could cause them to weaken under political strain.

Transformation

After 1994, judges were no longer appointed in secret by ministers and the president. They now had to sit through publically aired interviews by the Judicial Service Commission, which then made recommendations to the president. The judges appointed under apartheid were retained for a smooth transition and stability, but they became subject to the Constitution like everyone else.[31]

The judiciary has since attempted to transform itself from the white male preserve that it used to be into a body that represents the demography of the South African population. Out of 227 judges, 82 are female and 145 male, and just under two-thirds are black.[32]

The Commission for Gender Equality, the government's equal rights watchdog, found in a 2016 report that there were structural problems lower down that resulted in fewer women being considered for the judiciary. For example, at that time there were at least twice as many male lawyers as female, and three times as many male advocates.[33]

Transformation has also caused racial friction. In 2004 and 2011, race rows erupted in the Western Cape division after white male candidates, who some felt were very suitable for the job as they came from activist backgrounds, were overlooked for appointment because more black judges were needed.[34]

Table 5: landmark and important Constitutional Court judgments

1995	Outlawing the death penalty: S v Makwanyane and Another	Capital punishment was found to be inconsistent with the Interim Constitution and any other law, and it was made illegal.
1999	Right to vote: August and Another vs Electoral Commission and Others	Prisoners challenged the Independent Electoral Commission over their right to vote, and the court ruled that all prisoners should be able to vote.
2000	Right to housing: Government of the Republic of South Africa and Others v Grootboom and Others	The judgment established what the right to housing means for the poor. However, Irene Grootboom, who went to court after she was evicted from her home in the middle of winter, failed to secure a home.
2000	Separation of powers: South African Association of Personal Injury Lawyers v Heath and Others	The court ruled that Judge Willem Heath could not head the Special Investigating Unit, and therein fulfil the role of both investigator and judge.
2001	Right to safety: Carmichele v	Alix Carmichele turned to the

	Minister of Safety and Security and Another	courts after she was attacked by a man out on bail for violent crimes. The Constitutional Court ruled that the state had the obligation to protect women.
2002	Right to health: Minister of Health and Others v Treatment Action Campaign	The government was forced to remove restrictions which prevented Nevirapine, which impedes mother-to-child-transmission of HIV, from being used at public health facilities in a case brought by the Treatment Action Campaign.
2006	Freedom of religion: MEC for Education, KwaZulu-Natal and Others v Pillay	The Constitutional Court ruled that a Hindu girl could wear a nose stud to school in accordance with her religion.
2012	Recognising the limits to the court's power: National Treasury and Others v OUTA and Others	In a less popular ruling, the Constitutional Court overturned a High Court ruling that granted an interim order barring the government from charging e-tolls on some Johannesburg freeways. The court ruled it was a matter of policy, not rights, and should be handled by the government.
2016	Constitutional obligations of a president: EFF and Others v Speaker of the National Assembly and Others	In a case brought by the opposition party Economic Freedom Fighters, Jacob Zuma was ruled to have failed in his presidential duty of upholding, protecting and defending the Constitution because of the way he failed to

		heed a constitutionally-mandated report on public spending on his private home.
2017	Constitutional obligations of ministers: SASSA and Another v Minister of Social Development and Others	Then minister of social development, Bathabile Dlamini, was ordered to ensure that the administration of the social welfare grants of more than 10 million people be corrected. The minister was accused of failing to do her job, and she had to bear a fifth of the costs for the case herself.

Breaking the criminal justice system

While the Constitutional Court has epitomised the best of South Africa's legal system, the rest of the criminal justice system has had a turbulent ride in the past two and a half decades, especially when it has tried to prosecute politicians.

The first—and so far the only—politician to go to jail following South Africa's multi-billion rand Arms Deal, concluded in 1999, was former ANC chief whip and chairperson of parliament's defence committee, Tony Yengeni. In 2003, Yengeni was convicted of fraud for receiving a Mercedes Benz four-wheel drive from a company involved in the Arms Deal. He was subsequently embittered at having to bear the burden of guilt for the corrupt deal alone. Many in the party apparently sympathised with him, carrying him on their shoulders into the gates of Cape Town's high security Pollsmoor Prison, where he served just four months of his four-year sentence. Later allegations emerged that he in fact received millions of rands in bribes, but he wasn't charged with this.[35]

President Zuma's corruption charges also relate to the Arms Deal, but so far he has successfully escaped court. This is despite his financial advisor, Schabir Shaik, being found guilty of corruption and fraud in 2005. State prosecutors started noticing 'serious political interference' during Shaik's prosecution, which caused them grave concern. They, among others, questioned why Zuma, as the alleged recipient of the bribes, wasn't on trial together with him.[36] The judgment against Shaik implicated Zuma so convincingly that Mbeki 'released' him 'from his responsibilities as deputy president of the republic and member of cabinet'.[37] Zuma's fight to stay out of jail then started in earnest. His battle has spared no one, and has lasted for over a decade; eventually, in 2009, he became president and used his powers to dismantle the criminal justice system and the judiciary.

The political stakes of this fight were so high that when Zuma was accused in 2005 of raping the daughter of a friend who had also been involved in the fight against apartheid, he claimed that the Mbeki camp had set him a honey trap. He was acquitted, but not before giving detailed testimony about the intercourse that took place, exposing his belief that a shower after the deed would protect him against HIV/AIDS. His erroneous belief was deeply ironic, as he chaired the South African National AIDS Council as well as the Moral Regeneration Movement during his time as deputy president. The High Court judge added to Rudyard Kipling's famous poem 'If' in his 'not guilty' verdict: 'And if you can control your body and your sexual urges, then you are a man my son.'[38]

Just as the liberation movement used the courts during struggle days to fight against apartheid, Zuma used his trials to drum up sympathy for himself. He would address an army of militant supporters outside the court, and sing his trademark struggle song, 'Awuleth' Umshini Wami' ('Bring my machine gun').[39] The media wrote of his demise, but he defied predictions in 2007 when he was voted ANC president.

Nine months later, the court set aside a decision to prosecute Zuma for corruption, citing Mbeki's interference with the prosecution. This decision was overturned by the Supreme Court of Appeal a year later, but by that time the ANC had long since removed Mbeki from his position as president and replaced him with ANC deputy leader Kgalema Motlanthe.

The first step to keeping Zuma out of jail was to disband the Scorpions, an independent FBI-style unit, set up in 1999 amidst extreme concern about organised crime. Much of its focus was on the government's multi-billion rand Arms Deal, concluded in 1999, and it assembled the best of the country's crime-fighters.[40] It did, however, make a number of enemies by engaging in high-profile swoops on lawbreakers, often strategically leaked to the media. Those who felt its sting accused the Scorpions of doing Mbeki's political bidding.

A month before the 2009 general elections, the acting national director of public prosecutions, Mokotedi Mpshe, announced that the charges against Zuma would not be pursued.[41] It was only in April 2016, after a lengthy court battle by the Democratic Alliance, that a court ruled that Mpshe had: 'found himself under pressure ... and consequently made an irrational decision'. The case against Zuma was resumed. But in the seven intervening years, Zuma systematically dismantled the police and the national prosecuting authority in an effort to prevent them from pursuing the charges.

He appointed people he considered loyalists, most of them from his KwaZulu-Natal home province: a new police chief to replace Mbeki's police chief, who was suspended for corruption; and a new head of the unified intelligence service and of the Hawks unit, which replaced the Scorpions and was placed directly under the control of the police. Zuma also appointed a new director of public prosecutions, Menzi Simelane, who would toe the line. Former prosecutor turned Democratic Alliance MP

Glynnis Breytenbach explained her disillusionment in her colourful tell-all book: 'He told us, bluntly, that he was there to implement the policy of the ruling party. Which, if you want to prosecute independently, was vomit-inducing. He didn't say a thing about the law, the Constitution. Fuck all.'[42]

Many of Zuma's appointments were considered weak, and didn't last long. The new police chief was fired three years into the job after an irregular lease scandal. The prosecutions boss, Simelane, lasted less than two years before a court declared him unfit for office because he lied to a Commission of Inquiry. The next prosecutions boss was also forced to leave just over a year later because he'd had previous brushes with the law. The Hawks and intelligence heads were dropped by Zuma when their personal loyalty came into question.[43]

Zuma's attempt to change the Constitutional Court was less successful. Before he took office, he said that the status of the Constitutional Court justices had to be reviewed because they 'were not God'. After he became president, Zuma questioned why minority judgments had 'more logic than the one that enjoyed the majority', and said that the way the court worked had to change.[44]

When the chief justice position became vacant after the retirement of Pius Langa in 2009, Zuma overlooked Langa's deputy, Dikgang Moseneke, who had been critical of him. Instead, he appointed Sandile Ngcobo, who had once written a favourable minority judgment in a case concerning Zuma, and whom he—mistakenly—thought could be an ally. Justice Ngcobo's term as Constitutional Court justice lasted until 2011, and Zuma then nominated Mogoeng Mogoeng.[45] Many in the legal establishment anticipated that Mogoeng, a religious traditionalist, would submit to Zuma, but this was not to be. In March 2016, Mogoeng delivered the Nkandla judgment about Zuma's homestead, which was so scathing that it would have ended Zuma's career if he had respected the courts enough to heed the ruling and step down. The court found that Zuma's failure to comply with the Public Protector's report on Nkandla, which ordered him to pay back the public money spent on non-security upgrades, was 'inconsistent with his obligations to uphold, defend and respect the Constitution as the supreme law of the Republic'—as he had sworn to do in his oath of office.[46]

Zuma made the same 'mistake' when he appointed Thuli Madonsela as Public Protector—a constitutionally-mandated ombudsman. She produced two damning reports that helped bring his presidency to an early end. Zuma had spent at least R250 million in government money for upgrades to his private Nkandla homestead in rural KwaZulu-Natal, which her 2014 report found were not all for security upgrades, as he had claimed. Her second report detailed how a family of business-men, the Guptas, whom Zuma called his friends, had corrupted numerous officials and politicians, including Zuma himself. The inquiry she recommended, led by judge Raymond Zondo, has heard evidence implicating many in Zuma's immediate circle in corrupt acts, but it has also extended beyond that and deep into the governing ANC more broadly.

Holding Zuma to account for Nkandla was a slow process, delayed by an unwillingness by ANC MPs and the prosecuting service to act. While Madonsela had been meticulous in her investigations, her powers only went as far as recommending a course of action.

ANC leaders preferred to believe Zuma's defence that all of the Nkandla spending was indeed to ensure his security. Madonsela stated that Zuma had to pay back the money for whatever didn't qualify as such. The police minister, Nathi Nhleko, was ordered to determine the amount, and he loyally concluded that Zuma didn't owe a cent. The public, though, had difficulty believing that the numerous dwellings, amphitheatre, swimming pool, cattle kraal, chicken run and tuck-shop, managed by one of his wives, were solely meant to keep him safe.

MPs adopted the police minister's report, which effectively let Zuma off the hook, after watching a video in which the police minister went to Nkandla to demonstrate how water could be pumped from the swimming pool to put out fires—to the tune of 'O Sole Mio'. Amazingly, the MPs appeared to have bought the improbable story that the 'fire pool' was built for security purposes.

Zuma's state security minister, David Mahlobo, was even more diligent in trying to shield Zuma from blame. He went on to probe claims that Madonsela was a CIA agent. It was a classic ploy to discredit her, because this would have been almost impossible to prove, and she—and the American Embassy in Pretoria—denied the allegations.

While the national prosecuting authority was lax in pursuing Zuma or any of his acolytes whenever corruption was exposed, they hounded his critics vigorously. In October 2016, the prosecutions boss announced that he would press charges against former finance minister Pravin Gordhan over an alleged illegal authorisation of an early retirement. A few months later, the charges were withdrawn after it became apparent that the case had no chance of success.

In parliament, the opposition Economic Freedom Fighters took to fighting the issue the loud way, by disrupting sittings with chants of 'pay back the money' every time Zuma appeared in the legislature. They also went beyond these slogans to the Constitutional Court, after parliament failed to take the recommended remedial action. In March 2016, the court ruled that Zuma had failed in his duty of upholding, protecting and defending the Constitution. Zuma laughed off the judgment and apologised for any 'confusion' he might have caused, adding that what he had done was within the law at the time because the Constitutional Court had not yet ruled on it.[47]

ANC leaders continued to line up behind Zuma, and the party's MPs used their parliamentary majority to resist repeated motions of no confidence in him. This prompted the EFF and three other opposition parties to go to court again in December 2017.[48] The court gave parliament 120 days to institute impeachment procedures, but before the time was up Zuma resigned of his own accord, on Valentine's Day.[49]

Getting justice back on track

Nelson Mandela faced two adverse rulings in the Constitutional Court when he was president, but mindful of his long struggle for equality under the law, he reflected positively on these: 'These two examples clearly demonstrated that in the new South Africa there is nobody, not even the President, who is above the law, that the rule of law generally, and in particular the independence of the judiciary should be respected.'[50]

Ramaphosa worked closely with Mandela during the transition to democracy. Not only does he have a deep understanding of the Constitution which he helped to shape, but he also appreciates the values of strong institutions, especially of a strong economy. Many have asked whether Ramaphosa would have enough guts and the requisite support to follow through on his tough anti-corruption talk. The Commission of Inquiry chaired by deputy chief justice Raymond Zondo has heard startling claims of corruption and state capture, implicating a large number of prominent ANC leaders. The number of cases could clog the court system for years to come, and the prosecuting authority would need to be beefed up, particularly after the recent mass exodus of experienced prosecutors.

Ramaphosa would, however, lose credibility if he didn't make good on his vow to clean up governance. But he is a slow operator. Towards the end of his first year in office, he announced a former senior legal advisor to the prosecutor of the International Criminal Court, Shamila Batohi, as the new prosecutions head following a transparent interview process, which was a first. Justice experts, opposition parties and the media hailed her appointment as a demonstration of Ramaphosa's commitment to the rule of law.

Still, the big fish is Zuma. Much of Ramaphosa's support came from those who want to see the former president brought to book. Zuma left in his wake a pile of legal bills for the presidency's account, amounting to several million rands. In December, a court ruled that he was liable for these bills, but Zuma appealed the ruling. In the meantime, the bills are mounting up. Zuma's trial on corruption charges is underway, and his style so far has been to use every mechanism possible to delay the legal process, despite repeatedly clamouring for his day in court. He has used his court appearances to rally supporters, who regularly come out in great numbers. Former allies and accomplices such as Shaik, who was released from prison early on medical parole, could testify against him.[51]

10

CIVIL SOCIETY

THE PUSH FROM OUTSIDE

Protests have become an almost daily occurrence in South Africa. Frustrated by substandard living conditions or a lack of municipal services, the poor take to the streets, sometimes violently, as a last resort to make their voices heard.

On 7 April 2017, though, things were different. Thousands of people rose up in the four biggest cities—Pretoria, Durban, Johannesburg and Cape Town—a few days after a surprise late-night cabinet shake-up by then president Jacob Zuma saw the very capable finance minister, Pravin Gordhan, replaced by a hapless newcomer. The middle classes—of all races—took leave from work and left their comfort zones to make their displeasure known, brandishing posters saying: 'Zuma must go.' Not since the days of apartheid had so many South Africans gathered so widely to protest against a government.

The National Treasury was considered to be the last stronghold against efforts by Zuma and his associates, inside government and also in business, to illegally divert state money to their pockets in a project South Africans termed 'state capture'. Economic disaster loomed, and two ratings agencies downgraded the country to junk status. 'The devastating impact of this unexpected announcement on the South African economy is estimated to be approximately R500 billion,' Gordhan later testified.[1]

The marches were organised under the Save South Africa campaign, a loose conglomeration of civil society organisations, politicians, businesses and individuals opposing Zuma's leadership. Some months later, they got their way when Cyril Ramaphosa was elected president of the ANC. He took over the country's presidency after Zuma was pushed to resign a few weeks after. Civil society had stopped Zuma from destroying the country, just as it had with the apartheid government twenty-three years before.

The apartheid years

Some of the earliest resistance against slavery and racism in the colonial years came from missionaries and humanitarians. They wanted slavery abolished, but Boer farmers and British settlers who owned slaves resisted.[2] More than a century later, it was again clerics and those in organised religion who stood together to fight the injustices of the apartheid system, even as some churches were using the notion of God's 'chosen people' to justify the government's apartheid ideology.

Amongst these protesters were the World Council of Churches, who took a stance against apartheid after the Sharpeville Massacre in 1960, where sixty-nine people were killed after police shot at protesters; the white Afrikaans-speaking cleric Beyers Naude, who founded the Christian Institute in 1963 to foster interracial reconciliation; and the group of mainly black theologians from Soweto who issued the Kairos Document in 1985, which challenged some churches on their lukewarm response to the vicious policies of the apartheid state during the state of emergency.[3]

CIVIL SOCIETY

The South African Council of Churches, an interdenominational forum of about three dozen church groups, was founded in 1968 and became one of the most prominent and moral anti-apartheid voices. It aimed to unite churches to fight for democracy, countering those supporting apartheid.[4] The organisation has endured for more than half a century, and again played an important role by condemning corruption in the very ANC government that it had fought to put in place. Important figures from its ranks such as Archbishop Emeritus and Nobel Peace Prize laureate Desmond Tutu and the Reverend Frank Chikane again emerged to speak out, just as they did in the apartheid years.

There are also civil society organisations from the same time that have endured. One of the oldest is the Black Sash, established in 1955 by middle class white women protesting against the disenfranchisement of black voters. Their initial focus was on constitutional issues, but they later included the moral, legal and socio-economic issues around racial discrimination. They organised marches with other women's organisations, and also set up advice offices where people could get free paralegal advice.[5] The organisation still lobbies government and litigates around socio-economic issues.

Legal rights became important weapons of the disenfranchised. By the 1970s a number of non-governmental public interest law organisations emerged to champion human rights, such as the Legal Resources Centre, established in 1978 and headed by Arthur Chaskalson, who became democratic South Africa's first chief justice in 1994. The centre mounted direct challenges to apartheid legislation, such as the pass laws and the Group Areas Act.[6] Trade unionists also resorted to the law as they debated the strategic pros and cons of obtaining statutory recognition.

Civil society organisations cooperated closely, but operated largely independently of mainstream and banned political organisations like the ANC in the 1970s. Along with the Black Sash, organisations like the Release Mandela Campaign, the Soweto Parents Crisis Committee and the Detainees' Parents Support Committee were prominent. Although the government accused these civil society organisations of terrorism, they found it hard to prove this in court.[7]

By the mid-1980s, civil society moved closer to the ANC by associating with the United Democratic Front (UDF), which came to represent the liberation movement inside the country while the ANC was banned. At this time, there was a low-level war in South Africa between the government and those who opposed apartheid, and mass resistance broke out into the open. At the UDF's launch in 1983, one of its founders, Cape Town activist and cleric Allan Boesak, called for a 'united front of churches, civic associations, trade unions, student organisations and sports bodies' to fight oppression. There was ample support for his call. The UDF—with the help of funding from foreign sources in Europe and elsewhere—reintroduced an awareness of the rights called for by the 1955 Freedom Charter, rallying around the slogan 'UDF unites, apartheid divides'.[8] The UDF had support from activists of all races and was formed initially to focus on opposing the Tricameral Parliament, which allowed Coloured and Indian people nominal political participation but excluded black African people.

The UDF was allowed some breathing space as the government relaxed some of its restrictions against political organisation, due to pressures from within the country and internationally. Outdoor political meetings were banned, but indoor meetings and conferences were allowed. The media—including the alternative press and community papers—also increasingly reported on anti-apartheid opposition with impunity.[9]

Rights rhetoric by the UDF and its 400 civic, church, student and trade union affiliates in the 1980s played an important role in delegitimising the apartheid government.[10] The Congress of

South African Trade Unions, founded in 1985, organised strikes against apartheid laws and foregrounded workers' rights, and it provided the UDF with much-needed impetus when at times the latter group struggled to organise meetings and protest marches.[11]

The UDF had its final conference in 1991, after the unbanning of the ANC and other liberation organisations. ANC stalwart Walter Sisulu told delegates the UDF had indeed 'decisively turned the tide against the advances made by the [National Party] regime'. It had tipped the power from the apartheid regime towards the liberation movements.[12]

Exit apartheid, enter AIDS

Soon after South Africa achieved the democratic transition anti-apartheid activists had fought for, the country was faced with a significant new challenge. AIDS became a major issue worldwide in the 1980s, and African countries were hit the hardest. It started spreading apparently out of control in South Africa, especially with exiles returning from neighbouring countries where the prevalence of the disease was high. Due to the massive stigma, many preferred to live in ignorance rather than have themselves tested for the virus.[13]

A young activist who joined the anti-apartheid struggle as a child, Zackie Achmat, rose to prominence during this time. *The New Yorker* described him as 'the most important dissident in the country since Nelson Mandela'.[14] Achmat, a gay rights activist and co-founder of the Treatment Action Campaign (TAC) in 1998, took on the life-and-death issue of drug pricing. He was HIV-positive himself, and refused to go on treatment while it was still out of reach of the majority of patients. Anti-retroviral medication was cheap to manufacture, but patents held by international drug companies meant that it was unaffordable for the poor and even the middle class. At the time, it was believed that tens of millions of Africans could face death from a disease they could not afford to treat.[15]

The fight against HIV/AIDS proved, however, to be tough in new and complex ways. South Africa is a conservative society, and combating AIDS involved difficult and uncomfortable conversations about sex and sexuality. It also pitted former comrades against one another.

In the early 1990s, civil society organisations worked with ANC—and later government—leaders on developing South Africa's AIDS prevention policy. When the TAC was founded, it expected to continue that work, but it came up against Thabo Mbeki, who made it clear that he believed the dissidents on HIV/AIDS soon after he became president in 1999. Mbeki also believed AIDS drugs were toxic and should not be provided by the public health system. Sexual complexities also came into play. In a 2001 speech, Mbeki took aim against activists, saying that TAC protesters considered Africans 'germ carriers and human beings of a lower order' who were unable to subject their 'passions to reason'.[16] Mbeki, who spent most of the apartheid years in exile, had no first-hand experience of the way organisations like the UDF organised against apartheid. He was distrustful of foreign-funded NGOs, which he believed pursued Western, rather than African, agendas. Many activists to this day blame him for hundreds of thousands of AIDS-related deaths.

On drugs prices, civil society activists argued that a new way of thinking was needed in business and politics. Initially their arguments were considered outlandish, but as a result of relentless campaigning they soon had sympathy amongst ordinary people in South Africa and abroad. They challenged the government's views in court. In 2001, the TAC brought a court case against the minister of health, Manto Tshabalala-Msimang, which would make Nevirapine available in the public health system to HIV-positive pregnant women, to prevent their babies from being infected too. Justice Edwin Cameron, a legal activist at the centre of the HIV/AIDS battle, wrote in his memoirs years later that activists were 'heavy-hearted' about approaching the courts, because many supported the ANC and had associations with former activists who were now in government.[17] Some activists even had to be persuaded that court action was not treasonous, but legitimate to pursue in a democracy.[18]

Cameron reflected on the broader successes of the activists:

> They revolutionised our understanding that poor people have the right to proper healthcare. And today their arguments are widely accepted amongst health care planners, governments, international organisations and even drug companies. What changed the moral landscape was the principled, ingenious, high-energy assault the TAC and its allies around the world launched on the drug companies for their immoral exploitation of AIDS drug patents.[19]

Mark Heywood, another lifelong activist who led the University of the Witwatersrand's AIDS Law Project and co-founded the TAC with Achmat, said that there was 'continuity between the struggle against apartheid and the struggle to prevent and treat HIV infection. Freedom is vital for dignity and autonomy, the opportunity to be and become. It is meant to offer equality. This is what people in the liberation struggle had fought and died for'.[20]

Just like the struggle against apartheid, the fight against drug prices went global. The TAC reached out to international HIV/AIDS NGOs in 2001 after it joined a court case, on the side of the government, that was brought by Big Pharma and cited Nelson Mandela as the first respondent. The pharmaceutical companies were unhappy with government legislation to create competition in the market and to bring down medicine prices. The pricing of essential medicines became 'perhaps the first globally co-ordinated human rights campaign of the 21st century,' Heywood wrote. New technologies such as the internet and email helped with this. Writer John le Carre and singers Annie Lennox and Bono joined in. The court case was won and the price of anti-retroviral medicine fell dramatically.[21]

Heywood remarked that the 'new struggle' differed from the anti-apartheid struggle in many respects. 'The difference from the old struggle was that activists were being killed, not by apartheid's bullets or the hangman's noose, but by a virus that had become treatable. And people were dying in greater and greater numbers.' By 2003, in the TAC's estimation, 600 people a day were dying of HIV/AIDS. Unlike the old apartheid government, HIV does not discriminate on the basis of race, 'but it took full advantage of inequality and class,' Heywood wrote.[22]

The TAC used the tactics of civil disobedience, copying the ANC's defiance campaigns in the 1950s, in an attempt to spur Mbeki to action. At the launch of their campaign on 21 March 2003—Human Rights Day—protesters carried posters of Mbeki saying 'Wanted for not stopping 600 HIV/AIDS deaths every day'. They also took old struggle songs and reworded them with reference to the TAC and anti-retroviral treatment. The courts forced the government to start making AIDS drugs available on the public health system, and, soon after this, Mbeki's power started waning. Jacob Zuma took over as party leader and president in 2007. By that time cabinet, with the help of the TAC, had written a national strategic plan for health for the next few years, and the official policy set a target of enrolling 2.5 million people on anti-retroviral treatment by 2011.[23]

State capture shock

Zuma's administration initially came as a relief to HIV/AIDS activists. Even though he appeared to be ignorant, testifying during his rape trial in 2006 (in which he was acquitted) that he had taken a shower after unprotected sex to prevent HIV infection, his administration pushed for the public roll-out of medicine. Life expectancy started steadily increasing, from a low of fifty-two years for men and fifty-six years for women in 2006 to sixty-one years for men and sixty-seven for women in 2018.[24] His minister of health, Aaron Motsoaledi, 'out-activisted the activists with his passion and determination to defeat Aids,' Heywood wrote.[25]

With the AIDS cause taken up by government, Heywood's AIDS Law Project shut up shop in 2010, morphing into a bigger social justice organisation called Section27 (this refers to the section of the Constitution which deals with socio-economic rights). Section27 was immediately controversial when it, together with the TAC and about fifty other organisations, took part in a civil society conference organised by labour federation Cosatu in what was essentially an attempt to counter Zuma and the corruption that was surfacing under his administration. The ANC lashed out, calling Section27 'foreign-funded agents of imperialism masquerading as civil society advocates' who were trying to discredit and dislodge the governing party.[26] Conference organisers said that the gathering was merely an attempt to 'rediscover unity amongst civil society organisations', which had been working separately on service delivery, human rights and accountability issues.[27] The follow-up conferences never happened, but this one planted the seeds for trade unions and civil society to make common cause in attempts to oust Zuma seven years later.

After initially adopting a wait-and-see attitude to Zuma's first year in power, civil society organisations started organising in 2010 when there was an attempt to introduce measures for greater secrecy around government. The Protection of State Information Bill—or Secrecy Bill, as it was named by the media—would give government officials the right to classify, in the national interest, government information as 'top secret'. It was a broad bill, and also criminalised whistleblowing and investigative journalism.[28] In 2011 a majority of ANC MPs voted to pass it, despite vigorous campaigning by a newly-founded NGO, the Right2Know Campaign. They continued pushing back against the bill, which was mothballed.

Graft became a growing concern under Zuma's presidency. Zuma himself faced numerous corruption charges before he became president, but the National Prosecuting Authority dropped these on political grounds (the charges have since been reinstated). The first major scandal of Zuma's presidency happened when he tried to pass off millions of rands worth of upgrades—at taxpayers' expense—to his rural Nkandla homestead in KwaZulu-Natal as security upgrades. The second was when it became apparent that the Gupta family of businessmen were his friends for the personal benefits they—and Zuma's family—could improperly derive from his office.[29]

When labour federation Cosatu, now an affiliate of the ANC, launched Corruption Watch in 2012, it was therefore a political act. Graft had permeated the entire government system, right down to the traffic cops and immigration officials, and very little of this was getting prosecuted. Apart from speaking out about transparency and accountability, Corruption Watch also investigated the instances of corruption that were reported to it before quietly handing these cases over to the authorities.[30]

Despite growing calls for Zuma to go, he was re-elected ANC president by a gathering of party members at the end of 2012. Most of the eighty leaders on the ANC's powerful National Executive Committee were reliant on Zuma for jobs as ministers, and it became clear that, as with the apartheid government, it would be tough to fight corruption just from within. Outside pressure was needed.

Media reports exposing misdeeds involving Zuma, the Gupta family or their associates appeared weekly. Insiders, like former finance minister Pravin Gordhan, urged the South African public to find patterns in these reports and to 'join the dots'. It became clear that the instances of fraud and corruption were linked and formed part of a bigger project by Zuma and his kitchen cabinet that became known as state capture.

In 2017, in the run-up to the ANC's elective conference in December, three things happened that at last started turning opinions within the ANC against Zuma. First, there were the churches, which had become increasingly concerned about the moral effects of Zuma's leadership. Early in 2017, the South African Council of Churches released its Unburdening Panel draft report. This came about after the body offered a confessional space for those who might have been involved in the state capture project, or who might have knowledge of it, to speak freely without the fear of prosecution or persecution.

Second, there were the local academics, who compiled their own report which corroborated a lot of what the churches had said. They teamed up for two months to 'join the dots', as Gordhan had urged, resulting in the release of a report in May 2017 entitled 'Betrayal of the Promise'. Much of what was in this report had been in the public domain already, but the stark reality of the bigger picture was at last beginning to hit home.

Third, there was the media. Unlike during the apartheid years, journalists now enjoyed constitutional protection and could report freely, despite occasional attempts to muzzle them. An entire computer server with an enormous amount of confidential emails and documents from a Gupta-owned company was leaked to the media and published by investigative journalism NGO the amaBhungane Centre for Investigative Journalism, as well as online publication the *Daily Maverick*. Much of what became known as #GuptaLeaks served as proof for the contents of the 'Betrayal of the Promise' report. It also corroborated information that had been in the public domain already but had, up to then, been denied by the implicated parties. Some of the leaks also contained new information.

The authors of 'Betrayal of the Promise' later wrote in a book about their experience, entitled *Shadow State: The Politics of State Capture*, that these three events finally 'triggered a groundswell that effectively changed the public narrative from one of isolated instances of corruption into one about a systemic process of state capture coordinated by a power elite committed to an explicit political project'.[31]

Much of the momentum had already started with the release of Public Protector Thuli Madonsela's State of Capture report in October 2016, which recommended the setting up of a Commission of Inquiry into state capture and corruption.[32] The political response to the report was muted, except for attacks on Madonsela—rather bizarrely accusing her of being a foreign agent—by cronies of Zuma.

At the same time, Zuma's firing of Pravin Gordhan as finance minister in April 2017 sparked marches across the country of a magnitude last seen in apartheid South Africa. These were organised under the banner of new organisations alongside old struggle stalwart leaders such as Save South Africa and Future South Africa. Sixteen months before, a similar move saw a capable finance minister—Nhlanhla Nene—replaced by a former municipal mayor for a weekend, before Zuma was reprimanded by party leaders and Gordhan was appointed. Zuma's tampering with the finance ministry, and the ensuing financial chaos, triggered a fierce response from the middle classes. They were also emboldened by the effectiveness of student action against university tuition fees, prohibitively high to the majority, which started in October 2015 and continued months after. The #FeesMustFall hashtag was changed into #ZumaMustFall on social media and posters.

The way journalists, social movements, trade unions, legal aid centres, NGOs, the churches and academics united to mobilise against state capture was reminiscent of the way civil society fought apartheid in the 1980s. Ideologically disparate groups and people came together, with one thing in common: a broad support for the Constitution, for democracy and for a modern, professional administration.[33] This time, however, the political war was waged within—and for—the state administration. Civil society groupings used litigation and marches, and they lobbied ANC leaders in an attempt to change the narrative that the criminality in government could be justified as a necessary instrument for radical economic change to one of local, black ownership.[34]

Business associations were also mobilised, such as Business Leadership South Africa, a collection of CEOs which issued press statements openly critical of government. They also raised funds to support various anti-state capture campaigns, including the movement against public relations agency Bell Pottinger, which was funded by the Guptas to flame divisions in South Africa by pushing propaganda on social media. Business even aligned with trade unions and the South African Communist Party to push Zuma out.[35]

Those around the Zuma administration presented opposition to him as either the work of the racist acolytes of 'white monopoly capitalism'—political and social forces opposed to 'radical economic change'—or those working to benefit outside forces.[36] The 'foreign agents' label isn't new, and stems from the fact that civil society organisations are mostly reliant on foreign funding sources—often pro-democracy philanthropists and governments—because of a lack of a large-scale philanthropic culture locally.

Zuma lost power nationally after Cyril Ramaphosa was elected ANC leader at the party's December 2017 conference. Ramaphosa, whose supporters were behind some of the efforts by civil society to dislodge Zuma, took over the country's presidency in February 2018 after party seniors convinced Zuma to resign. Since then, many of the demands by organisations like Save South Africa, such as the restoration of a credible criminal justice system, the appointment of a commission into state capture, and steps to clean up corruption in government and state-owned enterprises, have been met.[37]

Ramaphosa's presidency isn't all good news. Zuma still appears to be in charge of patronage networks in his home province, KwaZulu-Natal, and almost half of those in the ANC's top leadership did not support Ramaphosa's election as party leader and are still actively working against him. Meanwhile, in civil society the 'Ramaphosa effect' could soon see many NGOs out of pocket because, in the view of the funders, the moment of crisis has passed. 'There's a concern about a social justice funding crisis because of the Ramaphosa effect,' Fatima Hassan, former director of the Open Society Foundation, which has funded many civil society organisations and journalism outfits, told *Daily Maverick* journalist Rebecca Davis. 'There was a moment when people realised we needed to fund a free media—but the minute Cyril [Ramaphosa] was appointed, that dissipated,' Hassan said. 'You create even greater threats to sustainability if your funding is dependent on who's occupying political office,' she warned, adding: 'Democracy is like a bath—you have to do it every day.'[38]

11

VIOLENT POLITICS IN A VIOLENT SOCIETY

South African politics takes place against a background of violence. The ruptures of the apartheid era have been carried over into post-apartheid society, leaving the country with a tragic reputation for abuse of women, beatings and murder. Police record some 650,000 victims of violence a year.[1] 'South Africa is one of the most violent and unsafe countries in the world', was how a newspaper headline summed up the situation.[2] There is little trust in the police and over 500,000 private security guards are employed by firms and individuals—more than twice the number of police officers.[3] The cost of this private militia is put at $3.7bn a year.

This climate of violence is carried over into political life. Outside of South Africa this is little understood. Most international observers assume that the miracle of the reconciliation ushered in by Nelson Mandela and Archbishop Desmond Tutu with the 'Rainbow Nation' still prevails. Yet there is no disputing that political murders and intimidation now disfigure South African politics. Violence and intimidation are a threat to the democratic process. Unless these issues are confronted, there is a clear risk that the legitimacy of elections will be undermined.

In June 2016, the then minister of police, Nkosinatphi Nhleko, announced that a special police task team had been established to investigate and prevent political killings.[4] 'We have noted with serious concern the incidents of killings, particularly where political figures are victims or where the killings are being linked to the upcoming local government. A situation like this cannot be allowed to continue, especially in the context of democracy,' he said in a statement. A year later, Nhleko reported that the killings continued, as did the work of the special task team, which consisted of seven detectives, five crime intelligence officers, four members of the Hawks and eleven members of the taxi violence task team.[5]

No details of any prosecutions by Nhleko were published, nor have the findings of the police task team been made public. This failure has left the public in the dark about the scale of the problem. At least as worrying is the failure of the police to prosecute those involved in these murders. Following a spate of political killings in 2016, the political commentator Gareth van Onselen observed: 'In every case, the police have said the motive for the killing is unknown, although politics has not been ruled out. In every case, no arrests have been reported and the police have asked the public to come forward with information.'[6] The analyst David Bruce calculated in 2014 that of 120 political killings he uncovered, just 10 per cent may have led to a conviction.[7]

Others put the scale of the violence even higher. One broadcaster said that they had catalogued 450 political murders in KwaZulu-Natal alone between 1994 and 2013. Yet fewer than one in ten of these murders resulted in successful convictions.[8]

Violence within the ANC

What is clear from the analysis is that, until recently, most of the violence and murder has been carried out within the

ANC. This was reflected in an *Economist* headline about KwaZulu-Natal: 'A most violent region: South Africa's ruling party is at war with itself'.[9]

These internal conflicts are reflected almost weekly in the press. On 11 May 2018, Musawenkosi 'Maqatha' Mchunu was turning into his driveway in the Pietermaritzburg area of KwaZulu-Natal at 7.00pm when he was ambushed by gunmen who fired several shots at him.[10] He was shot multiple times and was rushed to hospital, but he died from his wounds. Mchunu was an ANC regional branch convenor. The killing, although hardly rare, was sufficiently worrying to the ANC for President Ramaphosa and several other leading ANC cadres to visit his family.[11] In this instance, the killing appears to have been politically rather than financially motivated. Mchunu was a leading Ramaphosa supporter, in a region where most ANC branches support former president Jacob Zuma.[12]

Internal ANC violence is often part of a struggle for political influence—a means of gaining access to government contracts.[13] Politics is frequently (but by no means exclusively) driven by corruption. Opponents inside the party have been killed, since political power is a sure path to wealth and influence. Attaining office, by whatever means, grants access to privilege and resources with which to reward oneself and one's family and dependants. It is this system of corruption and patronage that has fuelled the intra-ANC killings. This is accepted by the party. ANC general secretary Gwede Mantashe is quoted as saying that: 'The reality is that selection of candidates for council is always a life-and-death issue.'[14] But this pattern of internal ANC murders is now changing. More recently, members of the Democratic Alliance have also been killed.[15]

Murders have become an entrenched element of South African politics. Three trends could increase this threat in the coming years. Firstly, as the ANC has begun to lose control of some areas of the country it has taken a less tolerant attitude towards the opposition. In 2006, the party lost control of Cape Town to a coalition led by the Democratic Alliance.[16] The ANC's response was less than democratic: it attempted to use administrative means to dislodge the DA. When this failed, it took to the streets, declaring that it would make Cape Town 'ungovernable'.[17] This tactic proved ineffective. In recent years, the ANC in the Cape has been dogged by internal strife, while the DA has continued to grow. In 2009, the DA took the Western Cape, the first time the ANC had lost a province. The ANC escalated its attacks. Mfuzo Zenzile, secretary of the ANC Youth League in the Cape Town region, acknowledged in 2012 that he had issued threats against the elected government: 'Our memorandum said we'd make the city and province ungovernable if our demands were not met in seven days,' he declared.[18]

This use of incendiary language by leading members of the ANC and, it must be added, by the Economic Freedom Fighters of Julius Malema, has done little to bolster the country's democratic structures.

Another, even more chilling, development has taken place in recent years: the emergence of the hired assassin. Mark Shaw and Kim Thomas of the University of Cape Town produced a paper titled 'The Commercialization of Assassination: "Hits" and Contract Killing in South Africa, 2000–2015'.[19] Thomas and Shaw recorded just over 1,000 individual cases of assassination or attempted assassination. By no means were all of them political. 'Where there is a cross-over between the involvement of state and criminal actors in perpetrating such violence, or cooperating in ways that facilitate violent outcomes, the position is particularly serious,' says Shaw. 'The result is a blurred distinction between the licit and the illicit, with a resulting replacement of trust with violence, or with the threat thereof.'[20]

In his book *Hitmen for Hire: Exposing South Africa's Underworld*, Mark Shaw explained the devastating toll murders have taken on the political system: 'The system of assassinations is a vicious political cycle: it empowers those whose power comes from the gun, and disempowers those who rely on their standing and capacity for delivery. Unchecked in South Africa it will undermine the very foundations of the democratic system.'[21] Since these reports were produced, there has been further evidence of a rising tide of political killings. In March 2018, there was a fresh investigation from the University of Cape Town and the Global Initiative against Transnational Organized Crime.[22] This showed a rising number of political killings and assassinations since 2013.

It is the combination of these trends—the association of political murders with corrupt practices and internal party disputes; the erosion of ANC support and the externalisation of violence once used to settle scores within the ANC; and, finally, the rise of the professional hitman—that makes elections so dangerous. It would be a mistake to reach apocalyptic conclusions, but it would equally be irresponsible to ignore these warning signs.

Lessons from the 2014 general election

In recent years, the ANC has begun to turn its violence outwards towards its political opponents. The mainly Zulu Inkatha Freedom Party and its rival, the breakaway National Freedom Party, have been involved in conflicts. The Democratic Alliance has already lost councillors, and this trend is on the rise. But not all political violence involves killings. To look at the pressures under which political parties are placed, the researcher David Bruce conducted anonymous interviews with victims of political intimidation, coming largely from parties being intimidated by the ANC. Two cases involved intimidation of Democratic Alliance (DA) supporters and one of the Economic Freedom Fighters (EFF).[23]

An interviewee from the DA in Mpumalanga described such an incident:

> So we would hold an event in a given community, let's say 20, 30, 40 community members would arrive, the ANC would make sure that they are at the same venue at the same time also with 20–30 people to come and just make noise and disrupt you so that you physically can't speak because of the noise interference. I had one in Delmas two months ago where we had to cancel the entire day's tour because the ANC literally followed us around with cars and the moment we stopped at a venue in a park somewhere, we started calling people together to come and talk to us, the ANC will come and surround us and prevent the people from talking to us.[24]

Another interviewee from the DA in the iLembe district north of Durban cited the following incident:

> Look, we actually had alerted the community and members of the DA that we were going to be having this gathering on Wednesday ... when we arrived there were ANC members who gathered just down the road from where we were supposed to be. When we started with our meeting their group kept growing ... and then as we wrapped our meeting they came to us singing and toyi-toying and they started bashing our cars [and] insulting people.[25]

The interviewee from the EFF had this to say:

> All EFF meetings have been disrupted, and they have been disrupted in this manner ... So there is a pattern ... You have people who are wearing ANC T-shirts. In a huge turnout, we have never addressed less than two thousand people where we've been, without posters and all those things. All you say is 'EFF is going to have a meeting and Julius is gonna address'. People come in huge numbers. And you see a group of seven ANC people wearing T-shirts, howling. And you ask them, 'What is your problem, we want to have our meeting.' [They respond] 'No, this is our community we cannot be removed. Freedom of this ... blah blah blah. 'If you are here then you must allow us to have our own meeting, and without you interfering

with that.' And they will become rowdy, even violent, even aggressive. In one instance one of the girls that was a part of the group literally hit my beret to the ground. I think they want to portray us as violent. That invites us to physically, you get what I mean, because if you hit my beret, obviously EFF members attach significance to the beret, and their leadership. So perhaps that's their strategy to collapse our meetings and then the report is that we beat people up in meetings. So, that is what would happen. In Pretoria for instance, they were literally throwing things at us, bottles and what. And the police were useless.[26]

South Africa has a reputation of holding free and fair elections. This is a fair generalisation, but it is not entirely accurate.[27] Bruce came to this conclusion: 'Intimidation continues to have an impact on the degree to which people in South Africa, most notably in poorer communities, feel free to openly support or even engage with political parties that are not dominant in the areas in which they live.'[28]

Although the ANC, as a party, may seem dormant when there is no election to be fought, it certainly conducts its election campaigns in an impressive fashion. Drawing on a legitimacy born out of a century of working for the rights of the African people, the party is capable of mobilising its core supporters across the country. While its support among ethnic minorities may have declined, and its leadership is no longer peppered with white, Coloured and Indian faces, it continues to win the backing of the majority of the African population.

Anyone travelling beyond the white suburbs of Cape Town into the predominantly African suburb of Khayelitsha during the 2014 election could not fail to be struck by the degree of ANC support. DA posters on the lampposts were few and far between. On election day itself, ANC t-shirts were ubiquitous in African areas, although the DA and other opposition parties also had supporters who wore their party's colours. In part, this was because the ANC simply distributed more t-shirts than its opponents. As one report put it: 'The African National Congress took its national election campaign to Botshabelo in the Free State on Sunday with ANC deputy president Cyril Ramaphosa conducting street visits. Ramaphosa left a trail of yellow t-shirts, walking down a street in L-section in Botshabelo, handing out shirts and greeting people.'[29]

This reflected the ANC's vast spending power. No official statements are provided by any of the parties about their election budgets, but unofficial estimates by the DA suggested that the ANC outspent its main rival by four or five to one. In part, this is the result of the ANC's highly effective investment arm, Chancellor House, which channels funds into the party from government contracts.[30] This diversion of public funds to fund the party has been repeatedly criticised. For example, in April 2014, on the eve of the election, it was revealed that the ANC had taken control of a supplier to the state electricity corporation, Eskom.[31] Advocate Paul Hoffman, head of the Institute for Accountability in Southern Africa, described the deal as 'illegal' in terms of the Constitution. He warned that 'this means money received from a state-owned entity will go straight into the coffers of the ANC ... No other party has the temerity to enter into deals like this, where they are both [player and referee]'.

The ANC has managed to augment its resources by tapping those of the state. This was discussed in an editorial in the *Mail & Guardian*:

> A reason why the ANC has managed its gravity-defying levitation, despite disillusionment within the ranks and derision outside them, is the power of incumbency. The ANC holds the goodies bag and has no hesitation dolling [sic] out taxpayer funded lollipops to keep the kiddies happily distracted ... At the most crass level, it has been the distribution of state funded food parcels, blankets and T-shirts at ANC political rallies. The DA is taking the ANC and the SA

Social Security Agency to court to halt this 'grotesque and continued abuse' of taxpayer funds.

A variation on this theme are newspaper advertisements and roadside billboards paid for by government departments, such as those ostensibly lauding the service achievements of the Gauteng provincial government, but dressed in ANC colours and using minimally tweaked ANC slogans. Such outrageous tactics, tried and tested by Zanu-PF in Zimbabwe, haven't raised as much as an eyebrow at the Independent Electoral Commission (IEC).[32]

On 7 April 2014, with the election campaign well under way, the DA's leader, Helen Zille, held a press conference to highlight the issue.[33] She drew the media's attention to a range of abuses involving the use of government resources for party political advantage. Zille described the government's *'Fetsa Tlala'* ('End Hunger') programme as little more than a fig leaf for ANC election campaigning and political patronage. The programme, with a budget of nearly R2 billion, included the distribution of tens of thousands of 'Fetsa Tlala' t-shirts to the public. The t-shirts, printed in ANC colours, had President Zuma's face on the front against the backdrop of an ANC flag. On the back were the words, 'We have a good story to tell'—the ANC election slogan. Zille also questioned the hiring of dozens of giant advertising hoardings in Gauteng, along major highways. Again, the adverts were in ANC colours and displayed only slightly edited versions of the ANC's election slogans. The DA calculated that the fifty-one advertising billboards in Gauteng were displayed at a cost of over R2 million a month, paid for by the province, not the party. Photographs of the billboards and examples of the 'Fetsa Tlala' t-shirts emblazoned with Jacob Zuma's face were provided to the media.

The ANC also suggests (quietly) that if another party is elected the system of social grants upon which so many black Africans rely for their income might be removed. This is not true, but it would appear to be a persuasive tactic. Hard evidence for voters' fears that this would be so is, naturally, difficult to arrive at. A survey by the University of Johannesburg's Centre for Social Development in Africa (CSDA) indicated that just under half of voters were not aware that the pensions and disability grants they received were theirs by right.[34] The numbers involved are huge; nearly 16 million people receive such grants:

> Summarising the study, Professor Yoland Sadie described the role of social grants in deciding voter behaviour as important, even if it was not decisive.[35] In this regard the legacy of voter identification of political parties as historically representing 'black' or 'white' sections of the population was not insubstantial...social grants can provide an incentive for people to vote for the ANC, since a large proportion of grant-holders who support the party do not think that 'they will continue receiving the grant when a new party comes to power.

Use of state resources (via advertising hoardings, newspaper advertisements and food parcels at rallies) and suggestions that grants and pensions might be at risk if a voter supported an opposition party would appear to be effective weapons in the ANC's armoury.

Media abuse

These financial resources bolster the ANC, but so too does the role of the state broadcaster, the SABC. The SABC is the largest newsgathering organisation in the country, with three of the four national free-to-air television stations and eighteen regional and national radio stations. It also broadcasts in all of South Africa's eleven official languages, plus Khoisan tongues !Xu and Khwe. It also has a long and sad history of exploitation as the tool of the ruling party. Although it is modelled on the BBC, the apartheid government used the SABC as a tool of propaganda.[36] The ANC has followed in their footsteps. This unfortunate fact was reflected in an article by Anton Harber, former editor of the *Mail & Guardian* and professor of journalism at the University of the Witwatersrand. Titled 'South Africa: SABC Is Key Weapon in ANC's Arsenal', the article concluded that the SABC was 'one of the party's most potent weapons', since it has a far larger audience than any other media.[37]

Broadcasting in all of South Africa's major languages, the SABC can reach parts of the population that others simply cannot:

> That is why the ANC has so much to say about the inadequacies of the print media, but is so silent on problems at the SABC, which can be relied on to block opposition adverts, play down Nkandla and pursue the ANC narrative. It is why it was prepared to lend R1.5bn to the SABC and give only a few million for the Media Development and Diversity Agency to support community media.[38]

This is not the first time that the ANC's use of the SABC has been highlighted. Susan Booysen suggested that the party has used the broadcaster to bolster its image in previous elections: 'The ANC expertly uses the public broadcaster, the South African Broadcasting Corporation (SABC), to feed supporting information, in particular in terms of government activities and statements by top-government figures in the run-up to elections.'[39]

Concerns about the SABC fall into two categories: bias and political advertising. The question of bias has been raised by many parties. For example, in 2014 the Congress of the People (COPE) accused the then chair of the SABC, Ellen Tshabalala, of encouraging an audience to vote for the ANC. 'We have always suspected that the SABC has the ANC's back, and our suspicions have now been confirmed without a shadow of doubt,' the statement read.[40] Similarly, the Pan African Congress youth wing accused the SABC of being 'the mouthpiece of the ANC'.[41]

More serious were the accusations against the SABC of censorship, for its refusal to air (or 'flight', as South Africans say) the party political broadcasts of the opposition parties. The DA was most severely affected, but it was not alone. Julius Malema's Economic Freedom Fighters complained of the same treatment.[42] The DA's commercial was refused permission twice by the SABC. The broadcaster claimed that the advert might incite violence against the police, that it used false information and that it attacked another party. Media Monitoring Africa scrutinised the arguments, rebutting them all.[43] The issue became something of a cause celebre in the media. One commentator erupted in anger, declaring: 'Hlaudi [Hlaudi Motsoeneng, the SABC chief operating officer], play the damn commercial!'[44] The SABC finally relented and broadcast the material, but considerable damage had already been done. In any election, timing is critical and days were lost as the lawyers wrangled over the complaints. These incidents did little to enhance the SABC's reputation.

That the state broadcaster is biased is bad enough. The fact that sections of the rest of the media are under the control of the ANC makes this far more serious. The ANC has adopted a range of measures directly out of the old apartheid playbook, when newspapers were established to support the state and journalists were funded or bribed to back the regime. The ANC initiative was to establish a media company friendly to the party with the assistance of supporters of President Zuma, and then to feed resources to it from the SABC. The aim was to fund a newspaper and a television company owned by the Gupta family, close allies of the president.[45] This began with the establishment of *The New Age* newspaper. 'The New Age, the pro-government newspaper owned by the Gupta family scored some R125 million in advertising in 2012, almost R75 million of it from government, parastatal or government-linked organisations. Not too bad for a brand-new newspaper that in 2012 didn't even have certified circulation figures,' concluded the veteran journalist Mandy de Waal in 2013.[46]

Matters did not end there. After the Guptas established their television channel ANN7 in 2013, it is alleged that the SABC began siphoning off money to pay for the venture. Evidence of this was provided by Vuyo Mvoko, one of four SABC journalists who made presentations to the parliamentary enquiry.[47] 'What SABC executives haven't informed you about is they have allowed SABC money to be used to build a rival channel—ANN7,' he explained. Mvoko alleged that the SABC paid for the production and broadcasting of breakfast briefings that regularly featured cabinet ministers and President Jacob Zuma. None of the cash they made went to the SABC, despite the considerable sums made from sponsorship and the charges made for attending the breakfasts. He said that the SABC was paying for its rival: 'It's the SABC that has to pay for its [own] downfall and to build this alternative channel.' The South African *Sunday Times* headline said it all: 'SABC "built up" Gupta rival television station'.[48]

These decisions had a catastrophic impact on the finances of the SABC. In 2015 Gavin Davis, a Democratic Alliance MP and a member of the Portfolio Committee on Communications, warned that the SABC was in crisis, 'the scale of which is only starting to become clear', and that it was 'facing financial ruin'.[49] His warnings were dismissed as scaremongering. Yet just two years later, this dire prediction had come true. Even the SABC's own spokesman, Kaizer Kganyago, accepted that the organisation's finances were 'under pressure'; the broadcaster was by this point funding its activities from its reserves.[50] But Kganyano placed the blame on external causes—including the state of the global economy and a parliamentary enquiry into the fitness of the SABC board to hold office. However, members of staff suggested that the situation was far worse. 'We're not even sure [if] we can pay salaries at month's end,' said one insider. 'Hlaudi's chickens have come home to roost,' said another.[51]

The parliamentary enquiry heard further allegations that the Guptas had only established ANN7 after failing to seize control of the SABC's news production, and that journalists critical of these events had been investigated by the State Security Agency.[52] The decision to bring in state security was—allegedly—taken by Motsoeneng.[53] The measures he ordered were draconian: state security agents went to one SABC employee's home village to interview locals about his lifestyle. The agents also demanded that certain members of staff take polygraph tests.[54]

Seizing critical newspapers

The third tactic adopted by the ANC was to take control of important independent newspapers. In August 2013, the first indications of what was taking place began to emerge. 'Independent News & Media South Africa, expected to change hands for R2-billion later this month, could find itself under the effective control of the South African government and two mystery Chinese investors', reported the *Mail & Guardian*.[55] It soon emerged that the report was accurate. Venerable newspapers, including the *Cape Argus*, the *Cape Times*, *The Mercury* (Durban), *The Star* (Johannesburg) and *Pretoria News*, had changed hands. Two Chinese companies—the China International Television Corporation and the China-Africa Development Fund, domiciled for tax purposes in the tax haven of Mauritius—had taken 20 per cent of the company. South Africa's state-owned Public Investment Corporation (PIC) had bought a 25 per cent stake, using Government Employee Pension Fund money. The remaining 55 per cent of Independent was to be held by a consortium led by Cape Town businessman Iqbal Survé, and his company Sekunjalo Investment Holdings. The Sekunjalo consortium was to include both a broad-based component and a number of politically linked people and organisations.[56]

The *Cape Times* editor, Alide Dasnois, was sacked, apparently for failing to deal with the death of Nelson Mandela in a manner which Surve approved of.[57] She had rushed out a special 'wrap-around' tribute to the president, but argued that she had no time to change the front page. Her supporters suggested that Surve's action had more to do with the story that appeared on the front of the paper, reporting the Public Protector's report into a controversial tender awarded to a Surve company. Dasnois was vindicated, but did not regain her position. Soon readers began complaining that the *Cape Times* was biased against the opposition Democratic Alliance, which runs the city; the party was routinely accused of being racist.[58] The overall impact was to deaden the instincts of the journalists employed on the papers. As Anton Harber concluded: 'The new chief executive, Dr Iqbal Surve, moved quickly against independent and critical voices on some of his newspapers.'[59]

Black ops

There was one final tactic employed by the ANC: media manipulation during elections. A covert 'war room' was set up on behalf of the party during the 2016 local elections, with a budget of R50 million to create false narratives favouring the ANC and targeting opposition parties. AmaBhungane, an investigative website, explained what took place: 'A covert team, initially known as the War Room, intended to "disempower DA and EFF campaigns" and set a pro-ANC agenda using a range of media, without revealing the ANC's hand.' This included the establishment of a seemingly independent news site and chat show, using 'influencers' on social media, and a plan to print fake opposition party posters.[60] The ANC attempted to suggest that it was not involved with the operation when the issue was raised in court following the non-payment of one of the contractors, but few believed the denials. As the commentator Ranjeni Munusamy put it: 'This is not only about the criminal acts and big personalities being shamed. It is also about the erosion of trust and further diminishing of the ANC's credibility ... The ANC cannot simply wash its hands or throw someone under the bus.'[61]

Election day

Events on election day itself indicated why it is difficult to regard the 2014 election as an entirely legitimate reflection of the will of the people. The former chair of the Electoral Commission, Pansy Tlakula, made it plain that electioneering was forbidden on 7 May—the day of the election itself. 'No political events can take place on voting day,' she told reporters. 'Campaigning finished at midnight last night.'[62] Travelling around the townships surrounding Cape Town throughout election day, it was evident that this ruling was extensively and openly flouted.

As the day drew to a close, cavalcades of cars, with loudspeakers blaring out party songs and supporters waving flags from the windows, could be seen touring up and down the streets. Outside polling stations, crowds, some more than a hundred strong, dressed in party colours and waving ANC flags, danced less than a metre from the long lines of men and women waiting patiently to cast their votes. When this was brought to the attention of the police and the representatives of the Electoral Commission at the stations, they either shrugged their shoulders or said that they did not have the resources to deal with these violations of the regulations.

The Electoral Commission appears to have little appetite for tackling such transgressions. It also refused to intervene in other election-related issues, including the bitter debate between the opposition parties and the SABC. There is a suspicion among the opposition that the commission is less than equitable in its treatment of their parties or members. This is reflected in the interviews undertaken for Bruce's Community Agency for Social

Enquiry report, which suggested that the commission was biased in favour of the ANC because of the partisan nature of the civil servants that it uses as its representatives at polling stations. This was the view of a member of the Inkatha Freedom Party:

> We are not happy as the IFP about the fact that IEC is using teachers as you know presiding officers, because teachers belong to SADTU, because SADTU is a strategic partner of the ANC. Each time there is going to be an election SADTU goes public to say that they are committed to ensuring that the ANC wins the elections. Now if you use such people to manage the processes of the elections then those processes are bound to actually attract question marks from other people.[63]

Another interviewee, this time from COPE, had this to say:

> Remember most of them are civil servants and largely teachers, who are members of SADTU. With each election, SADTU declares its unwavering support for the ANC. Whilst he or she is employed by the IEC, to deliver impartial elections, on the other hand they've got a mandate from their trade union, which is an ally of the ANC, to deliver votes for the ANC.[64]

The commission appears to take a narrow interpretation of its responsibilities, only acting to ensure that what happens directly within the polling stations and at the counting centres is in line with good practice. This despite its mandate from the Constitution, which calls for the Electoral Commission to 'manage' the elections in accordance with national legislation, and to 'ensure that those elections are free and fair'.[65] It would not be impossible for the commission to use this constitutional requirement to act more robustly and ensure that the environment in which the elections take place is far more conducive to the unrestricted expression of the will of the people of South Africa—the right for which they fought so hard.

Predicting the future is, of course, a mug's game, but we can draw upon past experience. Jakkie Cilliers and Ciara Aucoin of the Institute for Security Studies concluded a survey of prospects in the coming years with this chilling conclusion:

> South Africa is likely to experience significantly increased social instability in the next two years, mainly in the form of higher levels of violent protests, as the factional battles in the ANC plays out. On the current path violent protests will escalate, and we forecast particularly high levels of violence within the ANC in the run-up to the December 2017 National Conference as well as more general social and community violence in the run-up to the 2019 provincial and national elections.[66]

The political commentator Gareth Van Onselen went further: 'As the ANC implodes, as factionalism intensifies and as a culture of patronage and nepotism turns in on itself, it is not unreasonable to ask: how long until a senior member of the executive or the national government administration is assassinated?'[67] These predictions were made during the Zuma presidency. It is too early to say how the situation will alter now that Cyril Ramaphosa is in charge.

12

THE MAKING OF PRESIDENT RAMAPHOSA

In December 2017, the ANC met to decide who should replace Jacob Zuma as their leader. Since the party dominated parliament, whomever it chose would also become president of the country. Two serious candidates stood a real chance of election. The first, Dr Nkosazana Dlamini Zuma, had much to recommend her. A former minister of health under Nelson Mandela and minister of foreign affairs under Thabo Mbeki, she had gone on to lead the African Union Commission. She also had a solid track record as a 'struggle activist' who served her time in exile during apartheid. However, Dlamini Zuma had one fatal flaw: she was Jacob Zuma's former wife. Everyone inside the ANC knew (or thought they knew) that she was his proxy—his guarantee that he would not be sent to jail for corruption once he left office.

Up against Dlamini Zuma was Cyril Ramaphosa. There was much about him that was not appealing to ANC members. Yes, he was a black African—essential in a party that today has an almost exclusively African membership. But his was not the solid ANC or South African Communist Party pedigree of his predecessors. In the 1990s Ramaphosa's background was tainted by his support of the Black Consciousness Movement in his youth. He had not joined the ANC underground or gone into exile, and during the 1970s he had risen through the trade unions, not the armed struggle. He was also from a minority ethnic group, unlike Mandela and Mbeki (Xhosa) or Zuma (Zulu). As a Venda, he didn't have a substantial tribal base. And he carried the stain on his reputation of association with the worst police atrocity since the end of apartheid—the Marikana massacre of August 2012, when thirty-four miners were gunned down. The killings reinforced the sentiment that he had become too close to the business community. In the propaganda deployed by his opponents, he was a representative of 'monopoly capital'.

None of this worked in his favour. Ramaphosa was, from an ANC loyalist's perspective, just not really 'one of us'. Yet, in their hour of need, with the country on the brink of catastrophe, the ANC turned to Ramaphosa. The figure who had for years been derided as the 'nearly man' of South African politics was finally chosen to run the country, despite winning by the narrowest of margins. In making this choice, the ANC gave the presidency to one of the shrewdest, most able politicians of his generation.

The early years

Born on 17 November 1952 on the outskirts of Johannesburg, Cyril Ramaphosa went to school there before studying law at the University of the North (now the University of Limpopo). A supporter of the late Steve Biko's Black Consciousness Movement, he spent periods in jail before he qualified. This included eleven months in solitary confinement in the notorious Pretoria Central Prison in 1974.[1]

Rather than practising law, Ramaphosa joined the fledgling trade union movement. The unions were just being rebuilt in the 1970s after years of oppression, but one bastion of industry resisted all attempts at union organisation—the gold and diamond mines, on which the wealth of South Africa had been built. Giant mine compounds, home to thousands of men, were sealed behind barbed wire and armed guards. Ramaphosa saw that the way to the men was through organising the clerical staff—some of whom lived in the neighbouring townships, moving between home and the mines. He also presented himself to management as a reasonable man, with whom they could do a deal. Despite this, the going was tough. Dressed in a brown leather jacket, recruiting members by day and sleeping rough by night, Ramaphosa built the union. Its membership rose from 6,000 to 350,000 in just ten years. This process was not without significant strife. In August 1987, Ramaphosa led his union out on strike. Lasting three weeks, the strike was the largest the country had ever seen. Thousands lost their jobs, but the union remained intact. Ramaphosa's verdict was simple: 'They have not won and we have not lost.'[2] It took the union and the industry months, if not years, to recover, but Ramaphosa had made his point: he and his members were a force to be reckoned with.

Fighting management was vital for the mineworkers, but they were also living in an apartheid state and this posed political challenges that had to be answered. The National Union of Mineworkers had been allied to a black consciousness federation, but Ramaphosa moved it to the Federation of South African Trade Unions (FOSATU), which was committed to a non-racial perspective. Then, in 1985, he helped to align the union alliance with the ANC, with the founding of the Congress of South African Trade Unions (COSATU). For the first time since the 1960s, the ANC had a functioning trade union wing, with the mineworkers as its most powerful component.

Into politics and out again

Ramaphosa had brought an enormously valuable gift to the party. His work with the United Democratic Front, the civic organisation that fought apartheid on the streets and in the townships, cemented Ramaphosa's status within the party. When Nelson Mandela emerged from prison in 1991, his wife Winnie was on his left; Cyril Ramaphosa was on his right. Ramaphosa became the ANC's first secretary general after it was unbanned.

With his legal background and trade union experience, Ramaphosa made an ideal negotiator with the white government over the future constitution of the country. He had Roelf Meyer as his opposite number. They bonded well despite their differences, even going on a trout-fishing expedition together. Meyer, no fisherman, described how Ramaphosa helped to extract a hook from his finger with a pair of pliers.[3] 'Roelf, there's only one way to do this,' Ramaphosa said to Meyer. 'If you've never trusted an ANC person before, you'd better get ready to do so now.' Handing Meyer a bottle of whisky, Ramaphosa wrenched the hook from Meyer's finger with a pair of pliers. On this episode the trust between the two men was said to have been built. The veteran commentator Steve Friedman believed that Ramaphosa had succeeded in extracting more from the ruling National Party than they had wished to offer: 'The National Party no longer had a veto over decisions. With a stroke of a pen South Africa changed from apartheid to majority rule.'[4]

It became apparent that Ramaphosa was among those who might replace Mandela when the latter stepped down after just one term as president. Yet when Mandela resigned in June 1999, Ramaphosa did not succeed him. At the time, there was much speculation that Ramaphosa had been forced out of politics—that he had been outgunned by Thabo Mbeki, who had the support of the ANC's powerful former exile community. 'Not entirely true,' Ramaphosa now says about suggestions that he was shunted out of politics and into business. 'It was my choice.'[5] His entry into business was made easier by a group of black businessmen who were looking for associates. He became the deputy chairman of an investment holding company: New Africa Investments Limited, or NAIL. Led by Mandela's former doctor, Nthato Motlana, NAIL was designed to fill the gap in the South African economy left by years of racist policies that blocked black advancement. Motlana and his colleagues did not just want to enrich themselves, but to form a bridgehead into the business community for people of colour who had been denied the opportunity down the generations. Motlana remarked that Ramaphosa would do himself no political harm by entering this world—quite the opposite. 'You will have enough money to be incorruptible,' he told Ramaphosa, who was apparently less than amused by the comment.[6]

However, Motlana proved to be right. Ramaphosa joined NAIL at just the time when the giant Anglo American corporation, led by the Oppenheimers, was considering disposing of some of its assets. Anglo American rightly saw that it needed to bring some black businesspeople into the circle of white wealth if they were to survive. The strategy—sometimes dubbed 'elite capture' by its critics—was a success. Although Ramaphosa later complained that Anglo American had kept its most prized assets, the platinum mines, when it disposed of some of its holdings, NAIL went from strength to strength. It soon owned a major stake in everything from newspapers to breweries and food producers. For a group of men who had gone into business with very little capital, this was an astonishing achievement. By 2005, the company was worth R1.7 billion.[7]

Ramaphosa also founded his own investment company, the Shanduka group. His shrewd business sense and his political links meant that he became the preferred choice for white investors looking for a black partner. As time went by, criticism began to emerge that Black Economic Empowerment inevitably saw the same black figures benefiting from the deals. At the request of Mbeki, Ramaphosa led an enquiry into how this might be remedied. This led to the Broad-Based Black Economic Empowerment Act of 2003. Just how effective it really was in broadening the pool of beneficiaries is open to question: South Africa remains among the most unequal societies in the world. The end of apartheid had seen the circle of wealth widened to include Africans, Indians and Coloureds, but the elite remained no less exclusive.

While he was making his way in the world of business, Ramaphosa maintained his political ties. At the 1997 ANC conference, for example, he topped the poll for the party's powerful National Executive Committee.[8] Relations between Ramaphosa and Mbeki were less than cordial after the latter became president in June 1999. In April 2001, tensions within the ANC burst into the open, with Steve Tshwete, the minister of security, accusing Ramaphosa—together with two other senior party members, former Mpumalanga premier Mathews Phosa and former Gauteng premier Tokyo Sexwale—of involvement in a plot to oust Mbeki.[9] The Reuters news agency reported that the three of them were alleged to have accused Mbeki of having a hand in the assassination of the highly popular party member, and veteran of the armed struggle, Chris Hani.[10] The allegations were bizarre, and were rejected by the accused, but they did reveal deep divisions within the party. The *Guardian*'s Chris McGreal reported:

> The ANC said that as a result of the accusations it was concerned about the safety of Mr Mbeki and the three men accused of plotting against him. But in a confused statement, it tried to blame the allegations of dissent in the party on the press, even though the investigation was ordered by one of the ANC's cabinet ministers.[11]

The allegations shook Ramaphosa to the core. 'It was scary,' he later recalled. 'I started having visions of being arrested, being put before a court for treason and I thought "This is when the revolution eats its own children".'[12] Ramaphosa took the issue to Mandela, who advised him to keep calm and promised to intervene with Mbeki. But Mbeki refused to bend, going on television to confirm that an investigation was under way. It was neither the first, nor the last, strange allegation of plots inside the ANC, some of which have involved outside powers and intelligence services.[13] Like others, it gradually evaporated, leaving the whiff of subversion and deepening mistrust in its wake. The bridges between Ramaphosa and Mbeki had truly been burned.

Deputy president

Ramaphosa continued in business, while maintaining his strong links with the party. It was as chairman of the ANC's disciplinary appeals committee that he oversaw the expulsion of the party's youth leader, Julius Malema, in 2012. Malema went on to launch his own party, the Economic Freedom Fighters, but the ANC had managed to rid itself of a troublesome firebrand. As the year drew to a close, Ramaphosa took the decision to stand as deputy president of the ANC under Jacob Zuma. For the party, he represented someone with a wealth of experience who could act as a link to the emerging black business elite. In December 2012 he was duly elected, winning by a larger margin than Zuma himself. After the 2014 election, Zuma decided also to appoint Ramaphosa as deputy president of South Africa. Ramaphosa had emerged at the centre of South African life as a multi-millionaire and the apparent successor to Zuma. Major hurdles still lay ahead.

The first was the Marikana massacre of August 2012. When the police opened fire on mostly unarmed strikers (one miner probably had a pistol) they committed the worst atrocity since the end of apartheid. Ramaphosa had not ordered the massacre, but as a shareholder in the platinum mine via his holdings in Lonmin, as a member of the board and—above all—as chair of the company's transformation committee, he was seen as being in some way responsible for what took place. In a series of phone calls and emails with government ministers and the police, Ramaphosa appeared to have encouraged a tougher stance against the miners. A commission of enquiry finally decided he could not have known how the police would react, or that they would launch such a brutal and poorly planned operation. It was a finding that rang somewhat hollow for many South Africans. It does not take great familiarity with the police to know that they have a long history of using excessive force. The Marikana massacre was hardly an uncharacteristic or unforeseeable event.

The second hurdle was the question of how to deal with the myriad accusations of corruption against Jacob Zuma and his allies, the Gupta brothers. As deputy president, Ramaphosa had a ringside seat as the country was engulfed by the mass of suspect deals that were finally described as 'state capture'. His wealth meant he had neither a need for nor an interest in participating in this frenzy of abuse, but as reports in the media poured forth he had to decide how to respond. For the most part he kept his head down, biding his time, as the situation deteriorated. Finally, he could remain silent no longer. In October 2016, it was revealed that the Guptas had offered the deputy finance minister, Mcebisi Jonas, millions of rands to work for them as they set about controlling state finances. Ramaphosa protested that 'the ANC is not for sale', but he was careful not to name Zuma.[14] Matters deteriorated still further. The minister of finance, Pravin Gordhan, had been a strong critic of the Guptas. He was attacked; smeared with allegations that he had overseen unauthorised and illegal investigations while head of the tax authorities. This was followed by allegations that Gordhan was plotting with foreign powers to unseat Zuma.[15] It was a classic Zuma ploy to undermine and then to attack his opponents.

A fight to the death

In March 2017, as Gordhan arrived in London to try to reassure foreign investors, Zuma ordered him home the moment he got off the plane.[16] Without consulting his ANC colleagues, Zuma acted, and Gordhan was fired. For Ramaphosa, matters had come to a head and he went public. 'I raised my concern and objection on the removal of the Minister of Finance, largely because he was being removed based on an intelligence report that I believe had unsubstantiated allegations,' Ramaphosa stated.[17] As his biographer rightly concludes, Ramaphosa had crossed the Rubicon. 'By publicly breaking with Zuma over an executive decision for the first time, Ramaphosa had effectively thrown his hat in the ring ... From this point on, it would be a fight to the death—in the political sense, of course—between Zuma and Ramaphosa.'[18]

The divisions within the ANC deepened as the party began to consider who should succeed Zuma as its leader at the December 2017 conference. While several other leadership candidates emerged, it soon became clear that there were two distinct camps. On the one side was Jacob Zuma, who supported his former wife, Nkosazana Dlamini Zuma; on the other was Ramaphosa and his allies. For Zuma, it was essential that Dlamini Zuma win. He might have divorced her many years ago, in 1998, but she was his 'get out of jail free' card—the one person who could ensure that he was not held to account for the myriad cases of corruption he faced. Whether she saw her candidacy in different terms is another matter.

The clash between the camps was immediately the primary political issue facing the country, taking up acres of newspaper space. Opinion formers within the ANC were wooed assiduously—particularly the leaders of each province, since they were seen as the key to the votes at the conference. Money and promises of positions in government were said to have been used across the country. Ramaphosa won the trade union support and the backing of the Communist Party. Dlamini Zuma had the backing of the ANC women's and youth organisations. There were bitter clashes at many of the regional party conferences at which delegations were chosen. Ramaphosa won five of the ANC's provincial delegations while Dlamini Zuma took four, but these four included KwaZulu-Natal, which has the largest ANC membership in the country.

In the end, the decision went down to the wire. There were dark rumours of financial inducements for delegates to vote for Dlamini Zuma, with allegations that public funds were tapped in an attempt to secure a victory for the president's slate.[19] According to the head of the Independent Police Investigative Directorate, Robert McBride, R54 million was siphoned off from police funds for the purpose.[20]

Despite this, Ramaphosa managed to win—but only just. His margin of victory was 179 votes out of the total 4,701 votes that were cast. He won partly because courts ruled against some delegates who might have favoured his rival, and because others saw the way the wind was blowing and went over to the winning side. Jacob Zuma, who had been assured by his supporters that Dlamini Zuma would win, sat stony-faced. There were celebrations on the streets of Soweto. South Africans, on the whole, breathed a huge sigh of relief. Yet Ramaphosa's win was so circumscribed that he had to be extraordinarily careful about how he proceeded to reform the country. Of the top six posts in the ANC, only three were in his camp. He only had a very narrow majority on the National Executive. Some thirty-six of the eighty-strong Executive had been in the Zuma camp.[21]

Ramaphosa was certain of the loyalty of just twenty-nine. He would have to proceed very cautiously indeed in sweeping away the orgy of corruption.

Nor did Zuma take his defeat lying down. Despite losing the vote for the leadership of the ANC, he did not immediately resign the presidency of the country. He was not just fighting to hold off impending court cases, but for the future of his family. His children had benefited enormously from his position, and been given a string of lucrative positions. In 2014, Zuma's daughter Thuthukile was appointed to a position as chief of staff in the office of the minister of telecommunications and postal services, with an annual salary of R1 million. The position was never advertised. Another daughter, Gugu Zuma-Ncube, was given a bailout by the City of Durban so she could continue producing a Zulu-language television series. His nephew Khulubuse was involved in a series of financial scandals, some of which ended with miners driven into poverty and taking their own lives. The biggest beneficiary was Zuma's son Duduzane, who joined the Guptas to plunder Eskom and other state-owned enterprises.[22] Little wonder that the president fought to the end. Those close to Zuma warned that any attempt to remove him as president would be resisted. 'It will cause havoc,' declared a group associated with him.[23]

Ramaphosa persevered, slowly and carefully, but as he did so tensions rose. There were even dark rumours of mutiny by troops who had served with Zuma during the liberation struggle. An ANC member of parliament was quoted as saying that he had 'heard that Zuma was planning to declare a state of emergency, and cordon off the parliamentary precinct and arrest MPs'.[24] This plan was apparently foiled when the generals refused to cooperate, indicating their loyalty to the constitutional process. The Communist Party accused Zuma of being at the heart of a 'counter-revolutionary fightback', as Ramaphosa attempted to dismantle what the party described as 'the networks of parasitic looting of public resources that flourished under the patronage of former president Jacob Zuma'.[25]

Despite all of this, Ramaphosa did succeed in finally forcing Zuma to step down, even though it took the threat of impeachment to achieve it.[26] On 15 February 2018, Ramaphosa was sworn in as the fifth president of South Africa since the end of apartheid. He had fulfilled an ambition that had long been denied him.

13

THE 2019 ELECTION LEAVES THE COUNTRY STIRRED, NOT SHAKEN

A win, and a loss, for the ANC

It was a Sunday morning in early January, and there was a strong wind in the seaside city of Durban, the third biggest in South Africa. The usually punctual Cyril Ramaphosa was made to wait a couple of hours for the wind to subside before it was safe enough to step onto the stage set up in the Moses Mabhida Stadium and launch the ANC's massive birthday rally. It doubled as the launch of the party's manifesto, ahead of the 8 May election just four months away. The ten stadiums built for the 2010 FIFA World Cup in cities across the country have come in handy for the ANC's rallies. So far, it is the only party with enough money and supporters to fill them.

Hot on Ramaphosa's heels, former president Jacob Zuma followed him into the stadium. Ramaphosa received an excited but polite reception from the crowd, whereas they went wild for Zuma. The province of KwaZulu-Natal, of which Durban is the economic capital, is Zuma's home ground, but this wasn't quite the scenario Ramaphosa's supporters had hoped for. They wanted party supporters to unite behind Ramaphosa, but many in the party felt that Zuma had been less than fairly treated when he was forced to resign almost a year earlier. Underdogs tend to do well in South African politics.

With the ANC's majority in the elections still almost a given, party infighting characterised its campaign. Indeed, this took precedence over its battle with smaller parties such as the DA, which has been trying to build a support base by recruiting unhappy ANC voters, and the EFF, which has attracted younger voters as well as black middle-class professionals and businesspeople frustrated with the ANC. Many disillusioned ANC supporters have simply started staying away from the polls. The question wasn't who the winner would be, but whether Ramaphosa would be able to assert himself within the party by reining in Zuma's supporters, and prosecuting those who had looted state resources over the nine years of his predecessor's governance.

The manifesto itself contained the usual promises of jobs in a country where unemployment is rife (specifically, it pledged a modest doubling of the annual rate of employment creation to 275,000), continued grants, more houses, and running water and sanitation in all communities. It promised land expropriation without compensation, but cautiously added that the conditions would have to be clearly defined. Ramaphosa also promised to continue with his drive to attract international investment, which he initiated soon after becoming president in February 2018.

Ramaphosa's stark admission that the party had failed its country during Zuma's presidency (although it did not mention him by name) is the kind of move that would kill a party's campaign in more highly contested circumstances. Given the ANC's internal divisions, its failures in government, and the corruption it had tolerated on both national and local levels, Ramaphosa had to find a way to reinvent the party's image.

'We accept that mistakes have been made and, in some critical areas, progress has stalled,' he said. 'This is a moment of renewal. It is an opportunity to restore our democratic institutions and return our country to a path of transformation, growth and development.'[1] Ramaphosa repeated this message throughout his campaign. Visiting the small settlement of Mqanduli in the rural Eastern Cape, he said: 'Let us show the world and the whole country that the people of South Africa want change, they are voting for change to move forward, so that we can continue with our work as the ANC to improve the lives of our people.'[2]

As propaganda, it worked. Many ANC supporters interviewed on the campaign trail cited these promises as the reason they would vote for the party again, even though it had, by its own admission, let them down. Even the chattering classes were persuaded. Veteran journalist Peter Bruce argued that Ramaphosa—who has the support of only just over half of the eighty-six-strong National Executive Committee of his party—needed as many votes as possible to give him the legitimacy to pursue a reform agenda in government.[3] Ramaphosa polled higher than the party itself in some surveys.[4]

The biggest question throughout the election campaign was whether the ANC would support Ramaphosa in his implementation of this agenda, and, if not, whether he would be strong enough to effect his reforms. One of the ANC's major election promises was that it would fight corruption—and not for the first time. In 2014, Zuma had promised to boost the capacity of corruption-fighting agencies. Ironically, he did exactly the opposite, decimating the National Prosecuting Authority and elite crime-fighting agency the Hawks.[5] Five years later, Ramaphosa's manifesto promised that the ANC would clean up the corruption of the Zuma years and 'put an end to state capture, restore the integrity of public institutions and tackle corruption, while ensuring that government has the capacity, resources and people to serve citizens effectively'. It added: 'We are also determined to show no tolerance in the fight against corruption and misconduct within the ANC.'[6]

The election took place against the backdrop of a Commission of Inquiry into state capture, headed by Deputy Chief Justice Raymond Zondo and instituted by Zuma himself. The commission started its work towards the end of 2018, and its explosive revelations continually punctuated the ANC's campaign. It served as a reminder both of how the ANC had flouted its previous election promises, and how it was beginning to implement its new ones. Opposition parties used the information that emerged from the commission in their campaigns. For example, the EFF manifesto launch in February coincided with the revelation, disclosed by a whistleblower from security company Bosasa, that a shopping list of chicken pieces, lamb and alcohol, as well as an expensive handbag, had been given to former water and sanitation minister Nomvula Mokonyane in exchange for various favours. The company had also sponsored many ANC events. EFF supporters at the rally held up a naked female mannequin, representing the minister, with the words 'pay back Bosasa' and 'ANC thupa, it's coming' (warning the ANC that a beating was in the offing).

Despite these handicaps the ANC was victorious, as polls had indicated in the run-up to the voting. The exact figure had been hard to predict because it depended on turn-out. Some ANC supporters punished the party by staying away, while others voted for opposition parties. The ANC therefore won 57.5 per cent of the vote—down from the 62 per cent it got under Zuma in 2014, which itself had fallen from an all-time high of almost 70 per cent under Mbeki a decade before that.[7] But only 65.1 per cent of registered voters participated, the lowest ever figure in a South African election.

The most nail-biting outcome was in Gauteng, where the party got 50.19 per cent of the vote, dropping by four percentage points and barely scraping a majority in the provincial legislature, while the most shocking drop was in Zuma's home province of KwaZulu-Natal, where its share fell by over eleven percentage points to 54.2 per cent. In private, Zuma's supporters blamed this outcome on the way that the ANC had unseated him from the presidency. They also expressed dissatisfaction with Ramaphosa, arguing that while his supporters cited poor electoral performance as a reason for getting rid of Zuma, it was Ramaphosa who had now delivered the worst ever results for the party. ANC secretary general Ace Magashule, a fierce opponent of Ramaphosa, declared that the president could not take credit for the party's majority: 'The people who made us win the elections are volunteers, communities and people who love the ANC. The ANC has never been about an individual.'[8] The attack on Ramaphosa was neither subtle nor concealed.

On the other hand, the ANC's elections head Fikile Mbalula openly speculated—supported by opinion polls—that if Zuma had remained president and his faction had won the 2017 leadership contest in the ANC (via his former wife, Nkosazana Dlamini Zuma, whom Ramaphosa subsequently attempted to win over by appointing her a minister in his cabinet), the party's vote share could have dropped as low as 40 per cent. In 2016, the ANC won 55 per cent in the municipal elections.[9]

Opposition parties will continue to capitalise on these divisions; Julius Malema took a fresh shot during his party's post-election press conference by stating that Ramaphosa had performed worse than Zuma. 'The entire capitalist establishment, including international media tried to impose Ramaphosa on the people of South Africa,' he said. 'The reality is that despite being presented as the best of the best, Ramaphosa performed worse than Jacob Zuma, meaning that to ordinary people, Ramaphosa is no better than Zuma.'[10] His analysis might not be factually sound, but many of his followers, and of those sympathetic to Zuma, believe this.

Whatever Zuma's supporters felt, and despite its record of corruption and abuse, just over half of all South Africans still vote for the ANC. Travelling around the rural areas it is not hard to see why. While many places have been neglected, most have water, electricity and sanitation—necessities to which they seldom had access under apartheid. People living in decent homes, even if the electricity sometimes fails, don't forget that in a hurry. The power cables strung out across the country speak volumes to the voters. So too do the social security payments, which are vital to many African families. The pension or disability grant of R1,700 a month (£100) is not much to live on but it helps many to survive, and the ANC has succeeded in convincing many of its recipients that any other party might remove this safety net.

There are many in places like the Eastern Cape, still an ANC heartland, who continue to support the party, even if they do so reluctantly. Asanda Qosha, who lives in a village on the outskirts of King William's Town, is a self-employed builder. 'The ANC is the only vehicle for people to get out of poverty,' he explained. At the same time, he has no illusions about the party. 'The ANC is very corrupt. It really bothers me. They are robbing our poor: that's why there's no housing, roads or clinics.'[11] Some consider the ANC akin to family. Nomvelile Ngxokile's house in the tiny coastal town of Port St Johns was flooded by heavy rains, just before the elections. Even though this was partly due to the ineptness of the local ANC-run council, she said that she would stick with the ANC. 'ANC is our home. If ANC has got a problem, we're supposed to sit and talk because it's our home, we're not going to leave this home because your home's got mistakes. We're supposed to sit and talk.'[12]

The Democratic Alliance grinds to a halt

One person who has broken with a family tradition of supporting the ANC is Mmusi Maimane, who has led the opposition

Democratic Alliance (DA) since 2015. The 2019 election was the 38-year-old's first national and provincial campaign. The party's support had been on an upward trajectory in the preceding decade, reaching 22.23 per cent in 2014. The 2016 result was even more phenomenal: the DA's total share of the national vote climbed by about four percentage points, and the party instituted mayors, in cooperation agreements with other opposition parties, in three formerly ANC metros.

However, the DA's final rally in Soweto, south-west of Johannesburg, the weekend before the elections, was poorly attended, and although it looked good on television it lacked sparkle in real life. The campaign had become shrill by that point, and had fallen back on controversial (but previously marginally successful) scare tactics used in earlier elections, with a last batch of posters urging voters to vote DA so as to prevent an ANC–EFF coalition from coming to power. With Ramaphosa's popularity outstripping that of the ANC in opinion polls, the DA repeatedly reminded voters that Ramaphosa was part of a party which, by its own admission, was riddled with corruption.

At the rally, Maimane told the crowds to be as brave as the South African athlete Caster Semenya, who was in the midst of a fresh storm about her testosterone levels. He said they should have the courage to change the party that they voted for. 'I know this is hard for those who have only ever known one party. I was in that position too once, but looking back now, embracing change was the best thing I ever did,' he said. 'I'm not asking you to marry me, I'm merely asking you to employ a government with a proven track record.'[13]

His pleas fell on deaf ears. The DA's share of the vote fell by 1.5 per cent, to 20.8 per cent. The party had tried to appeal to black voters by supporting black economic empowerment, while Maimane contentiously vowed to take on 'white privilege'.[14] In the end, however, its black vote grew by only 0.4 per cent to

4.7 per cent, according to elections analyst Dawie Scholtz.[15] The ANC lost 5.8 per cent of the black electorate's votes, but it was the EFF that took most of them, gaining 5.5 per cent among black voters.

The biggest blow was the DA's loss of an estimated 470,000 votes to the Freedom Front Plus (FF Plus), which appealed to white voters on the right who felt that the DA wasn't voicing their concerns about land redistribution, the murder of white farmers, and black economic empowerment, among other things.[16] Under Zuma, a DA campaigner explained, white voters 'outsourced' politics to the DA because they considered the party a potent weapon against the former president. With Zuma gone and the noise around him subsiding, they had some space to reconsider whom to support.[17] Others in the party blamed Maimane for scaring off this demographic, and for failing to sufficiently inspire black voters. He laid low in the days immediately after the elections, but indicated that he accepted responsibility for the party's failure to make progress.[18] However, his supporters in the party hierarchy rallied around him by declaring that the party took 'collective responsibility' for its electoral losses.[19]

Helen Zille, who was Maimane's predecessor as party leader and was brought out towards the end of the DA's campaign to appeal to those who were contemplating turning to the FF Plus, has argued that it is what she terms 'identity politics' that is eating into DA support. She argued:

> Our job is to build a new majority on the basis of a common set of values, among people who genuinely want one South Africa for all (unlike—for example—the EFF that wants South Africa for one race only).

> We are a party for people who are committed to addressing the real problems preventing economic growth, improved education, and social progress, without seeking to scapegoat minorities.

It is fallacious to present the key issue in SA as a dichotomy between 'black poverty' and 'white privilege'. The face of privilege has been transformed by a predatory ANC/EFF elite that has looted the country and set us on the road to ruin. The DA should not pander to this analysis.[20]

Zille is a hero in some constituencies, but her tweets have been criticised by some within the party for undermining Maimane's leadership. In 2017, she was made to apologise for a series of tweets which appeared to justify colonialism (although she claimed they did nothing of the kind). She was subsequently ordered to withdraw from DA decision-making structures.[21] Two years later, however, she defended the tweets again in the run-up to the elections. In the wake of the DA's dismal performance among voters, Zille then caused another Twitter storm by terming the corruption of the governing ANC an example of 'black privilege'.

This has prompted a harsh backlash, even within her own party. Mbali Ntuli, the DA's young, black head of elections in KwaZulu-Natal (the only province where the DA did grow in 2019), lashed out on Twitter and, without naming Zille, accused her of being 'tone deaf' and not engaging 'with the masses' on the ground during the campaign.[22] This was clearly untrue. Zille repeatedly took the campaign into black areas of the Cape, and was often warmly received by those she met.

Another huge issue for the party was the way it dealt with Patricia de Lille, its mayor in Cape Town and a seasoned politician with a reasonable support base. She resigned after accusations of maladministration followed by a disciplinary process riddled with politics and inconsistencies, and went on to launch a party of her own, named GOOD. She took two seats nationally and one in the Western Cape, where the DA lost two seats.

Establishing the best way forward represents a dilemma for the DA. As political journalist Pieter du Toit suggests, the party may have lost its best opportunity to make progress:

The biggest indictment of the party's leadership team is the fact that it showed a singular inability to profit from the ANC's debauchery over the last five years. If the DA cannot establish itself as a viable alternative to the ANC in a period of grand corruption, capture and the Zuma government's destruction, when will it be able to do so?[23]

This is a fair reflection on the DA's 2019 campaign, but it is also important not to ignore the party's successes. It remains the official opposition; it continues to speak for more than one in five South Africans; and it has a party hierarchy and membership that truly reflects the racial composition of the country.

The Economic Freedom Fighters: gaining big while remaining small

One of the biggest winners in this election was the Economic Freedom Fighters (EFF), whose leadership is young, brash and vocal. The party, which has caused much disruption to parliamentary sittings when it hasn't got its way, came close to doubling its twenty-five seats, adding another nineteen, although its percentage of the vote was only 10.8 per cent.[24] Its voter base tends to be younger, but registration for voting, and turnout, among this constituency is low. Many South Africans would also confess that, while they want to see the energetic and disruptive EFF represented in parliament, they do not want to see it in government.

The party is vocal on social and other media, and has also been successful in forcing the ANC to shift government policy towards its own on several fronts. The ANC's position on nationalising land without compensation has become more similar to the EFF's, and it has also reacted to EFF campaigns to reduce the fees for university education, increasing the number of students exempted from paying for their studies.

The EFF has moved from being the biggest opposition party in only one province, Limpopo, to three provinces, adding Mpumalanga and the North West. This will give Malema's party the chance to show that it is more than just an oppositional force, and can actually contribute to the political process. This opportunity has also presented itself in Gauteng, where the ANC has the slimmest of majorities (50.2 per cent of the vote).[25] The EFF could work with the rest of the opposition to hold the ANC to account (it is already working with the DA to govern the metro councils of Johannesburg and Pretoria), or it could decide to cooperate with the ANC in government instead.

Apart from its usual rallies, pamphleteering, and a large number of simple, well-branded posters (Malema's face on a red background, accompanied by the words 'son of the soil'), the EFF campaigned simply by maintaining a physical presence, with members wearing red t-shirts or trademark red berets in social spaces. It also often used ambush tactics, such as pamphleteering on street corners near ANC campaigns. Supporters were even once heard singing outside a home in a community on the West Rand, near Johannesburg, while Ramaphosa made door-to-door visits.

Instances of violence and intimidation between EFF and ANC supporters did not make headlines as they did in 2014, although heated exchanges and chair-throwing between the EFF and smaller radical parties made some televised debates impossible. EFF leaders afterwards condemned the violence.[26] The party was slower, however, to condemn the intimidation of journalists. During the campaign, Malema doxed talk show host and political commentator Karima Brown by tweeting a screenshot of a message from her, containing her phone number, after she accidentally sent editorial instructions to an EFF WhatsApp group. Despite condemnation from other journalists, he did not remove the tweet straight away. As a result, Brown received a series of personal calls, insults, and threats of murder and rape.[27]

Malema also enjoyed a small victory in March, when the South African Human Rights Commission made the contentious ruling that some of his utterances over the past few years had not constituted hate speech. This included an instance where he told a crowd of supporters that the party would not call for the slaughter of white people, 'at least for now'.[28] Much of the EFF's power is wielded through the threat of violence. On election day, along with most of the other opposition parties, it raised concerns about double voting. Malema told a press conference held after the elections that the Independent Electoral Commission (IEC) should modernise its systems before the 2021 local government elections. 'Its incapacity and incompetence will lead to violence and an unworkable political environment,' he said.[29]

The EFF wasn't spared internal controversies ahead of the poll either, of the variety that occur in most parties when they are nominating candidates to the legislatures. An MP who didn't obtain a good position on the nominations list wrote a letter claiming that Malema had failed to account for the R2 million he collected from the party's public representatives in party levies every month.[30] The party was also haunted throughout the election by a banking scandal from which it was said to have benefited.[31]

On a personal level, however, it was a difficult election for Malema, who first lost his aunt in the early stages of campaigning, and weeks later, shortly before election day, also lost the grandmother who had raised him, whom he was very close to.[32] Messages of condolence poured in to Malema from across party lines.

The other beneficiaries

The mainly white, conservative Freedom Front Plus, which has a leadership dominated by Afrikaans-speaking men, was perhaps the biggest winner of the election—albeit with a very low starting point—and more than doubled its seats in the National Assembly, going from four to ten. One of these seats will be occupied by Wynand Boshoff, the grandson of former prime minister and architect of apartheid Hendrik Verwoerd. Its 2.4 per cent share of the vote was a 0.2 per cent improvement on its previous high point in 1994, when it won votes from former National Party supporters.

The Freedom Front Plus played on white fears that their position in the country was being eroded and adopted the slogan 'fight back', which was printed on myriad posters and displayed on lampposts in towns and cities beyond the party's traditional strongholds in mainly rural inland provinces.[33] One prominent example of this perceived loss of standing was the abolition of Afrikaans as the official language in several universities (including Stellenbosch—the alma mater of most Afrikaner prime ministers and presidents).There was also recently an incident in Schweizer-Reneke, a small rural town, in which a school teacher was incorrectly accused of racism. The DA jumped on the bandwagon and as a result lost every single voting district in the town, as well as damaging its support base nationally.[34] Fears of land expropriation without compensation by the governing party, and a sense that the DA was unclear on where it stood on the matter, have helped to win the party further votes.

The Inkatha Freedom Party (a mainly Zulu party) also did well in the elections. It took fourteen seats, an increase of four, apparently profiting from the collapse of rival splinter party the National Freedom Party, as well as unhappiness with the ANC amongst Zuma supporters in its KwaZulu-Natal heartland.[35]

Free and fair, but uninspiring

South Africa's sixth election since the end of apartheid saw nearly 17.7 million people out of a registered total of 26.2 million vote at 22,924 polling stations.[36] More than 9 million eligible voters, two-thirds of them younger than thirty, did not bother to register to vote at all, despite the bulk of the IEC's marketing directly targeting young voters.[37] Out of forty-eight parties on the longest ever ballot paper in a democratic South Africa, only fourteen made it to parliament—still the highest number since 1994.

The election was not without its flaws. It turned out that some were able to remove the supposedly indelible mark which was made on all voter's thumbs when they cast their votes. Some attributed this to substandard materials due to cuts in the IEC's budget.[38] Voters were not confined to voting in the district where they were registered, which enabled people to fraudulently vote more than once, but also contributed to shortages at certain polling stations. A handful of people were prosecuted for voting more than once. However, the statistician-general sampled the results of 1,020 voting stations and found that the influence on the final results would have been negligible.

Voters abroad—only allowed to vote following a court order in 2009—also posed a problem. A total of 29,334 people were registered to vote abroad, but that is a small fraction of those who qualify. In order to register and vote, there were various forms to fill in and present at South African embassies and high commissions, sometimes far away from the cities where expats live. There were also some concerns about voters having to place their votes in two envelopes, with the outer layer marked with their name and identity number for audit purposes. This meant that the secrecy of these votes could be compromised. Apart from the staff of these government institutions, most voters abroad supported the opposition.

Even though there was a general feeling that the elections were free and fair, there was concern about how little interest South Africans showed in participating. As one commentator, Dawie Scholtz, put it:

> This was an exceptionally low-turnout election; an almost shockingly low-turnout election compared to previous national elections. South Africa has never had a national election with less than 70%

overall turnout. In 2014, turnout was 72.5%. The overall turnout for the 2019 national election (including all overseas voters who filled in VEC10 forms), is 65.1%. This is much lower than anticipated and influenced the election outcome significantly.[39]

Post-mortems of the election by official bodies, as well as opposition parties, are likely to look seriously at how to get young people more interested in participating in South Africa's fledgling democracy in the future. As with all of the country's elections, it will be extensively analysed and debated. But one fact should not escape anyone's attention: the outcome—despite imperfections—did reflect the wishes of South Africa's voters. It was not decided by the president in advance of the vote, with ballot boxes stuffed and sealed before anyone had gone to the polls. The new parliament will be made up of MPs who can genuinely say that they are the representatives of their people. On the African continent that is—sadly—something of a rarity. It took South Africans more than a century to achieve, and it still merits celebration.

NOTES

1. INTRODUCTION: EXTRAORDINARY COUNTRY, CONTRASTING LIVES

1. Elmon Tshikhudo, 'Vhembe's burning', *Limpopo Mirror*, 16 August 2013, https://www.limpopomirror.co.za/articles/news/20721/2013–08–16/vhembes-burning, last accessed 8 April 2019.
2. Mpho Dube, '"VBS killings" trouble SACP', *The Sowetan*, 3 February 2019, https://www.sowetanlive.co.za/sundayworld/news/2019-02-03-vbs-killings-trouble-sacp/, last accessed 8 April 2019.
3. Kyle Cowan, 'Explosive report into VBS Mutual Bank reveals large-scale "looting"', News24, 10 October 2018, https://www.news24.com/SouthAfrica/News/explosive-report-into-vbs-bank-reveals-large-scale-looting-20181010, last accessed 8 April 2019.
4. Joseph Cotterill, 'South Africa: How Cape Town beat the drought', *Financial Times*, 2 May 2018, https://www.ft.com/content/b9bac89a-4a49-11e8-8ee8-cae73aab7ccb, last accessed 8 April 2019.
5. Canny Maphanga, 'Helping the next Zondo—deputy chief justice and good samaritan uplift poor youth', News24, 13 January 2019, https://www.news24.com/SouthAfrica/News/helping-the-next-zondo-deputy-chief-justice-and-good-samaritan-uplift-poor-youth-20190113, last accessed 8 April 2019.

2. A BRIEF HISTORY

1. 'Nomination for the assignation of Grade I Status for the Porterville

Galleon Rock Art, Porterville, Western Cape', South African Heritage Resources Agency, 31 May 2017, http://www.sahra.org.za/sahris/cases/nomination-assignation-grade-i-status-porterville-galleon-rock-art-porterville-western-cape, last accessed 8 April 2019.

2. 'The San', South African History Online, http://www.sahistory.org.za/article/san, last accessed 8 April 2019.

3. 'When, why and where the first African farmers settled in Southern Africa', South African History Online, http://www.sahistory.org.za/article/when-why-and-where-first-african-farmers-settled-southern-africa, last accessed 8 April 2019.

4. H. B. Thom (ed.), *Journal of Jan van Riebeeck*, 3 vols, Cape Town: A. A. Bakema for the Van Riebeeck Society, 1952–58, pp. 195–6.

5. Richard Elphick and Hermann Giliomee (eds), *The Shaping of South African Society, 1652–1840*, Cape Town: Maskew Miller Longman, 1989, p. xvii.

6. Simon Hall, 'Farming Communities of the Second Millennium: Internal Frontiers, Identity, Continuity and Change', in Carolyn Hamilton, Bernard Mbenga and Robert Ross (eds), *The Cambridge History of South Africa, Volume 1: From Earliest Times to 1885*, Cambridge: Cambridge University Press, 2010, pp. 146–7.

7. Hermann Giliomee, 'The Eastern Frontier, 1770–1812', in Richard Elphick and Hermann Giliomee (eds), *The Shaping of South African Society, 1652–1840*, Cape Town: Maskew Miller Longman, 1989, p. 421.

8. Gerald Groenewald, 'Slaves and Free Blacks in VOC Cape Town, 1652—1795', *History Compass*, vol. 8/9 (2010), pp. 964–83.

9. Andrew Ross, *John Philip (1775–1851): Missions, Race and Politics in South Africa*, Aberdeen: Aberdeen University Press, 1986, p. 109.

10. Elizabeth Elbourne and Robert Ross, 'Combating Spiritual and Social Bondage: Early Missions in the Cape Colony', in Richard Elphick and Rodney Davenport (eds), *Christianity in South Africa: A Political, Social & Cultural History*, London: James Currey, 1997, p. 39.

11. *Report of Commission of Inquiry regarding Cape Coloured Population of the Union*, Pretoria: Government Printer, 1937, p. 212.

12. Ibid., p. 212.

13. Denis Judd and Keith Surridge, *The Boer War: A History*, London: John Murray, 2002, p. 20.

14. L. M. Thompson, *The Unification of South Africa, 1902–1910*, Oxford: Clarendon Press, 1960, p. 2.

15. This version of events is contested. Some historians suggest that English and Indian trade at Delagoa Bay from the 1760s onwards contributed to the *Mfecane*, but this alternative narrative is not widely accepted. See John Wright, 'Turbulent Times: Political Transformations in the North and East, 1760s–1830s', in *The Cambridge History of South Africa, Volume 1*, p. 214.

16. Ibid., p. 249.

17. Charles H. Feinstein, *An Economic History of South Africa*, Cambridge: Cambridge University Press, 2005, p. 57.

18. Hermann Giliomee, *The Afrikaners: Biography of a People*, London: Hurst and Company, 2003, p. 290.

19. Hermann Giliomee and Bernard Mbenga, *New History of South Africa*, Cape Town: Tafelberg, 2007, p. 159.

20. Ibid., p. 198.

21. D. Hobart Houghton and Jenifer Dagut, *Source Material on the South African Economy: 1860–1970. Vol. 1, 1860–1899*, Cape Town; London: Oxford University Press, p. 340.

22. See Duncan Innes, *Anglo American and the Rise of Modern South Africa*, London: Heinemann Educational Books, 1984, p. 48 ff. for a discussion of this issue.

23. Feinstein, *An Economic History of South Africa*, p. 63.

24. Andre Odendaal, *The Founders: The Origins of the ANC and the Struggle for Democracy in South Africa*, Auckland Park: Jacana, 2012, p. 189.

25. In 1860, after two centuries of hard toil, South Africa's farms had produced total exports worth just £2,500,000 a year. By the first half of the 1890s gold exports alone totalled £4,500,000 a year. See Feinstein, *An Economic History of South Africa*, p. 100.

26. Odendaal, *The Founders*, p. 24.

27. Brian Willan, *Sol Plaatje: South African Nationalist, 1876–1932*, Berkeley: University of California Press, 1984, p. 21.

28. Heather Hughes, *The First President: A Life of John L. Dube, Founding President of the ANC*, Auckland Park: Jacana, 2011, pp. 30–40.

29. Odendaal, *The Founders*, p. 38.

30. Ibid., p. 96.

31. Ibid., p. 100.

32. Ibid., pp. 43–44. The poem was published in *Isigidimi* in June 1882. Hoho is a reference to the mountain refuge from which Mgolombane Sandile resisted the British; he was killed there in 1878.

33. Judd and Surridge, *The Boer War*, p. 34.

34. G. H. L. Le May, *British Supremacy in South Africa, 1899–1907*, Oxford: Clarendon Press, 1965, p. 18.

35. Ibid., p. 31.

36. See J. S. Marais, *The Fall of Kruger's Republic*, Oxford: Clarendon Press, 1961, pp. 1–3 for a discussion of this issue.

37. Giliomee and Mbenga, *New History of South Africa*, p. 211. In 1897 the British decided to increase the garrison in South Africa to 8,000 men and twenty-four field guns. See Le May, *British Supremacy in South Africa*, p. 6.

38. Judd and Surridge, *The Boer War*, pp. 91–92.

39. Ibid., p. 60.

40. Giliomee, *The Afrikaners*, p. 252.

41. Judd and Surridge, *The Boer War*, p. 191.

42. Ibid., p. 193.

43. Giliomee, *The Afrikaners*, p. 255.

44. Ibid., pp. 260–62.

45. W. K. Hancock, *Smuts: The Sanguine Years, 1870–1919*, Cambridge: Cambridge University Press, 1962, p. 133.

46. Ibid., p. 155.

47. Andre Wessels (ed.), *Lord Kitchener and the War in South Africa, 1899–1902*, Stroud: Sutton Publishing for the Army Records Society, 2006, p. 197.

48. Hancock, *Smuts: The Sanguine Years*, p. 159.

49. Ibid., pp. 161–2.

50. Thomas Pakenham, *The Boer War*, London: Abacus, 1991, p. 572. Others give different figures. Elizabeth van Heyningen quotes the official figures from the monument to the women in the camps at 26,251 women and children and 1,676 men, but some have given even higher

figures. See Elizabeth van Heyningen, *The Concentration Camps of the Anglo-Boer War: A Social History*, Auckland Park: Jacana, 2013, p. 18.

51. Martin Plaut, *Promise and Despair: The First Struggle for a Non-Racial South Africa*, Johannesburg: Jacana, 2016, p. 64–67.

52. Colonel John Seely, Secretary of State for the Colonies, Clause 35 (Qualifications of Voters), House of Commons Debate, 19 August 1909, https://api.parliament.uk/historic-hansard/commons/1909/aug/19/clause-35-qualifications-of-voters, last accessed 16 April 2019.

53. *The Daily Mail*, 19 July 1909.

54. *Imperial Conference, Correspondence and Papers relating to a Conference with Representatives of the Self-Governing Dominions on the Naval and Military Defence of the Empire, 1909*, London: HMSO, 1909, Cmnd 4948.

55. *The Graphic*, 21 August 1909.

56. Odendaal, *The Founders*, p. 438.

57. Peter Walshe, *The Rise of African Nationalism in South Africa: The African National Congress, 1912–1952*, London: Hurst and Company, 1970, pp. 31–35.

58. Sol Plaatje, *Native Life in South Africa Before and Since the European War and the Boer Rebellion (1916)*, Johannesburg: Ravan Press, 1982, p. 21.

59. S. B. Spies, 'The Outbreak of the First World War and the Botha Government', *South African Historical Journal*, vol. 1, no. 1 (1969), pp. 47–48.

60. 'The SS Mendi—A Historical Background', SA Navy, http://www.navy.mil.za/newnavy/mendi_history/mendi_hist.htm, last accessed 16 April 2019.

61. Philip Bonner, 'South African Society and Culture, 1910–1948', in Robert Ross, Anne Kelk Mager and Bill Nasson (eds), *The Cambridge History of South Africa, Volume 2: 1885–1994*, Cambridge: Cambridge University Press, 2011, p. 298.

62. T. R. H. Davenport, *South Africa: A Modern History*, Toronto; Buffalo: University of Toronto Press, 1987, p. 313. Smuts had introduced a convoluted system of representation for Africans beyond the Cape in the 1920s, but it was largely disregarded by Africans.

63. 'The Leader of the Ossewa Brandwag: Johannes Frederik Janse van Rensburg', The O'Malley Archive, https://omalley.nelsonmandela.org/omalley/index.php/site/q/03lv02424/04lv02730/05lv02996/06lv03000.htm, last accessed 16 April 2019.

64. 'A History of the Springbok Legion', South African History Online, https://www.sahistory.org.za/article/history-springbok-legion, last accessed 16 April 2019.

65. Giliomee, The Afrikaners, p. 454.

66. Ibid., p. 470.

67. Nelson Mandela, Long Walk to Freedom, London: Little Brown, 1994, p. 104.

68. Tom Lodge, Mandela: A Critical Life, Oxford: Oxford University Press, 2006, p. 36.

69. Ibid., p. 43.

70. This remains a controversial, contested question. See Stephen Ellis, External Mission: The ANC in Exile, 1960–1990, London: Hurst and Company, 2012, p. 22 for a discussion of the issue.

71. Feinstein, An Economic History of South Africa, p. 151.

72. 'Defiance Campaign 1952', South African History Online, http://www.sahistory.org.za/topic/defiance-campaign-1952, last accessed 16 April 2019.

73. 'Treason Trial 1956–1961', South Africa History Online, https://www.sahistory.org.za/article/treason-trial-1956–1961, last accessed 16 April 2019.

74. Ellis, 'Chapter One: Call to Arms', in External Mission, pp. 1–39.

75. 'I am prepared to die', The Nelson Mandela Foundation, 20 April 2011, https://www.nelsonmandela.org/news/entry/i-am-prepared-to-die, last accessed 17 April 2019.

76. Lodge, Mandela, p. 171.

77. 'F. W. de Klerk's speech at the opening of Parliament 2 February 1990', The O'Malley Archive, https://omalley.nelsonmandela.org/omalley/index.php/site/q/03lv02039/04lv02103/05lv02104/06lv02105.htm, last accessed 17 April 2019.

78. 'South Africa's New Era; Transcript of Mandela's Speech at Cape Town City Hall: "Africa It Is Ours!"', New York Times, 12 February 1990,

http://www.nytimes.com/1990/02/12/world/south-africa-s-new-era-transcript-mandela-s-speech-cape-town-city-hall-africa-it.html? pagewanted=all, last accessed 17 April 2019.

79. 'Nelson Mandela's address to rally in Cape Town on his release from prison 11 February 1990', South African History Online, https://www. sahistory.org.za/archive/nelson-mandelas-address-rally-cape-town-his-release-prison-11-february-1990, last accessed 17 April 2019.

3. THE AFRICAN NATIONAL CONGRESS

1. Phumla Mkize, 'Stress is for whites—Zuma', *The Sowetan*, 16 April 2014, https://www.pressreader.com/south-africa/sowetan/20140416/ 282089159757889, last accessed 17 April 2019.

2. Anthony Butler, *The Idea of the ANC*, Auckland Park: Jacana, 2012, p. 10.

3. Prince Mashele and Mzukisi Qobo, *The Fall of the ANC: What Next?*, Johannesburg: Picador Africa, 2014, p. 2.

4. Bongani Ngqulunga, *The Man Who Founded the ANC: A Biography of Pixley ka Isaka Seme*, Cape Town: Penguin Random House South Africa, 2017.

5. 'Formation of the South African Native National Congress', South African History Online, https://www.sahistory.org.za/dated-event/for-mation-south-african-native-national-congress, last accessed 26 December 2018.

6. Renier Schoeman and Daryl Swanepoel, *Unity in Diversity: 100 Years of ANC Leadership (1912–2012)*, Johannesburg: BM Books, 2012, p. 23.

7. Ibid., p. 19.

8. Ibid., p. 26.

9. Ibid., pp. 47–52.

10. 'Continued resistance and internal criticism 1920s and 1930s', South African History Online, https://www.sahistory.org.za/topic/contin-ued-resistance-and-internal-criticism-1920s-and-1930s, last accessed 26 December 2018.

11. Schoeman and Swanepoel, *Unity in Diversity*, p. 45.

12. Ibid., p. 45.

13. Ibid., p. 73.

14. Ibid., p. 78.

15. Ibid., p. 118 and p. 130.

16. Ibid., p. 112.

17. Ibid., p. 146.

18. 'ANC and the early development of apartheid 1948–1950s', South African History Online, https://www.sahistory.org.za/topic/anc-and-early-development-apartheid-1948–1950s, last accessed 26 December 2018.

19. Ibid.

20. Schoeman and Swanepoel, *Unity in Diversity*, p. 137.

21. Ibid., p. 170.

22. Raymond Suttner, *The ANC Underground in South Africa, 1950–1976*, Auckland Park: Jacana, 2008, p. 32.

23. Ibid., p. 22.

24. Stephen Ellis, *External Mission: The ANC in Exile, 1960–1990*, London: Hurst and Company, 2012, pp. 25–26.

25. Schoeman and Swanepoel, *Unity in Diversity*, p. 172; Ellis, *External Mission*.

26. Mashele and Qobo, *The Fall of the ANC*, p. 74.

27. Schoeman and Swanepoel, *Unity in Diversity*, p. 174.

28. Suttner, *The ANC Underground*, p. 7 and p. 1.

29. Ibid., p. 3.

30. Ellis, *External Mission*, pp. 82–83.

31. Mashele and Qobo, *The Fall of the ANC*, p. 75.

32. Ibid., p. 74.

33. Suttner, *The ANC Underground*, p. 68.

34. Ibid., p. 159.

35. Schoeman and Swanepoel, *Unity in Diversity*, p. 208.

36. Ellis, *External Mission*.

37. The South African Democracy Education Trust, *The Road to Democracy in South Africa: Volume 1 (1960–1970)*, Pretoria: Unisa Press, 2010, p. 490.

38. Ellis, *External Mission*.

39. Schoeman and Swanepoel, *Unity in Diversity*, p. 212; Mashele and Qobo, *The Fall of the ANC*, p. 111.

40. Schoeman and Swanepoel, *Unity in Diversity*, p. 214.

41. 'South African Students Movement (SASM)', South African History Online, https://www.sahistory.org.za/article/south-african-students-movement-sasm, last accessed 27 December 2018.

42. Schoeman and Swanepoel, *Unity in Diversity*, p. 214.

43. Basia Cummings, Matthew Holmes and *Guardian* readers, '"My activism started then": the Soweto uprising remembered', *The Guardian*, https://www.theguardian.com/world/2016/jun/16/my-activism-started-then-the-soweto-uprising-remembered, last accessed 5 January 2019.

44. Schoeman and Swanepoel, *Unity in Diversity*, p. 214.

45. 'Armed struggle, the anti-apartheid struggle accelerates 1984–1990', South African History Online, https://www.sahistory.org.za/topic/armed-struggle-anti-apartheid-struggle-accelerates-1984–1990, last accessed 28 December 2018.

46. Schoeman and Swanepoel, *Unity in Diversity*, p. 217.

47. 'Armed struggle, the anti-apartheid struggle accelerates', South African History Online.

48. HSRC Press, '"I was angry and bitter": Chris Hani on the ANC's Decision to Suspend the Armed Struggle', *Sunday Times*, http://hsrcpress.bookslive.co.za/blog/2015/01/08/i-was-angry-and-bitter-chris-hani-on-the-ancs-decision-to-suspend-the-armed-struggle/, last accessed 29 December 2018.

49. 'Armed struggle, the anti-apartheid struggle accelerates', South African History Online.

50. Sisonke Msimang, 'Winnie Mandela's legacy: a renewed militancy in South Africa', *The Washington Post*, 4 April 2018, https://www.washingtonpost.com/news/global-opinions/wp/2018/04/04/winnie-mandelas-legacy-a-renewed-militancy-in-south-africa/?utm_term=.3c61772e3776, last accessed 28 December 2018.

51. Winnie Madikizela-Mandela, *491 Days: Prisoner Number 1323/69*, Johannesburg: Picador Africa, 2013, pp. 234–5.

52. Schoeman and Swanepoel, *Unity in Diversity*, p. 217.

53. 'Boipatong massacre—17 June 1992', South African History Online, https://www.sahistory.org.za/topic/boipatong-massacre-17-june-1992, last accessed 29 December 2018.

54. Allister Sparks, *Beyond the Miracle: Inside the New South Africa*, London: Profile Books, 2003, p. 262.

55. Schoeman and Swanepoel, *Unity in Diversity*, p. 251.

56. Sparks, *Beyond the Miracle*, p. 192.

57. Ibid., p. 188.

58. Ibid., p. 189.

59. Ibid., pp. 190–91.

60. Mashele and Qobo, *The Fall of the ANC*, pp. 5–7.

61. Ray Hartley, 'How Ramaphosa nearly became Nelson Mandela's deputy', *Sunday Times*, 12 November 2017, https://www.timeslive.co.za/sunday-times/news/2017-11-11-how-ramaphosa-nearly-became-nelson-mandelas-deputy/, last accessed 18 April 2019.

62. William Mervin Gumede, *Thabo Mbeki and the Battle for the Soul of the ANC*, Cape Town: Zebra Press, 2005, p. 341.

63. Sparks, *Beyond the Miracle*, pp. 264–66.

64. Sifiso Mxolisi Ndlovu and Miranda Strydom (eds), *The Thabo Mbeki I Know*, Johannesburg: Picador Africa, 2016, p. 346.

65. Kgolane Rudolph Phala, 'The Future of the ANC as a Ruling Party', *Umrabulo*, vol. 42, 2016, https://anc1912.org.za/docs/umrabulo_42_2016_ebook.pdf, last accessed 18 April 2019.

66. See also Chapter Five on the apartheid legacy and corruption.

67. 'The Arms Deal: What You Need to Know', Corruption Watch, 22 January 2014, https://www.corruptionwatch.org.za/the-arms-deal-what-you-need-to-know-2/, last accessed 6 January 2019.

68. 'Address by Zwelinzima Vavi, to the ANC Victory Celebrations', Congress of South African Trade Unions, 23 April 2009, http://www.cosatu.org.za/show.php?ID=199, last accessed 19 February 2019.

69. Frank Chikane, *Eight Days in September: The Removal of Thabo Mbeki*, Johannesburg: Picador Africa, 2012, p. 100.

70. Schoeman and Swanepoel, *Unity in Diversity*, p. 284.

71. 'President Thabo Mbeki Resigns', News24, 22 September 2008, https://www.news24.com/SouthAfrica/News/Mbekis-address-Full-text-20080921-2, last accessed 18 April 2019.

72. Ray Hartley, *Ragged Glory: The Rainbow Nation in Black and White*, Johannesburg; Cape Town: Jonathan Ball, 2014, p. 211.

73. '#GuptaLeaks: How Sun City had to fight the Guptas for wedding payment', News24, 6 June 2017, https://www.news24.com/SouthAfrica/News/guptaleaks-how-sun-city-had-to-fight-the-guptas-for-wedding-payment-20170606, last accessed 19 February 2019.

74. Scorpio and amaBhungane, '#GuptaLeaks: Emails offer further proof of Gupta racist attitudes', *Daily Maverick*, 9 June 2017, https://www.dailymaverick.co.za/article/2017-06-09-scorpio-and-amabhungane-guptaleaks-emails-offer-further-proof-of-gupta-racist-attitudes/, last accessed 19 February 2019.

75. Carien du Plessis and Andisiwe Makinana, 'Malema takes a swipe at Gupta family', Independent Online, 28 February 2011, https://www.iol.co.za/news/politics/malema-takes-a-swipe-at-gupta-family-1033211, last accessed 2 January 2019.

76. Ray Hartley, 'Book Extract: Ramaphosa and the massacre at Marikana', News24, 26 November 2017, https://www.news24.com/Books/book-extract-ramaphosa-and-the-massacre-at-marikana-20171126–2, last accessed 3 January 2019.

77. Hartley, *Ragged Glory*, p. 234.

78. *The New York Times* put this in perspective in a damning article: Norimitsu Onishi and Selam Gebrekidan, 'South Africa Vows to End Corruption. Are Its New Leaders Part of the Problem?', *New York Times*, 4 August 2018, https://www.nytimes.com/2018/08/04/world/africa/south-africa-anc-david-mabuza.html, last accessed 19 February 2019.

4. THE POLITICAL OPPOSITION

1. Jenni O'Grady, 'Detractors jealous of Zuma wit: ANC', Independent Online, 7 February 2011, https://www.iol.co.za/news/south-africa/gauteng/detractors-jealous-of-zuma-wit-anc-1022653, last accessed 18 April 2019; Ranjeni Munusamy, 'In the name of the Father: Jacob's law on politics and religion', *Daily Maverick*, 9 October 2013, https://www.dailymaverick.co.za/article/2013-10-09-in-the-name-of-the-father-jacobs-law-on-politics-and-religion/, last accessed 18 April 2019.

2. 'Our Vision', Democratic Alliance KwaZulu-Natal, http://www.dakzn.org.za/our-vision/, last accessed 18 April 2019.

3. Ibid.

4. 'What is the ANC?', African National Congress Eastern Cape, http://anceasterncape.org.za/about/what-is-the-anc/, last accessed 18 April 2019.

5. Ibid.

6. 'Minister defends welfare system', News24, 23 February 2010, http://www.news24.com/SouthAfrica/News/Minister-defends-welfare-system-20100223, last accessed 18 April 2019.

7. Jannie Rossouw, 'Why social grants matter in South Africa: they support 33% of the nation', The Conversation, 16 February 2017, https://theconversation.com/why-social-grants-matter-in-south-africa-they-support-33-of-the-nation-73087.

8. Democratic Alliance, 'Alternative Budget 2011/2012: A Budget to Address Poverty', February 2011, https://docs.google.com/viewer?a=v&pid=explorer&chrome=true&srcid=0B_-slGu8-FTxYmE0OTE1Z-mYtZmNjOS00OGRkLTk2NmUtM2E1ZGQ2OTZlNmE4&hl=en, last accessed 18 April 2019.

9. Ibid., Table 45.

10. 'ANC is denied two-thirds majority', BBC News, 25 April 2009, http://news.bbc.co.uk/1/hi/world/africa/8017713.stm, last accessed 18 April 2019.

11. Ben Maclennan, 'ANC slams "pale male" Cape executive', *Mail & Guardian*, 9 May 2009, https://mg.co.za/article/2009-05-09-anc-slams-pale-male-cape-executive, last accessed 18 April 2019.

12. Anna Majavu, 'Zuma put wives at risk of HIV—Zille', *The Sowetan*, 12 May 2009, https://www.sowetanlive.co.za/news/2009-05-12-zuma-put-wives-at-risk-of-hiv-zille/, last accessed 18 April 2019.

13. Carien du Plessis, Xolani Mbanjwa, Siyabonga Mkhwanazi and SAPA, 'Zille receives "reprimand of sorts" from DA', Independent Online, 14 May 2009, https://www.iol.co.za/news/politics/zille-receives-reprimand-of-sorts-from-da-443264, last accessed 18 April 2019.

14. Murray Williams, 'Zille extends olive branch to Zuma', Independent Online, 29 May 2009, https://www.iol.co.za/news/politics/zille-extends-olive-branch-to-zuma-444805, last accessed 18 April 2019.

15. Roger B. Beck, *The History of South Africa*, Westport; London: Greenwood Publishing Group, 2000, p. 138.

16. Helen Suzman, *In No Uncertain Terms: A South African Memoir*, London: Sinclair-Stevenson, 1993, p. 47.

17. Democratic Party, 'One Nation, One Future Manifesto', in *The Democratic Party Constitution & Policy*, 1993, p. 1.

18. Suzman, *In No Uncertain Terms*, p. 58.

19. Ibid., p. 25.

20. Ibid., p 181.

21. 'One Nation, One Future Manifesto', p. 1.

22. Suzman, *In No Uncertain Terms*, p. 287.

23. Jack Bloom, *Out of Step: Life-Story of a Politician—Politics and Religion in a World at War*, Johannesburg: Jack Bloom, p. 50.

24. Reports of the Independent Electoral Commission of South Africa, https://www.elections.org.za/content/Elections/Election-reports/, last accessed 19 April 2019. The 2011 local election vote is not directly comparable with the national elections of the previous years, but the percentage share of the vote is broadly indicative of DA support.

25. *Report of the Independent Electoral Commission of South Africa: National and Provincial Elections*, Pretoria: Electoral Commission of South Africa, 2 June 1999, p. 75.

26. Zwelethu Jolobe, 'The Democratic Alliance: Consolidating the Official Opposition', in Roger Southall and John Daniel (eds), *Zunami! The 2009 South African Elections*, Johannesburg: Jacana, 2009, p. 133.

27. Anthony Lemon, 'The Implications for Opposition Parties of South Africa's 2009 General Election', paper for presentation at the *Democratization in Africa* conference, Leeds University, 4–5 December 2009, p. 4.

28. Ibid., p. 78.

29. Tony Leon, *On the Contrary: Leading the Opposition in a Democratic South Africa*, Johannesburg; Cape Town: Jonathan Ball, 2008, p. 542.

30. Ibid., p. 535.

31. Jessica Piombo and Lia Nijzink, *Electoral Politics in South Africa: Assessing the First Democratic Decade*, New York; Basingstoke: Palgrave Macmillan, 2005.

32. Jolobe, 'The Democratic Alliance', p. 134.

33. *Report of the Independent Electoral Commission of South Africa: National*

and *Provincial Elections*, Pretoria: Electoral Commission of South Africa, 14 April 2004, p. 60.

34. 'History', The Democratic Alliance, https://www.da.org.za/why-the-da/history, last accessed 19 April 2019.

35. Andrew Harding, 'South African opposition parties to merge', BBC News, 15 August 2010, http://www.bbc.co.uk/news/world-africa-10981635, last accessed 19 April 2019.

36. Jolobe, 'The Democratic Alliance', p. 137.

37. Ibid., p. 143.

38. Helen Zille, 'DA no longer just a party of opposition', Politicsweb, 27 March 2011, https://www.politicsweb.co.za/opinion/da-no-longer-just-a-party-of-opposition—helen-zil, last accessed 19 April 2019.

39. Ian Neilson, 'Moody's reaffirms Cape Town's double-A credit rating', Politicsweb, 29 June 2011, https://www.politicsweb.co.za/opinion/moodys-reaffirms-cape-towns-doublea-credit-rating, last accessed 21 June 2019.

40. Department of Cooperative Governance and Traditional Affairs, *Basic Services Publication: Comparative Information on Basic Services*, 2009, http://www.sadelivery.co.za/files/delivery/resources/Basic%20Services%20Publication%20_for%20WEB.pdf, last accessed 19 April 2019.

41. 'Mantashe: ANC a "Cinderella party" in Western Cape', *Mail & Guardian*, 2 December 2010, http://www.mg.co.za/article/2010-12-02-mantashe-anc-is-a-cinderella-party, last accessed 19 April 2019.

42. Mandy Rossouw, 'Municipal poll jitters for the ANC', *Mail & Guardian*, 3 December 2010, http://www.mg.co.za/article/2010-12-03-municipal-poll-jitters-for-the-anc, last accessed 19 April 2019.

43. Nonkululeko Njilo, 'Helen Zille defends herself about undermining Lindiwe Mazibuko', *Business Day*, 20 July 2018, https://www.businesslive.co.za/bd/national/2018-07-20-helen-zille-defends-herself-about-undermining-lindiwe-mazibuko/, last accessed 31 May 2019.

44. '2014 National and Provincial Elections: National Results', Electoral Commission of South Africa, http://www.elections.org.za/content/elections/results/2014-national-and-provincial-elections—national-results/, last accessed 19 April 2019.

45. Faiez Jacobs and Zahir Amien, 'The DA: "The more things change, the more they stay the same"', *Daily Maverick*, 24 April 2018, https://www.dailymaverick.co.za/opinionista/2018-04-24-the-da-the-more-things-change-the-more-they-stay-the-same/, last accessed 19 April 2019.

46. Paul Herman, 'DA's race policy scares other parties—Maimane', News24, 7 April 2018, https://m.news24.com/SouthAfrica/News/das-race-policy-scares-other-parties-maimane-20180407, last accessed 19 April 2019.

47. Gareth van Onselen, 'How the ANC has blinded the media to its own racism', *Business Day*, 18 April 2018, https://www.businesslive.co.za/bd/opinion/columnists/2018-04-18-gareth-van-onselen-how-the-anc-has-blinded-the-media-to-its-own-racism/, last accessed 19 April 2019.

48. 'South Africa local elections: ANC loses in capital Pretoria', BBC News, 6 August 2016, http://www.bbc.co.uk/news/world-africa-36997461, last accessed 19 April 2019.

49. Crispian Olver, *How to Steal a City: The Battle for Nelson Mandela Bay, an Inside Account*, Johannesburg; Cape Town: Jonathan Ball, 2017, pp. 3–6.

50. Kristoff Adelbert, 'Building a legacy of reconciliation and progress—Athol Trollip', Politicsweb, 18 August 2016, https://www.politicsweb.co.za/opinion/building-a-legacy-of-reconciliation-and-progress—, last accessed 19 April 2019.

51. Luke Daniel, 'Democratic Alliance-led coalition breaks down in Nelson Mandela Bay', *The South African*, 3 August 2018, https://www.the-southafrican.com/democratic-alliance-coalition-breaks-nelson-man-dela-bay/, last accessed 19 April 2019.

52. 'Mashaba meets with Hawks over corruption in the City of Johannesburg', *Daily Maverick*, 30 January 2019, https://www.dailymaverick.co.za/article/2019-01-30-mashaba-meets-with-hawks-over-corrup-tion-in-the-city-of-johannesburg/, last accessed 19 April 2019.

53. Kevin Brandt, 'Patricia de Lille resigns as Cape Town mayor and DA member', Eyewitness News, 31 October 2018, https://ewn.co.za/2018/10/31/patricia-de-lille-announces-resignation-as-cape-town-mayor, last accessed 19 April 2019.

54. Greg Nicolson, 'Disciplining Zille: Helen Zille apologises, keeps premiership', *Daily Maverick*, 13 June 2017, https://www.dailymaverick.co.za/article/2017-06-13-disciplining-zille-helen-zille-apologises-keeps-premiership/, last accessed 19 April 2019.

55. Tshidi Madia and Mahlatse Mahlase, 'DA leaders pick sides amid confusion over party's decision to ditch BEE', *Mail & Guardian*, 7 August 2018, https://mg.co.za/article/2018-08-07-da-leaders-pick-sides-amid-confusion-over-partys-decision-to-ditch-bee, last accessed 19 April 2019.

56. Gwen Ngwenya, Resignation as Head of Policy of the Democratic Alliance, 18 January 2018, http://static.ow.ly/docs/resignation%20letter_8bJk.pdf, last accessed 19 April 2019.

57. Gareth van Onselen, 'The DA's own need for internal reform', Politicsweb, 3 October 2016, https://www.politicsweb.co.za/news-and-analysis/the-das-own-need-for-internal-reform, last accessed 19 April 2019.

58. By the chairman of the Anglo American corporation, Gavin Relly, as quoted in Themba Nzimande, *The Legacy of Prince Mangosuthu Buthelezi: In the Struggle for Liberation in South Africa*, Dartford: Xlibris, p. 27; and by former ANC chairperson Mosiuoa Lekota, as quoted in Arthur Konigkramer, 'Buthelezi: a freedom fighter unjustly vilified', *The Witness*, 8 August 2018, https://www.pressreader.com/south-africa/the-witness/20180808/281741270242011, last accessed 19 April 2019.

59. 'EFF's Ndlozi ripped to shreds for saying Buthelezi deserved Nobel peace prize', *The Citizen*, 29 August 2018, https://citizen.co.za/news/south-africa/2002138/effs-ndlozi-ripped-to-shreds-for-saying-buthelezi-deserved-nobel-peace-prize/, last accessed 19 April 2019.

60. 'Inkatha Freedom Party (IFP)', South African History Online, https://www.sahistory.org.za/topic/inkatha-freedom-party-ifp, last accessed 12 October 2018.

61. 'Our History', Inkatha Freedom Party, http://www.ifp.org.za/who-we-are/our-history/, last accessed 13 October 2018; 'Inkatha Freedom Party (IFP)', South African History Online.

62. 'Inkatha Freedom Party (IFP)', South African History Online.

63. 'The bargain that saved us in 1994', Independent Online, 27 April 2014, https://www.iol.co.za/sundayindependent/the-bargain-that-saved-us-in-1994–1680948, last accessed 12 October 2018.

64. Aubrey Matshiqi, 'KwaZulu-Natal adds to its history of factional rights', *Business Day*, 12 June 2018, https://www.pressreader.com/south-africa/business-day/20180612/281848644305377, last accessed 13 October 2018.

65. Paul Herman, 'IFP welcomes "giant step forward" for medical cannabis use', News24, 24 November 2016, https://www.news24.com/SouthAfrica/News/ifp-welcomes-giant-step-forward-for-medical-cannabis-use-20161124, last accessed 13 October 2018.

66. Andisiwe Makinana, 'The MP who cared', News24, 19 March 2017, https://www.news24.com/SouthAfrica/News/the-mp-who-cared-20170319–2, last accessed 19 April 2019.

67. 'News Makers 2016 | Mkhuleko Hlengwa', YouTube, 24 December 2016, https://www.youtube.com/watch?v=yHUy-rLuYbs, last accessed 13 October 2018.

68. Clive Ndou and News24, 'Buthelezi stepping down as IFP leader', News24, 30 October 2017, https://www.news24.com/SouthAfrica/News/buthelezi-stepping-down-as-ifp-leader-20171029, last accessed 19 April 2019.

69. Michiel Le Roux, *Misadventures of a Cope Volunteer: My Crash Course in Politics*, Cape Town: Tafelberg, 2010, p. 10.

70. Allister Sparks, *First Drafts: South African History in the Making*, Jeppestown: Jonathan Ball, p. 313.

71. SAPA, 'Shilowa "an ANC spy"', *Sunday Times*, 19 January 2011, https://www.timeslive.co.za/politics/2011-01-19-shilowa-an-anc-spy/, last accessed 14 October 2018.

72. Mosiuoa Lekota and Suzanne Venter, 'Lekota—a farmer for farmers', *Farmer's Weekly*, 28 November 2008, https://www.farmersweekly.co.za/archive/lekota-a-farmer-for-farmers/, last accessed 15 October 2018.

73. Carien du Plessis, 'Zuma calls Malema "leader in the making"', Independent Online, 26 October 2009, https://www.iol.co.za/news/politics/zuma-calls-malema-leader-in-the-making-462670, last accessed 5 June 2019.

74. 'ANCYL march moves from Sandton to Pretoria', Independent Online, 27 October 2011, https://www.iol.co.za/news/south-africa/gauteng/ancyl-march-moves-from-sandton-to-pretoria-1166416, last accessed 5 June 2019.

75. Xolani Mbanjwa, Carien du Plessis and Charl du Plessis, 'The end of Malema', News24, 5 February 2012, https://www.news24.com/SouthAfrica/Politics/The-end-of-Malema-20120205?cpid=2, last accessed 5 June 2019.

76. G. Nicolson and T. Lekgowa, 'Marikana: Malema's 2014 battle begins', *Daily Maverick*, 14 October 2013, https://www.dailymaverick.co.za/article/2013-10-14-marikana-malemas-2014-battle-begins/, last accessed 15 October 2018.

77. 'EFF launch: Marikana', YouTube, 16 October 2013, https://www.youtube.com/watch?v=hCa-k_CYV1g, last accessed 15 October 2018.

78. Lizeka Tandwa, 'Not all hurtful speech is hate speech—SAHRC after findings on Malema', News24, 27 March 2019, https://www.news24.com/SouthAfrica/News/not-all-hurtful-speech-is-hate-speech-sahrc-after-findings-on-malema-20190327, last accessed 7 June 2019.

79. SAPA, 'Malema wants Zim style land grabs', Fin24, 1 August 2013, https://www.fin24.com/Economy/Malema-wants-Zim-style-land-grabs-20130801, last accessed 7 June 2019.

80. Abigail Javier, 'Juju Valley: A "role model" for landowners', Entertainment Weekly, 26 April 2019, https://ewn.co.za/2019/04/26/juju-valley-a-role-model-for-land-owners, last accessed 7 June 2019.

81. Tom Head, 'Julius Malema: Five times his calls for "land grabs" got him in serious trouble', *The South African*, 12 December 2018, https://www.thesouthafrican.com/opinion/julius-malema-land-grabs-court-dec-2018/, last accessed 7 June 2019.

82. Ralph Mathekga, *When Zuma Goes*, Cape Town: Tafelberg, 2016, pp. 103–5.

83. 'Sars accepts Malema tax commitment', *The Herald*, 26 May 2014, https://www.heraldlive.co.za/news/2014-05-26-sars-accepts-malema-tax-commitment/, last accessed 15 October 2018.

84. Jenni Evans, 'Floyd Shivambu denies getting R10m from VBS', News24, 13 October 2018, https://www.news24.com/SouthAfrica/News/floyd-

shivambu-denies-getting-r10m-from-vbs-20181013, last accessed 20 April 2019.

85. 'We won't get to see EFF members naked in Parliament', eNCA, 5 February 2015, https://www.enca.com/south-africa/eff-allowed-wear-overalls-parliament, last accessed 7 June 2019.

86. 'Holomisa says his expulsion from ANC is confirmed', South African Press Association, 30 September 2016, http://www.justice.gov.za/trc/media%5C1996%5C9609/s960930b.htm, last accessed 20 April 2019.

87. 'Core Values', United Democratic Movement, http://udm.org.za/about/core-values/, last accessed 16 October 2018.

88. Mmakgomo Tshetlo, 'Why Bantu Holomisa has a stronger brand than his party the UDM', 702, 9 October 2017, http://www.702.co.za/articles/275564/why-bantu-holomisa-has-a-stronger-brand-than-his-party-the-udm, last accessed 16 October 2018.

89. Interview with Carien du Plessis, 5 August 2016.

90. 'Rev Kenneth Raselabe Joseph Meshoe', People's Assembly, https://www.pa.org.za/person/kenneth-raselabe-joseph-meshoe/, last accessed 16 October 2018.

91. 'Our Legacy', African Christian Democratic Party, https://www.acdp.org.za/our_legacy, last accessed 20 April 2019.

92. Ibid.

93. Tamar Kahn, 'Parliament rejects ACDP's abortion bill', *Business Day*, 6 September 2018, https://www.businesslive.co.za/bd/national/2018-09-06-parliament-rejects-acdps-abortion-bill/, last accessed 16 October 2018.

94. Motsoko Pheko, '60 years: How the "Freedom Charter" betrayed Africans', Pambazuka News, 22 July 2015, https://www.pambazuka.org/governance/60-years-how-freedom-charter-betrayed-africans, last accessed 16 October 2018.

95. 'Pan Africanist Congress (PAC)', South African History Online, https://www.sahistory.org.za/topic/pan-africanist-congress-pac, last accessed 16 October 2018.

96. Lubabalo Ngcukana, 'Behind the chaos at Sobukwe's funeral', City Press, 26 August 2018, https://city-press.news24.com/News/behind-the-chaos-at-sobukwes-funeral-20180825, last accessed 16 October 2018.

97. 'Welcome to the APC', African People's Convention, http://www.theapc.org.za/, last accessed 16 October 2018.

98. 'Azanian People's Organization (AZAPO)', South African History Online, https://www.sahistory.org.za/topic/azanian-peoples-organization-azapo, last accessed 16 October 2018.

99. 'Mission', Freedom Front Plus, https://www.vfplus.org.za/mission, last accessed 23 February 2019.

100. Andisiwe Makinana, 'FF Plus goes international with campaign to stop land expropriation', *Sunday Times*, 27 August 2018, https://www.timeslive.co.za/politics/2018-08-27-ff-plus-goes-international-with-campaign-to-stop-land-expropriation/, last accessed 23 February 2019.

5. CORRUPTION: THE LEGACY OF APARTHEID

1. Hennie van Vuuren, *Apartheid, Guns and Money: A Tale of Profit*, Johannesburg: Jacana, 2017, p. 2.

2. Ibid., p. 3.

3. Ibid., pp. 5–6.

4. Hennie van Vuuren and Michael Marchant, '7 Things We Learned About Apartheid Corruption From Apartheid, Guns and Money', HuffPost, 17 July 2017, https://www.huffingtonpost.co.za/hennie-van-vuuren/7-things-we-learned-about-apartheid-corruption-from-apartheid-g_a_23030055/, last accessed 24 January 2019.

5. Ibid.

6. Ibid.

7. Van Vuuren, *Apartheid, Guns and Money*, p. 157.

8. Ibid., p. 44.

9. Ibid., p. 8.

10. Van Vuuren and Marchant, '7 Things We Learned About Apartheid'.

11. 'What's the arms deal all about?', Corruption Watch, 15 January 2014, https://www.corruptionwatch.org.za/whats-the-arms-deal-all-about/, last accessed 24 January 2019.

12. 'Seriti in more trouble over arms deal probe', News24, 22 March 2013, https://www.news24.com/SouthAfrica/News/Seriti-in-more-trouble-over-arms-deal-probe-20130322, last accessed 20 January 2019.

13. Van Vuuren, *Apartheid, Guns and Money*, p. 45.

14. Ralph Mathekga, *When Zuma Goes*, Cape Town: Tafelberg, 2016, p. 48.

15. Bhorat et al., 'Betrayal of the Promise: How South Africa is Being Stolen', State Capacity Research Project, May 2017, https://pari.org.za/wp-content/uploads/2017/05/Betrayal-of-the-Promise-25052017.pdf, last accessed 20 April 2019; for more details, see Chapter Six, on the economy.

16. Bhorat et al., 'Betrayal of the Promise'.

17. Sam Sole and Stefaans Brümmer, 'Zuma in talks over ANC paper', *Mail & Guardian*, 30 April 2010, https://mg.co.za/article/2010-04-30-zuma-in-talks-over-anc-paper, last accessed 26 January 2019.

18. Lianne Friedman, 'How did Guptas qualify for BEE steel deal?', EconoServ, 25 August 2010, https://www.econoserv.co.za/how-did-guptas-qualify-for-bee-steel-deal/, last accessed 26 January 2019.

19. Helen Grange and Agiza Hlongwane, 'Zuma's billion rand gift', Independent Online, 12 September 2010, https://www.iol.co.za/news/zumas-billion-rand-gift-680446, last accessed 26 January 2019.

20. amaBhungane, 'Analysis: The R16bn "Gupta premium"—how the Transnet locomotive acquisition went from R38.6-bn to R54.5-bn', *Daily Maverick*, 3 June 2018, https://www.dailymaverick.co.za/article/2018-06-03-analysis-the-r16bn-gupta-premium-how-the-transnet-locomotive-acquisition-went-from-r38-6-bn-to-r54-5-bn/, last accessed 27 January 2019.

21. 'Project Spider Web: The full document', Politicsweb, 24 August 2015, https://www.politicsweb.co.za/documents/project-spider-web-the-full-document, last accessed 20 April 2019.

22. 'Mcebisi Jonas' full statement to state capture commission: "They would kill me"', News24, 24 August 2018, https://www.news24.com/Columnists/GuestColumn/mcebisi-jonas-full-statement-to-state-capture-commission-they-would-kill-me-20180824, last accessed 27 January 2019.

23. Bhorat et. al, 'Betrayal of the Promise', p. 15.

24. Willie Esterhuyse, *Endgame: Secret Talks and the End of Apartheid*, Cape Town: Tafelberg, 2012, p. 165.

25. Barry Gilder, 'Tackle all dimensions of corruption', Independent Online,

12 August 2012, https://www.iol.co.za/sundayindependent/tackle-all-dimensions-of-corruption-1360443, last accessed 3 February 2018.

26. Pieter du Toit, 'Bosasa scandal: ANC knew of "havoc" and they did nothing, Dennis Bloem tells Zondo commission', News24, 1 February 2019, https://www.news24.com/SouthAfrica/News/bosasa-scandal-anc-knew-of-havoc-and-they-did-nothing-dennis-bloem-tells-zondo-commission-20190201, last accessed 20 April 2019.

27. Prince Mashele and Mzukisi Qobo, *The Fall of the ANC: What Next?*, Johannesburg: Picador Africa, 2014, p. 76.

28. Van Vuuren, *Apartheid, Guns and Money*, p. 78.

29. Phillip de Wet and Mmanaledi Mataboge, 'Chancellor House: R266m for nine years of lies by ANC partner', *Mail & Guardian*, 26 September 2015, https://mg.co.za/article/2015-09-29-chancellor-house-r266-million-for-9-years-of-lies-by-anc-partner, last accessed 22 January 2019.

30. Van Vuuren, *Apartheid, Guns and Money*, p. 85.

31. Progressive Business Forum, http://www.pbf.org.za/index.php, last accessed 22 January 2019.

32. Justin Brown, 'Corporate SA buys into ANC's influence peddling scheme', Fin24, 24 December 2017, https://www.fin24.com/Economy/corporate-sa-buys-into-ancs-influence-peddling-scheme-20171224–3, last accessed 22 January 2019.

33. SAPA, 'Zille sent Atul Gupta thank you note for donation', *Mail & Guardian*, 30 January 2013, https://mg.co.za/article/2013-01-30-zille-sent-atul-gupta-thank-you-note-for-donation, last accessed 23 January 2019; Daniel Friedman, 'Links to cigarette smugglers no secret, says Malema', *The Citizen*, 10 July 2018, https://citizen.co.za/news/south-africa/1975301/links-to-cigarette-smugglers-no-secret-says-malema/, last accessed 20 April 2019.

34. These words are quoted by ANC and opposition politicians alike, and there is a widespread perception that Mandela said them, although AfricaCheck could find no actual record of it: 'Were these words about apartheid and the ANC uttered by Mandela?', AfricaCheck, 28 September 2017, https://africacheck.org/spot-check/were-these-words-about-apartheid-and-the-anc-uttered-by-mandela/, last accessed 29 January 2019.

35. Jay Naidoo, 'To my generation: Listen. Listen very carefully', *Daily Maverick*, 3 December 2012, https://www.dailymaverick.co.za/opinionista/2012-12-03-to-my-generation-listen-listen-very-carefully/, last accessed 29 January 2019.

36. Ibid.

37. Mandy de Waal, 'Apartheid and the Marikana murder charges: a common purpose indeed', *Daily Maverick*, 31 August 2012, https://www.dailymaverick.co.za/article/2012-08-31-apartheid-and-the-marikana-murder-charges-a-common-purpose-indeed/, last accessed 31 January 2019.

38. Andisiwe Makinana, 'Bheki Cele reveals "pathetic" corruption conviction statistics', *Sunday Times*, 21 January 2019, https://www.timeslive.co.za/politics/2019-01-21-cele-reveals-pathetic-corruption-conviction-statistics/, last accessed 29 January 2019.

39. Peter Fabricius, 'Investor countries' June 2018 memo to Pretoria sparks February 2019 diplomatic incident', *Daily Maverick*, 4 February 2019, https://www.dailymaverick.co.za/article/2019-02-04-investor-countries-june-2018-memo-to-pretoria-sparks-february-2019-diplomatic-incident/, last accessed 4 February 2019.

40. Peter Fabricius, 'Ramaphosa gives SA ambassadors a better story to sell', *Daily Maverick*, 24 October 2018, https://www.dailymaverick.co.za/article/2018-10-24-ramaphosa-gives-sa-ambassadors-a-better-story-to-sell/, last accessed 4 February 2019.

6. THE ECONOMY: EXPLAINING THE FAILURE TO THRIVE

1. Between 1912 and 1939, value added in private manufacturing rose from £8.9 million to £53.8 million. See Charles H. Feinstein, *An Economic History of South Africa*, Cambridge: Cambridge University Press, 2005, p. 2.

2. Johannes Fedderke and Charles Simkins, 'Economic Growth in South Africa Since the Late Nineteenth Century', Working Papers 138, Economic Research Southern Africa, 2009, p. 20, https://econrsa.org/papers/w_papers/wp138.pdf, last accessed 20 April 2019.

3. Carnegie Commission report, cited in Dan O'Meara, *Volkskapitalisme: Class, Capital and Ideology in the Development of Afrikaner Nationalism, 1934–1948*, Cambridge: Cambridge University Press, 1983, p. 26.

4. Feinstein, *An Economic History of South Africa* p. 120.

5. Ibid., p. 182.

6. Ibid., p. 123.

7. Ibid., p. 175.

8. Ibid., p. 176.

9. Ibid., p. 184.

10. Fedderke and Simkins, 'Economic Growth in South Africa', p. 20.

11. Adam Raphael, 'British Firms Pay Africans Starvation Rate', *The Guardian*, 12 March 1973.

12. Fedderke and Simkins, 'Economic Growth in South Africa', p. 26.

13. Patti Waldmeir, *Anatomy of a Miracle: The End of Apartheid and the Birth of the New South Africa*, London: Viking, 1997, p. 56.

14. Ibid., p. 56.

15. Feinstein, *An Economic History of South Africa*, p. 192.

16. Dani Rodrik, 'Understanding South Africa's Economic Puzzles', *Economics of Transition*, vol. 16, no. 4 (2008), pp. 769–97.

17. Feinstein, *An Economic History of South Africa*, p. 7.

18. Waldmeir, *Anatomy of a Miracle*, p. 133.

19. Hennie van Vuuren, *Apartheid, Guns and Money: A Tale of Profit*, Hurst, London, 2018, p. 34.

20. Waldmeir, *Anatomy of a Miracle* p. 213.

21. Ibid., p. 256.

22. William E. Jackson, Todd M. Alessandri and Sylvia Sloan Black, 'The Price of Corporate Social Responsibility: The Case of Black Economic Empowerment Transactions in South Africa', Working Paper, no. 2005–29, Federal Reserve Bank of Atlanta, p. 1.

23. Roger Southall, 'Ten Propositions about Black Economic Empowerment in South Africa', *Review of African Political Economy*, vol. 34, no. 111 (2006), p. 74.

24. Ibid., p. 74.

25. 'South Africa's Black Empowerment: The President Says It Has Failed', *The Economist*, 31 March 2010, https://www.economist.com/middle-east-and-africa/2010/03/31/the-president-says-it-has-failed, last accessed 20 April 2019.

26. Ibid.

27. 'GDP by Country: Statistics from the World Bank: South Africa', South Africa Data Portal, http://southafrica.opendataforafrica.org/mhrzolg/gdp-by-country-statistics-from-the-world-bank-1960–2016?country=South%20Africa, last accessed 20 April 2019.

28. Statistics South Africa reported that in the third quarter of 2017 unemployment stood at 27.7 per cent. The expanded unemployment rate, which includes those who wanted to work but did not look for a job, stood at 36.8 per cent. 'Quarterly Labour Force Survey', Statistics South Africa, http://www.statssa.gov.za/?p=10658, last accessed 20 April 2019.

29. Miriam Altman, 'Employment Scenarios to 2024', Human Sciences Research Council, 2007, http://www.hsrc.ac.za/en/research-data/view/3407, last accessed 20 April 2019.

30. 'Economic growth better than what many expected', Statistics South Africa, 6 March 2018, http://www.statssa.gov.za/?p=10985, last accessed 20 April 2019.

31. Vimal Ranchhod, 'Why is South Africa's unemployment rate so high?', GroundUp, 14 February 2019, https://www.groundup.org.za/article/why-south-africas-unemployment-rate-so-high/, last accessed 20 April 2019.

32. For further discussion of state capture, see Chapter Five.

33. Marianne Thamm, 'The core values that once illuminated the ANC now provide the moral backbone of Gordhan's Zondo submission', *Daily Maverick*, 8 November 2018, https://www.dailymaverick.co.za/article/2018-11-08-the-core-values-that-once-illuminated-the-anc-now-provide-the-moral-backbone-of-gordhans-zondo-submission/, last accessed 20 April 2019.

34. Commission of Inquiry into State Capture, https://www.sastatecapture.org.za/, last accessed 20 April 2019.

35. Bhorat et al., 'Betrayal of the Promise: How South Africa is Being Stolen', State Capacity Research Project, May 2017, p. 4, https://pari.org.za/wp-content/uploads/2017/05/Betrayal-of-the-Promise-25052017.pdf, last accessed 20 April 2019.

36. Stephen Grootes, 'With Moyane's dismissal, Ramaphosa's slo-mo revolution claims a crucial scalp', *Daily Maverick*, 2 November 2018,

https://www.dailymaverick.co.za/article/2018-11-02-with-moyanes-dismissal-ramaphosas-slo-mo-revolution-claims-a-crucial-scalp/, last accessed 20 April 2019; Andrew Cave, 'Deal that undid Bell Pottinger: inside story of the South Africa scandal', *The Guardian*, 5 September 2017, https://www.theguardian.com/media/2017/sep/05/bell-pottinger-south-africa-pr-firm, last accessed 20 April 2019.

37. Paul Burkhardt, 'Eskom Gets Some Breathing Room With $1.7 Billion Facility', Bloomberg, 28 February 2018, https://www.bloomberg.com/news/articles/2018–02–28/eskom-signs-1-7-billion-short-term-credit-facility-with-banks, last accessed 20 April 2019.

38. Carol Paton, 'Eskom to be split into three SOEs, Cyril Ramaphosa confirms in Sona', *Business Day*, 7 February 2019, https://www.businesslive.co.za/bd/national/2019-02-07-eskom-to-be-split-into-three-soes-cyril-ramaphosa-confirms-in-sona/, last accessed 20 April 2019.

39. Wendell Roelf, 'South African Airways says it needs capital injection "now"', Reuters, 24 April 2018, https://www.reuters.com/article/us-safrica-saa/south-african-airways-says-it-needs-capital-injection-now-idUSKBN1HV1ND, last accessed 20 April 2019.

40. Joseph Cotterill, 'South African Airways should be shut down, says Mboweni', *Financial Times*, 1 November 2018, https://www.ft.com/content/23ff2a6a-ddfd-11e8–8f50-cbae5495d92b, last accessed 20 April 2019.

41. Genevieve Quintal, 'R1-trillion nuclear deal was beyond SA's financial reach, says Pravin Gordhan', *Business Day*, 20 November 2018, https://www.businesslive.co.za/bd/national/2018-11-20-r1-trillion-nuclear-deal-was-beyond-sas-financial-reach-says-pravin-gordhan/,   last accessed 20 April 2019.

42. Victor Sulla and Precious Zikhali, 'Overcoming Poverty and Inequality in South Africa: An Assessment of Drivers, Constraints and Opportunities', Working Paper, Washington, D.C.: World Bank Group, 2018, p. 89.

43. Ibid., p. 62.

44. Hanna Ziady, 'Companies hoarding R1.4-trillion in cash', *Business Day*, 3 August 2017, https://www.businesslive.co.za/bd/economy/2017-08-03-companies-hoarding-r14-trillion-in-cash/, last accessed 21 April 2019.

45. Guy Johnson, Amogelang Mbatha and Ntando Thukwana, 'Ramaphosa Lauds Success of South Africa's Investment Drive', Bloomberg, 26 October 2018, https://www.bloomberg.com/news/articles/2018-10-26/south-africa-s-investment-drive-ahead-of-target-president-says, last accessed 21 April 2019.

46. Jason Burke, 'Ramaphosa says corruption inquiry shedding light on dark period in South Africa', *The Guardian*, 1 November 2018, https://www.theguardian.com/world/2018/nov/01/ramaphosa-says-corruption-inquiry-shedding-light-on-dark-period-in-south-africa, last accessed 21 April 2019.

47. Alexander Winning and Tiisetso Motsoeneng, 'Goldman forecasts South African economic rebound in 2019', Reuters, 3 October 2018, https://www.reuters.com/article/us-safrica-economy-goldman-sachs/goldman-forecasts-south-african-economic-rebound-in-2019-idUSKCN1MD1FP, last accessed 21 April 2019.

48. 'South Africa Economic Update: Jobs and Inequality', World Bank, 2018, http://pubdocs.worldbank.org/en/798731523331698204/South-Africa-Economic-Update-April–2018.pdf, last accessed 21 April 2019.

49. Ibid., p. vii.

50. Ibid., p. 36.

51. Paul Burkhardt, 'First Big Oil and Gas Discovery Made Offshore of South Africa', Bloomberg, 7 February 2019, https://www.bloomberg.com/news/articles/2019–02–07/total-discovery-opens-new-petroleum-province-off-south-africa, last accessed 21 April 2019.

52. Tim Cohen, 'So, speaking of economics, what happened to that R1.5-trillion?', *Daily Maverick*, 19 June 2019, https://www.dailymaverick.co.za/article/2019-06-19-so-speaking-of-economics-what-happened-to-that-r1-5-trillion/, last accessed 22 June 2019.

7. LAND AND AGRICULTURE: THE THORNIEST TOPICS

1. 'South Africa—Agricultural Sector', Export.gov, 25 October 2018, https://www.export.gov/article?id=South-Africa-agricultural-equipment, last accessed 21 April 2019.

2. 'Abstract of Agricultural Statistics', Department of Agriculture, Forestry and Fisheries, 2017, https://www.daff.gov.za/Daffweb3/Portals/0/

Statistics%20and%20Economic%20Analysis/Statistical%20Information-tion/Abstract%202017.pdf, last accessed 21 April 2019.

3. Ed Stoddard, 'Explainer: South Africa's ANC to "test constitution" on land expropriation', Reuters, 22 May 2018, https://af.reuters.com/article/africaTech/idAFKCN1IN1LY-OZATP, last accessed 21 April 2019.

4. 'Malema Vows to Fight for Land Revolution in South Africa', iAfrica, 12 September 2018, https://www.iafrica.com/malema-vows-to-fight-for-land-revolution-in-south-africa/, last accessed 21 April 2019.

5. Economic Freedom Fighters, 'No land ownership for black or white—EFF policy', Politicsweb, 2 March 2018, https://www.politicsweb.co.za/documents/no-land-ownership-for-black-or-white—eff-policy, last accessed 21 April 2019.

6. News24, 'Professor Ben Cousins tells land summit "At least 60% of commercial farmland will have to be distributed"', Institute for Poverty, Land and Agrarian Studies, 24 August 2018, https://www.plaas.org.za/news/professor-ben-cousins-tells-land-summit-least-60-commercial-farmland-will-have-be-distributed, last accessed 21 April 2019.

7. Lameez Omarjee, 'ANC reaches resolution on land reform', Fin24, 20 December 2017, https://www.fin24.com/Economy/anc-reaches-resolution-on-land-reform-20171220, last accessed 21 April 2019.

8. 'Read in Full: President Ramaphosa's announcement on land expropriation, job creation', *Mail & Guardian*, 1 August 2018, https://mg.co.za/article/2018-08-01-read-in-full-cyril-ramaphosa, last accessed 21 April 2019.

9. Jan Gerber, 'It's "moral cretins" EFF vs "white monopoly capital" Cosatu', News24, 5 September 2018, https://www.news24.com/SouthAfrica/News/its-moral-cretins-eff-vs-white-monopoly-capital-cosatu-20180905, last accessed 21 April 2019.

10. Andries Mahlangu, 'Cyril Ramaphosa's land shock unravels rand recovery, currency plunges 16c in an hour', *Business Day*, 1 August 2018, https://www.businesslive.co.za/bd/markets/2018-08-01-cyril-ramaphosas-land-shock-unravels-rand-recovery-currency-plunges-16c-in-an-hour/, last accessed 21 April 2019.

11. Ana Monteiro, 'South Africa Land Prices Drop 32% on Land-Reform Change, Drought', Bloomberg, 10 September 2018, https://www.

bloomberg.com/news/articles/2018–09–10/south-africa-land-prices-drop-32-on-land-reform-change-drought, last accessed 21 April 2019.

12. 'Exclusive: "This is no land grab", writes Cyril Ramaphosa', *Business Day*, 24 August 2018, https://www.businesslive.co.za/bd/opinion/2018-08-24-exclusive-this-is-no-land-grab-writes-cyril-ramaphosa/, last accessed 21 April 2019.

13. 'The Distribution of Land in South Africa: An Overview', Institute for Poverty, Land and Agrarian Studies, http://www.plaas.org.za/sites/default/files/publications-pdf/No1%20Fact%20check%20web.pdf, last accessed 21 April 2019.

14. Burgert Gildenhuys, 'State controlled land in four maps', MapAble, 6 March 2018, http://www.mapable.co.za/single-post/2018/03/06/State-controlled-land-in-four-maps, last accessed 21 April 2019.

15. Sol Plaatje, *Native Life in South Africa Before and Since the European War and the Boer Rebellion (1916)*, Johannesburg: Ravan Press, 1982, p. 21.

16. Lawrine Platzky and Cherryl Walker, *The Surplus People: Forced Removals in South Africa*, Johannesburg: Ravan Press, 1985, p. 30; quoted in Marc Wegerif, Bev Russell and Irma Grundling, *Still Searching for Security: The Reality of Farm Dweller Evictions in South Africa*, Johannesburg: Nkuzi Development Association and Social Surveys, 2005, p. 28.

17. 'The Story of the First Two "Coloured" Governors at the Cape—Simon and Willem', Camissa People: Cape Slavery and Indigene Heritage, 17 May 2016, https://camissapeople.wordpress.com/2016/05/17/the-story-of-the-first-two-coloured-governors-at-the-cape-simon-willem/, last accessed 21 April 2019.

18. 'Strategic Plan 2011–2014', Department of Rural Development and Land Reform, 2011, p. 40.

19. 'Annual Report 2009–2010', Department of Rural Development and Land Reform, 2011, p. 27.

20. African National Congress, 'The Reconstruction and Development Programme: A Policy Framework', Johannesburg: Umanyano, paragraph 2.4.1.

21. Hopewell Radebe, 'Call for land reform clarity', *Business Day*, 1 July

2011, www.pressreader.com/south-africa/business-day/20110701/282
686158860247, last accessed 21 April 2019.

22. 'Speech by the Minister of Rural Development and Land Reform, Gugile Nkwinti (MP) at the debate on the State of the Nation Address—"Building vibrant, equitable, and sustainable rural communities"—National Assembly', South African Government, 19 February 2013, https://www.gov.za/speech-minister-rural-development-and-land-reform-gugile-nkwinti-mp-debate-state-nation-address-0, last accessed 21 April 2019.

23. M. A. Aliber, 'Land Redistribution for Agricultural Development: Case Studies in Three Provinces', HSRC, October 2003, http://www.hsrc.ac.za/en/research-outputs/view/867, last accessed 21 April 2019.

24. Edward Lahiff, '"Willing Buyer, Willing Seller": South Africa's Failed Experiment in Market-Led Agrarian Reform', *Third World Quarterly*, vol. 28, no. 8 (2007), p. 1590.

25. 'Black farmers selling land back to whites', News24, 31 August 2011, http://www.news24.com/SouthAfrica/Politics/Black-farmers-selling-land-back-to-whites-20110831.

26. South African Press Association, 'Government-bought farms collapse', 02 February 2007, https://groups.google.com/forum/#!topic/soc.culture.south-africa/jEyFHUOZjOs%5B1–25%5D, last accessed 22 June 2018.

27. Bongani Mthethwa, 'Farms collapse as land reform fails', *Sunday Times*, 1 March 2009, https://www.pressreader.com/south-africa/sunday-times-1107/20090301/284374080279378, last accessed 21 April 2019.

28. 'What Nkwinti said on land reform', Politicsweb, 7 March 2010, http://www.politicsweb.co.za/politicsweb/view/politicsweb/en/page71656?oid=164364&sn=Detail, last accessed 21 April 2019.

29. Tara Weinberg, 'The Contested Status of "Communal Land Tenure" in South Africa', Institute for Poverty, Land and Agrarian Studies, May 2015.

30. Tshidi Madia, 'Traditional leaders act like village tin-pot dictators—Motlanthe', News24, 19 May 2018, https://www.news24.com/SouthAfrica/News/traditional-leaders-act-like-village-tin-pot-dictators-motlanthe-20180519, last accessed 21 April 2019.

31. Sonwabile Mnwana, 'Why giving South Africa's chiefs more power adds to land dispossession', The Conversation, 4 April 2018, https://theconversation.com/why-giving-south-africas-chiefs-more-power-adds-to-land-dispossession-93958, last accessed 21 April 2019.

32. Weinberg, 'The Contested Status of "Communal Land Tenure"', p. 16.

33. Monde B. Makiwane and Dan OD Chimere-Dan (eds), 'The People Matter: The State of the Population in the Eastern Cape', Research and Population Unit, Eastern Cape Department of Social Development, 2010, pp. 15–16.

34. 'State of Local Government in South Africa: Overview Report', National State of Local Government Assessments, Working Documents, Department of Cooperative Governments and Traditional Affairs, 2009, p. 77.

35. Alex Duval Smith, 'Apartheid land reforms in chaos as blacks sell farms back to whites', The Independent, 3 September 2011, https://www.independent.co.uk/news/world/africa/apartheid-land-reforms-in-chaos-as-blacks-sell-farms-back-to-whites-2348437.html, last accessed 22 April 2019.

36. Wendell Roelf, 'South Africa land reform panel swamped with submissions, asks for delay', Reuters, 27 September 2018, https://www.reuters.com/article/us-safrica-land/south-africa-land-reform-panel-swamped-with-submissions-asks-for-delay-idUSKCN1M720X, last accessed 22 April 2019.

37. Ferial Haffajee, 'ANC Floats New Deal On Land Expropriation Without Compensation', HuffPost, 22 May 2018, https://www.huffingtonpost.co.za/2018/03/28/anc-floats-new-deal-on-land-expropriation-without-compensation_a_23397146/, last accessed 22 April 2019.

38. Ibid.

39. 'The Freedom Charter', South African History Online, https://www.sahistory.org.za/article/freedom-charter, last accessed 26 April 2019.

8. EDUCATION: THE WEAKEST LINK

1. 'South Africa has one of the world's worst education systems', The Economist, 7 January 2017, https://www.economist.com/middle-east-and-africa/2017/01/07/south-africa-has-one-of-the-worlds-worst-education-systems, last accessed 22 April 2019.

2. Education 'worse than under apartheid', News24, 23 March 2012, https://www.news24.com/SouthAfrica/News/Education-worse-than-under-apartheid-20120323, last accessed 22 June 2019.

3. SAPA, 'Bantu education was better: academic', *Sunday Times*, 15 August 2013, https://www.timeslive.co.za/news/south-africa/2013-08-15-bantu-education-was-better-academic/, last accessed 22 April 2019.

4. Brian Willan, *Sol Plaatje, A Life of Solomon Tshekisho Plaatje, 1876–1932*, Johannesberg: Jacana, 2018, p. 18 ff.

5. Xolani Qubeka, 'Why the legacy of Bantu Education lingers on', *Cape Times*, 5 May 2017, https://www.pressreader.com/south-africa/cape-times/20170505/282059096906550, last accessed 26 April 2019.

6. 'The Freedom Charter', South African History Online, https://www.sahistory.org.za/article/freedom-charter, last accessed 26 April 2019.

7. Zandile P. Nkabinde, *An Analysis of Educational Challenges in the New South Africa*, Lanham; New York; Oxford: University Press of America, 1997, p. 44.

8. Yusuf Sayed, 'The Case of Teacher Education in Post-Apartheid South Africa: Politics and Priorities', in Linda Chisholm (ed.), *Changing Class: Education and Social Change in Post-Apartheid South Africa*, London: Zed Books, 2004, p. 248.

9. Melanie Smuts, 'Bad education: it starts with how we train teachers', *Daily Maverick*, 4 April 2018, https://www.dailymaverick.co.za/opinionista/2018-04-04-bad-education-it-starts-with-how-we-train-teachers/, last accessed 22 April 2019.

10. Ashley Westaway, 'Towards an Explanation of the Functionality of South Africa's "Dysfunctional" Schools', paper presented to the Melon Media and Citizenship group, School of Journalism, Rhodes University, May 2015, p. 8.

11. African National Congress, *A Policy Framework for Education and Training*, Braamfontein: ANC Education Department, 1994, http://www.africa.upenn.edu/Govern_Political/ANC_Education.html, last accessed 22 June 2019.

12. Corene de Wet and Charl Wolhuter, 'A Transitiological Study of Some South African Educational Issues', *South African Journal of Education*, vol. 29, no. 3, 2009, p. 360.

13. 'A South African Curriculum for the Twenty First Century', Report of the Review Committee on Curriculum 2005, 31 May 2000, http://citeseerx.ist.psu.edu/viewdoc/download?doi=10.1.1.364.3411&rep=rep1&type=pdf, last accessed 22 April 2019.

14. Quoted in Mogamad Aslam Fataar, 'Education Policy Development in South Africa, 1994–1997', PhD thesis, University of the Western Cape, 1999, p. 157, https://etd.uwc.ac.za/handle/11394/1332, last accessed 20 March 2018.

15. Ibid., p. 215.

16. Paulo Freire's Educational Theory, New Foundations, 2018, https://www.newfoundations.com/GALLERY/Freire.html last accessed 22 June 2019.

17. Ken Harley and Volker Wedekind, 'Political Change, Curriculum Change and Social Formation, 1990 to 2002', in Chisholm, *Changing Class*, p. 202.

18. Ibid., p. 202.

19. Sipho Masondo, Dominic Mahlangu and Harriet McLea, 'Youth Sacrificed for OBE', *Sunday Times*, 6 July 2010.

20. Sesona Ngqakamba, 'The "real" matric pass rate is 37.6%—DA', News24, 4 January 2019, https://www.news24.com/SouthAfrica/News/the-real-matric-pass-rate-is-376-da-20190104, last accessed 22 April 2019.

21. Van der Berg et al., 'The Performance of Low Fee Independent Schools in South Africa—What Can Available Data Tell?', Stellenbosch Economic Working Paper 01/17, Research on Socio-Economic Policy, Department of Economics, University of Stellenbosch, 2017, p. 9.

22. 'Best private and public schools in South Africa: cost vs performance', BusinessTech, 9 February 2016, https://businesstech.co.za/news/lifestyle/111863/best-private-and-public-schools-in-south-africa-cost-vs-peformance/, last accessed 22 April 2019.

23. Van der Berg et al., 'The Performance of Low Fee Independent Schools', p. 10.

24. Dave Chambers, 'SA schooling is bottom of the class, Economist tells its readers', *Sunday Times*, 6 January 2017, https://www.timeslive.co.za/news/south-africa/2017-01-06-sa-schooling-is-bottom-of-the-class-economist-tells-its-readers/, last accessed 22 April 2019.

25. Milton Nkosi, 'Is South Africa's education system really "in crisis"?', *BBC News*, 29 January 2016, http://www.bbc.co.uk/news/world-africa-35427853, last accessed 22 April 2019.

26. Nic Spaull, 'Basic education thrown under the bus—and it shows up in test results', *Business Day*, 16 April 2018, https://www.businesslive.co.za/bd/opinion/2018-04-16-basic-education-thrown-under-the-bus—and-it-shows-up-in-test-results/, last accessed 22 April 2019.

27. 'South Africa has one of the world's worst education systems', *The Economist*.

28. City Press, 'Exclusive—Back to Bantu education?', News24, 27 January 2013, https://www.news24.com/Archives/City-Press/Exclusive-Back-to-Bantu-education-20150430, last accessed 22 April 2019.

29. 'Report of the Ministerial Task Team Appointed by Minister Angie Motshekga to Investigate Allegations into the Selling of Posts of Educators by Members of Teachers Unions and Departmental Officials in Provincial Education Departments', Department of Basic Education, 18 May 2016, https://nicspaull.files.wordpress.com/2016/05/dbe-2016-volmink-report.pdf, last accessed 22 April 2019.

30. Ibid., p. 18.

31. Ibid., pp. 122–23.

32. Aretha Linden, 'Six teachers in sex with pupils scandal', DispatchLive, 12 February 2018, http://www.dispatchlive.co.za/news/2018/02/12/six-teachers-sex-pupils-scandal/, last accessed 22 April 2019.

33. 'Report of the Ministerial Task Team Appointed by Minister Angie Motshekga', p. 22.

34. 'Editorial: Why Ramaphosa must tackle Sadtu', *Financial Mail*, 10 January 2019, https://www.businesslive.co.za/fm/opinion/editorial/2019-01-10-editorial-why-ramaphosa-must-tackle-sadtu/, last accessed 22 April 2019.

35. Ian Bunting, 'The Higher Education Landscape under Apartheid', in Cloete et al. (eds), *Transformation in Higher Education: Global Pressures and Local Realities*, Dordrecht; London: Springer, 2006, p. 35.

36. 'World University Rankings 2010–11', Times Higher Education World University Rankings, https://www.timeshighereducation.com/world-university-rankings/2011/world-ranking#!/page/0/length/25/sort_by/rank/sort_order/asc/cols/undefined, last accessed 22 April 2019.

37. Simamkele Dlakavu, 'Wits political studies post-graduate students: On a quest to revolutionise the academy', *Daily Maverick*, 19 December 2014, https://www.dailymaverick.co.za/opinionista/2014-12-19-wits-political-studies-post-graduate-students-on-a-quest-to-revolution-alise-the-academy/, last accessed 22 April 2019.

38. By 2011 some 74 per cent of students were Indian, Coloured and black African, yet only 32 per cent of the staff fell into these categories. Camalita Naicker, 'From Marikana to #feesmustfall: The Praxis of Popular Politics in South Africa', *Urbanisation*, vol. 1, no. 1 (2016), pp. 53–61.

39. Belinda Bozzoli, 'What happens when universities start to decay: The case of Unisa', *Daily Maverick*, 13 November 2018, https://www.dailymaverick.co.za/opinionista/2018-11-13-what-happens-when-universities-start-to-decay-the-case-of-unisa/, last accessed 22 April 2019.

40. 'Science Must Fall?', YouTube, 13 October 2016, https://www.youtube.com/watch?v=C9SiRNibD14, last accessed 22 April 2019.

41. Junior Bester, 'Protesters throw poo on Rhodes statue', Independent Online, 11 March 2015, https://www.iol.co.za/news/south-africa/west-ern-cape/protesters-throw-poo-on-rhodes-statue-1829526,   last accessed 22 April 2019.

42. Quoted in Francis B. Nyamnjoh, 'Black Pain Matters: Down with Rhodes', *Pax Academica*, nos 1 and 2 (2015), p. 55.

43. Jonathan Jansen, 'Prof Mayosi's suicide and the high cost of leadership at universities', *Rand Daily Mail*, 1 August 2018, https://www.busi-nesslive.co.za/rdm/lifestyle/2018-08-01-jonathan-jansen-prof-mayo-sis-suicide-and-the-high-cost-of-leadership-at-universities/, last acces-sed 22 April 2019.

44. Nic Spaull, 'Basic education thrown under the bus—and it shows up in test results', *Business Day*, 16 April 2018, https://www.businesslive.co.za/bd/opinion/2018-04-16-basic-education-thrown-under-the-bus—and-it-shows-up-in-test-results/, last accessed 22 April 2019.

45. Sean Mfundza Muller, 'Free higher education in South Africa: Cutting through the lies and statistics', *Mail & Guardian*, 25 January 2018, https://mg.co.za/article/2018-01-25-free-higher-education-in-south-africa-cutting-through-the-lies-and-statistics, last accessed 22 April 2019.

46. Prinesha Naidoo, 'SA's R172.2bn fee plan to pressure budget, WB says', Moneyweb, 22 January 2019, https://www.moneyweb.co.za/news-fast-news/sas-r172–2bn-fee-plan-to-pressure-budget-wb-says/, last accessed 22 April 2019.

9. JUSTICE AND THE LAW

1. Cases CCT 143/15 and CCT 171/15, Constitutional Court of South Africa, 2016, https://cdn.24.co.za/files/Cms/General/d/3834/24efe59 744c642a1a02360235f4d026b.pdf, last accessed 9 January 2019.
2. Lourens du Plessis, 'South Africa', in Gerhard Robbers (ed.), *Encyclopedia of Law and Religion: Volume 1, Africa*, Leiden: Brill, p. 268.
3. Edwin Cameron, *Justice: A Personal Account*, Cape Town: Tafelberg, 2014, p. 183.
4. 'SABC is allowed to broadcast Thatcher Case', South African History Online, https://www.sahistory.org.za/dated-event/sabc-allowed-broadcast-thatcher-case, last accessed 9 January 2019.
5. Lourens du Plessis, 'South Africa', in Gerhard Robbers (ed.), *Encyclopedia of Law and Religion: Volume 1, Africa*, p. 261.
6. Ibid., p. 262.
7. Ibid., p. 264.
8. Ibid., p. 267.
9. Saul Dubow, *South Africa's Struggle for Human Rights*, Auckland Park: Jacana, 2012, p. 43.
10. Ibid., p. 44.
11. Saul Dubow, 'Smuts, the United Nations and the Rhetoric of Race and Rights', *Journal of Contemporary History*, vol. 43, no. 1 (2008), p. 44.
12. Dubow, *South Africa's Struggle for Human Rights*, p. 68.
13. Ibid., p. 92.
14. Ibid., p. 117.
15. Cameron, *Justice*, p. 277.
16. Dubow, *South Africa's Struggle for Human Rights*, p. 122.
17. Ibid., p. 122.
18. See Chapter Seven on land and agriculture.
19. Glynnis Breytenbach, *Rule of Law: A Memoir*, Johannesburg: Pan Macmillan, 2017, p. 58.

20. Cameron, *Justice*, p. 22.
21. Ibid., p. 11.
22. 'Dean in South Africa Is Cleared On Appeal in Subversion Case', *New York Times*, 15 April 1972, https://www.nytimes.com/1972/04/15/archives/dean-in-south-africa-is-cleared-on-appeal-in-subversion-case-south.html, last accessed 22 April 2019.
23. Cameron, *Justice*, p. 29.
24. Ibid., p. 33.
25. Ibid., p. 36.
26. Ibid., p. 38.
27. Ibid., p. 40.
28. Ibid., p. 49.
29. See also Chapter Ten, on civil society.
30. 'Debate: Is there excessive "lawfare" in South Africa?', 702, 5 May 2017, http://www.702.co.za/articles/254963/debate-is-there-excessive-lawfare-in-south-africa, last accessed 17 January 2019.
31. Cameron, *Justice*, p. 111.
32. 'The make-up of South Africa's judiciary', Judges Matter, 29 March 2017, http://www.judgesmatter.co.za/opinions/south-africa-judges/, last accessed 17 January 2019.
33. 'Lack of Gender Transformation in the Judiciary: Investigative Report', Commission for Gender Equality, 2016, http://www.cge.org.za/wp-content/uploads/2016/12/CGE-Lack-of-Gender-Transformation-in-the-Judiciary-Investigative-Report-.pdf, last accessed 17 January 2019.
34. Angela Quintal, 'Tempers flare in judicial "race row"', Independent Online, 26 October 2004, https://www.iol.co.za/news/south-africa/tempers-flare-in-judicial-race-row-225172, last accessed 22 April 2019; and Glynnis Underhill, 'New race row divides judiciary', *Mail & Guardian*, 5 August 2011, https://mg.co.za/article/2011-08-05-new-race-row-divides-judiciary, last accessed 22 April 2019.
35. 'Who's who in the arms deal?', Corruption Watch, 20 January 2015, https://www.corruptionwatch.org.za/whos-who-in-the-arms-deal/, last accessed 18 January 2019.
36. Breytenbach, *Rule of Law*, p. 128.
37. Ray Hartley, 'How Zuma lost control—and the people who let him

down', *Sunday Times*, 11 February 2018, https://www.timeslive.co.za/sunday-times/opinion-and-analysis/2018-02-10-how-zuma-lost-control-and-the-people-who-let-him-down/, last accessed 18 January 2019.

38. Ibid.
39. Ibid.
40. 'Monograph 96: The Scorpions. Analysing the Directorate of Special Operations, Jean Redpath', Institute for Security Studies, 1 March 2004, https://issafrica.org/research/monographs/monograph-96-the-scorpions.-analysing-the-directorate-of-special-operations-jean-redpath, last accessed 18 January 2019.
41. Hartley, 'How Zuma lost control'.
42. Breytenbach, *Rule of Law*, p. 137.
43. Hartley, 'How Zuma lost control'.
44. Justice Sandile Ngcobo delivered a minority judgment in favour of Zuma in 2008 when he was the only one on the Constitutional Court bench who disagreed that the search-and-seizure warrants used by the Scorpions three years earlier to gather information from the offices of his lawyer, Mike Hulley, were legal.
45. Hartley, 'How Zuma lost control'.
46. Ranjeni Munusamy, 'Nkandla judgment: The Mastery of the Concourt vs the Invincibility of Jacob Zuma', *Daily Maverick*, 1 April 2016, https://www.dailymaverick.co.za/article/2016-04-01-nkandla-judgment-the-mastery-of-the-concourt-vs-the-invincibility-of-jacob-zuma/, last accessed 22 April 2019.
47. Hartley, 'How Zuma lost control'.
48. Claudi Mailovich, 'How we got to the ConCourt hearing Zuma's impeachment case', *Sunday Times*, 29 December 2017, https://www.timeslive.co.za/politics/2017-12-29-how-we-got-to-the-concourt-hearing-zumas-impeachment-case/, last accessed 18 January 2019.
49. 'Jacob Zuma resigns as president of South Africa', News24, 14 February 2018, https://www.news24.com/SouthAfrica/News/jacob-zuma-resigns-as-president-of-south-africa-20180214, last accessed 18 January 2019.
50. Lauren Segal and Sharon Cort, *One Law, One Nation: The Making of the South African Constitution*, Auckland Park: Jacana, 2011, p. 10.

51. Andre Jurgens, 'There are tales Schabir Shaik can tell...', *Sunday Times*, 16 October 2017, https://www.timeslive.co.za/politics/2017-10-16-there-are-tales-schabir-shaik-can-tell/, last accessed 18 January 2019.

10. CIVIL SOCIETY: THE PUSH FROM OUTSIDE

1. Marianne Merten, 'State Capture wipes out third of SA's R4.9-trillion GDP—never mind lost trust, confidence, opportunity', *Daily Maverick*, 1 March 2019, https://www.dailymaverick.co.za/article/2019-03-01-state-capture-wipes-out-third-of-sas-r4-9-trillion-gdp-never-mind-lost-trust-confidence-opportunity/, last accessed 22 April 2019.
2. Saul Dubow, *South Africa's Struggle for Human Rights*, Auckland Park: Jacana, 2012, p. 30.
3. Lourens du Plessis, 'South Africa', in Gerhard Robbers (ed.), *Encyclopedia of Law and Religion: Volume 1, Africa*, Leiden: Brill, p. 272.
4. 'Founding', South African Council of Churches, http://sacc.org.za/history/, last accessed 22 April 2019.
5. 'History of the Black Sash', Black Sash, https://www.blacksash.org.za/index.php/our-legacy/history-of-the-black-sash, last accessed 22 April 2019.
6. Dubow, *South Africa's Struggle for Human Rights*, p. 84.
7. Edwin Cameron, *Justice: A Personal Account*, Cape Town: Tafelberg, 2014, p. 29.
8. 'Turning the Tide: A chapter from the UDF. A history of the United Democratic Front in South Africa', South African History Online, https://www.sahistory.org.za/articles/turning-tide-chapter-udf-history-united-democratic-front-south-africa, last accessed 22 April 2019.
9. Ibid.
10. Dubow, *South Africa's Struggle for Human Rights*, p. 88.
11. 'Turning the Tide', South African History Online.
12. Ibid.
13. Cameron, *Justice*, p. 95.
14. Samantha Power, 'The Aids Rebel', *The New Yorker*, 11 May 2003, https://www.newyorker.com/magazine/2003/05/19/the-aids-rebel, last accessed 22 April 2019.

15. Cameron, *Justice*, p. 118.
16. Ibid., p. 131.
17. Ibid., p. 151.
18. Mark Heywood, *Get Up! Stand Up! Personal Journeys Towards Social Justice*, Cape Town: Tafelberg, 2017, p. 122.
19. Cameron, *Justice*, p. 118.
20. Heywood, *Get Up! Stand Up!*, p. 92.
21. Ibid., pp. 115–18.
22. Ibid., p. 137.
23. Ibid., p. 154.
24. 'Mid-year population estimates', Statistics South Africa, 2018, https://www.statssa.gov.za/publications/P0302/P03022018.pdf, last accessed 22 April 2019.
25. Heywood, *Get Up! Stand Up!*, p. 157.
26. Greg Nicolson, 'Section27: "Everywhere they need help—we just give them help"', *Daily Maverick*, 15 May 2013, https://www.dailymaverick.co.za/article/2013-05-15-section27-everywhere-they-need-help-we-just-give-them-help/, last accessed 22 April 2019.
27. Nonkosi Khumalo and Mark Heywood, 'ANC statement reminiscent of Mbeki-era paranoia—TAC/SECTION27', Politicsweb, 3 November 2010, https://www.politicsweb.co.za/documents/anc-statement-reminiscent-of-mbekiera-paranoia—ta, last accessed 22 April 2019.
28. Chipkin et al. (eds), *Shadow State: The Politics of State Capture*, Johannesberg: Wits University Press, 2018, p. 2.
29. See Chapter Five, on corruption.
30. Corruption Watch, https://www.corruptionwatch.org.za/, last accessed 22 April 2019.
31. Chipkin et al., *Shadow State*, p. xxv.
32. The Public Protector is one of six independent state institutions set up under the Constitution to support democracy and investigate public complaints about government abuses.
33. Chipkin et al., *Shadow State*, p. 1.
34. Ibid., p. 12.
35. Ibid., p. 10.
36. Ibid., p. 7.

37. Sipho Pityana, 'How civil society is taking the fight to government', News24, 20 October 2017, https://www.news24.com/Columnists/GuestColumn/how-civil-society-is-taking-the-fight-to-government-20171020, last accessed 22 April 2019.

38. Rebecca Davis, 'SA civil society veteran warns of the dangers of the "Ramaphosa effect"', Daily Maverick, 7 February 2019, https://www.dailymaverick.co.za/article/2019-02-07-sa-civil-society-veteran-warns-of-the-dangers-of-the-ramaphosa-effect/, last accessed 22 April 2019.

11. VIOLENT POLITICS IN A VIOLENT SOCIETY

1. Chandre Gould, 'Comment: Why is crime and violence so high in South Africa?', AfricaCheck, 17 September 2014, https://africacheck.org/2014/09/17/comment-why-is-crime-and-violence-so-high-in-south-africa-2/, last accessed 22 April 2019.

2. 'South Africa is one of the most violent and unsafe countries in the world', BusinessTech, 18 June 2015, https://businesstech.co.za/news/government/90808/south-africa-is-one-of-the-most-violent-and-unsafe-countries-in-the-world/, last accessed 22 April 2019.

3. Krista Mahr, 'High South African crime rates and low faith in police boost private security in Guateng', Financial Times, 13 May 2017, https://www.ft.com/content/ab7600e4-2068-11e7-b7d3-163f5a7f229c?mhq5j=e1, last accessed 22 April 2019.

4. African News Agency, 'Special police task force to probe political killings, says police minister', Financial Times, 5 June 2016, https://mg.co.za/article/2016-06-05-special-police-task-force-to-probe-political-killings-say-minister, last accessed 22 April 2019.

5. '2016 political violence in South Africa', eNCA, 27 July 2016, http://www.enca.com/south-africa/2016-political-violence-in-south-africa, last accessed 22 April 2019.

6. Gareth van Onselen, 'Political assassinations are on the rise', Rand Daily Mail, 29 February 2016, https://www.businesslive.co.za/rdm/politics/2016-02-29-political-assassinations-are-on-the-rise/, last accessed 22 April 2019.

7. David Bruce, 'Political Killings in South Africa: The Ultimate Intimidation', Institute for Security Studies Policy Brief, 3 November

2014, https://issafrica.org/research/policy-brief/political-killings-in-south-africa-the-ultimate-intimidation, last accessed 22 April 2019.

8. 'Hundreds of political killings left unsolved', eNCA, 20 July 2016, http://www.enca.com/south-africa/hundreds-of-political-killings-left-unsolved, last accessed 22 April 2019.

9. 'A most violent region: South Africa's ruling party is at war with itself', *The Economist*, 30 September 2017, https://www.economist.com/middle-east-and-africa/2017/09/30/south-africas-ruling-party-is-at-war-with-itself, last accessed 22 April 2019.

10. 'SAPS political violence task team probes murders of ANC and IFP members', Independent Online, 12 May 2018, https://www.iol.co.za/news/south-africa/kwazulu-natal/saps-political-violence-task-team-probes-murders-of-anc-and-ifp-members-14939632, last accessed 22 April 2019.

11. 'Ramaphosa arrives at the KZN home of slain ANC councillor', *The Citizen*, 14 May 2018, https://citizen.co.za/news/south-africa/1925899/ramaphosa-arrives-at-the-kzn-home-of-slain-anc-councillor/, last accessed 22 April 2019.

12. 'SAPS political violence task team probes murders of ANC and IFP members'.

13. See Mary de Haas, 'The Killing Fields of KZN: Local Government Elections, Violence and Democracy in 2016', *South African Crime Quarterly*, no. 57 (2016), pp. 43–53; Karl von Holdt, 'South Africa: The Transition to Violent Democracy', *Review of African Political Economy*, vol. 40, no. 138 (2013), pp. 589–604; and Jakkie Cilliers and Ciara Aucoin, 'Economics, Governance and Instability in South Africa', Institute for Security Studies Policy Brief, 19 June 2016, https://issafrica.org/research/papers/economics-governance-and-instability-in-south-africa, last accessed 22 April 2019.

14. Van Onselen, 'Political assassinations are on the rise'.

15. Two DA councillors have been shot around the time of writing: Xolile Gangxu—see Siyavuya Mzantsi, 'Reward offered after DA councillor shot dead', Independent Online, 21 June 2017, https://www.iol.co.za/capetimes/news/reward-offered-after-da-councillor-shot-dead-9909247, last accessed 22 April 2019; and Kingsol Chabalala—

see Hlengiwe Nhlabathi, 'Attempt to kill DA leader was "politically motivated"', News24, 20 August 2017, http://www.news24.com/SouthAfrica/News/attempt-to-kill-da-leader-was-politically-motivated-20170819, last accessed 22 April 2019.

16. 'History', Democratic Alliance, https://www.da.org.za/why-the-da/history, last accessed 22 April 2019.

17. The Democratic Alliance published a list of incidents of gradually escalating violence and intimidation. Democratic Alliance, 'Timeline of ANC & ANCYL's WCape ungovernability campaign', Politicsweb, 15 August 2012, http://www.politicsweb.co.za/party/timeline-of-anc—ancyls-wcape-ungovernability-camp, last accessed 22 April 2019.

18. Pretoria News, 'ANCYL charged after threat to make DA turf ungovernable', Independent Online, 2 August 2012, https://www.iol.co.za/pretoria-news/ancyl-charged-after-threat-to-make-da-turf-ungovernable-1355187, last accessed 22 April 2019.

19. Mark Shaw and Kim Thomas, 'The Commercialization of Assassination: "Hits" and Contract Killing in South Africa, 2000–2015', *African Affairs*, vol. 116, no. 465 (2017), pp. 597–620.

20. Natalie Simon, 'Rise of the hired hitman: assassinations and democracy in SA', News24, 18 November 2016, http://www.news24.com/Columnists/GuestColumn/rise-of-the-hired-hitman-assassinations-and-democracy-in-sa-20161118, last accessed 22 April 2019.

21. Mark Shaw, *Hitmen for Hire: Exposing South Africa's Underworld*, Johannesburg; Cape Town: Jonathan Ball, 2017, p. 67.

22. 'The Rule of the Gun: Hits and Assassinations in South Africa, January 2000 to December 2017', The Global Initiative Against Transnational Organized Crime, University of Cape Town, March 2018, https://assassinationwitness.org.za/wp-content/uploads/2018/03/The-rule-of-the-gun_Assassination-Witness.pdf, last accessed 22 April 2019.

23. David Bruce, 'Just singing and dancing? Intimidation and the manipulation of voters and the electoral process in the build-up to the 2014 elections', Community Agency for Social Enquiry, April 2014, https://www.nelsonmandela.org/uploads/files/intimidation-in-elections.pdf, last accessed 22 April 2019.

24. Ibid., p. 55.

25. Ibid., pp. 54–55.
26. Ibid., p. 56.
27. This is an edited version of an analysis by Martin Plaut, based in part on his personal experience of the election. See Martin Plaut, 'South Africa: How the ANC Wins Elections', *Review of African Political Economy*, vol. 41, no. 142 (2014), pp. 634–44.
28. David Bruce, 'Just singing and dancing?' p. 4.
29. Andre Grobler, 'Ramaphosa leaves yellow T-shirt trail', News24, 16 March 2014, https://www.news24.com/elections/news/ramaphosa-leaves-yellow-t-shirt-trail-20140316/comments, last accessed 22 April 2019.
30. See, for example, City Press, 'ANC's Chancellor House in secret R170m Eskom supplier deal', News24, 26 April 2014, https://www.news24.com/Archives/City-Press/ANCs-Chancellor-House-in-secret-R170m-Eskom-supplier-deal-20150430, last accessed 22 April 2019.
31. City Press, 'ANC's Chancellor House in secret R170m Eskom supplier deal'.
32. William Saunderson-Meyer, 'How the ANC's gravity-defying levitation is achieved', *Mail & Guardian*, 26 April 2014, http://www.thoughtleader.co.za/williamsaundersonmeyer/2014/04/26/how-the-ancs-gravity-defying-levitation-is-achieved/, last accessed 22 April 2019.
33. Helen Zille, 'How the ANC is abusing state funds for election campaigning', Politicsweb, 7 April 2014, https://www.politicsweb.co.za/party/how-the-anc-is-abusing-state-funds-for-election-ca, last accessed 22 April 2019.
34. Linda Ensor, 'Poor believe grants tied to party not state', *Business Day*, 23 May 2014, http://www.bdlive.co.za/national/2014/05/23/poor-believe-grants-tied-to-party-not-state, last accessed 22 April 2019.
35. Yolanda Sadie, 'What Motivates Poor People to Support a Particular Party?', Media briefing session at the Centre for Social Development in Africa and Department of Politics at the University of Johannesburg, 27 May 2014.
36. The National Party used the broadcaster to considerable effect after 1948: 'the ruling National Party has adroitly used the SABC as a tool

with which to dominate its political opposition and to reassure its own followers.' William A. Hachten and C. Anthony Giffard, *The Press and Apartheid: Repression and Propaganda in South Africa*, London; Basingstoke: Macmillan, 1984, p. 200.

37. Anton Harber, 'South Africa: SABC Is Key Weapon in ANC's Arsenal', AllAfrica, 9 May 2014, http://allafrica.com/stories/201405091653.html, last accessed 25 April 2019.

38. Ibid.

39. Susan Booysen, *The African National Congress and the Regeneration of Political Power*, Johannesburg: Wits University Press, 2011, p. 220.

40. COPE: Statement by the Congress of the People, SABC confirms it is the ANC's chief propagandist, 24 March 2014, https://www.polity. org.za/article/cope-statement-by-the-congress-of-the-people-sabc-confirms-it-is-the-ancs-chief-propagandist-24032014–2014–03–24, last accessed 22 June 2019.

41. Hulisani Mmbara, 'SABC is the mouthpiece of the ANC', Mayihlome News, 17 July 2009, http://mayihlomenews.co.za/?currentaffairs=sabc-is-the-mouthpiece-of-the-anc, last accessed 25 April 2019.

42. Sue Valentine, 'Broadcaster betrays South Africa's young democracy', The Media Online, 13 May 2014, http://themediaonline.co.za/2014/05/sabc-betrays-south-africas-young-democracy/, last accessed 25 April 2019.

43. MMA responds to possible censorship at the SABC, 11 April 2014, accessed 21 May 2014. http://www.mediamonitoringafrica.org/index. php/news/entry/mma_responds_to_possible_censorship_at_the_sabc/.

44. Richard Poplak, 'HANNIBAL ELECTOR: Hlaudi, play the damn commercial!', *Daily Maverick*, 30 April 2014, http://www.dailymaver-ick.co.za/article/2014-04-30-hannibal-elector-hlaudi-play-the-damn-commercial/, last accessed 25 April 2019.

45. The relationship between the president and the Guptas, and its impact on South African media, is covered in considerable detail in an article written by a pseudonymous writer who goes by the name Lily Gosam. See Lily Gosam, 'Zuma, the Guptas and the great media heist', *Rand Daily Mail*, 18 January 2017, https://www.businesslive.co.za/rdm/politics/2017-01-18-zuma-the-guptas-and-the-great-media-heist/, last accessed 25 April 2019.

46. Mandy de Waal, 'The New Age: A growing media empire, built with your money', *Daily Maverick*, 19 April 2013, http://www.dailymaverick.co.za/article/2013-04-19-the-new-age-a-growing-media-empire-built-with-your-money/#.UXDIvYUYLow, last accessed 25 April 2019.

47. Gaye Davis and Gia Nicolaides, 'Was SABC money used to fund Gupta-owned ANN7?', Eyewitness News, 13 December 2016, http://ewn.co.za/2016/12/13/sabc-said-to-have-funded establishment-of-gupta-owned-ann7, last accessed 26 April 2019; Bekezela Phakathi, 'SABC "built up" Gupta rival television station', *Business Day*, 13 December 2016, https://www.businesslive.co.za/bd/national/media/2016-12-13-sabc-built-up-gupta-rival-television-station/, last accessed 26 April 2019.

48. Phakathi, 'SABC "built up" Gupta rival television station'.

49. '"SABC in crisis, facing financial ruin," says DA', Channel24, 21 May 2015, http://www.channel24.co.za/TV/News/SABC-in-crisis-facing-financial-ruin-says-DA-20150521, last accessed 26 April 2019.

50. Charl Blignaut, 'SABC faces collapse', 19 March 2017, http://www.news24.com/SouthAfrica/News/sabc-faces-collapse-20170319-3, last accessed 26 April 2019.

51. 'Is This the Beginning of the End of the SABC?', City Press, 18 March 2017, quoted by Radio Islam News, http://www.radioislam.org.za/a/index.php/latest-news/20544-is-this-the-beginning-of-the-end-of-the-sabc.html, last accessed 22 June 2019.

52. '"Hlaudi has the president on speed dial"—Here's what you need to know from SABC inquiry', City Press, 13 December 2016, http://citypress.news24.com/News/hlaudi-has-the-president-on-speed-dial-heres-what-you-need-to-know-from-sabc-inquiry-20161213, last accessed 26 April 2019.

53. Charl Blignaut and Lloyd Gedye, 'Hlaudi calls in the spooks', News24, 27 November 2016, http://www.news24.com/SouthAfrica/News/hlaudi-calls-in-the-spooks-20161127-2, last accessed 26 April 2019.

54. Stephan Hofstatter, 'Secret purge: Hlaudi's dirty war at SABC', *Sunday Times*, 23 December 2016, http://www.timeslive.co.za/sundaytimes/stnews/2016/12/23/Secret-purge-Hlaudis-dirty-war-at-SABC, last accessed 26 April 2019.

55. Craig McKune and Sam Sole, 'Independent sale tightens media noose', *Mail & Guardian*, 8 August 2013, https://mg.co.za/article/2013-08-08-00-independent-sale-tightens-media-noose, last accessed 26 April 2019.

56. Craig McKune, 'Chinese companies scoop shares in Independent News', *Mail & Guardian*, 15 August 2013, https://mg.co.za/article/2013-08-15-chinese-companies-scoop-shares-in-independent-news, last accessed 26 April 2019.

57. Wim Pretorius, 'Cape Times must apologise to former editor—press ombudsman', News24, 1 August 2016, http://www.news24.com/SouthAfrica/News/cape-times-must-apologise-to-former-editor-press-ombudsman-20160801, last accessed 26 April 2019.

58. Ed Herbst, 'The Cape Times: from hero to zero', Politicsweb, 30 September 2015, http://www.politicsweb.co.za/news-and-analysis/the-cape-times-from-hero-to-zero, last accessed 26 April 2019.

59. Anton Harber, 'Op-Ed: Twenty-five years after Mandela's freedom, SA media struggle', *Daily Maverick*, 11 February 2015, http://www.dailymaverick.co.za/article/2015-02-11-op-ed-twenty-five-years-after-mandelas-freedom-sa-media-struggle/#.VNvpmHb7d7k, last accessed 29 April 2019.

60. Susan Comrie, 'Inside the ANC's "black ops" election campaign', amaBhungane, 24 January 2017, https://amabhungane.org/stories/inside-the-ancs-black-ops-election-campaign/, last accessed 26 April 2019.

61. Ranjeni Munusamy, 'Black Ops, alternative facts and damn lies: The ANC's escalating credibility crisis', *Daily Maverick*, 30 January 2017, https://www.dailymaverick.co.za/article/2017-01-30-black-ops-alternate-facts-and-damn-lies-the-ancs-escalating-credibility-crisis/#.WI8j9pKKSMk, last accessed 26 April 2019.

62. SAPA, 'No campaigning on Election Day—Tlakula', *The Citizen*, 7 May 2014, https://citizen.co.za/news/south-africa/172339/campaigning-election-day-tlakula/, last accessed 26 April 2019.

63. Bruce, 'Just singing and dancing?', p. 89.

64. Ibid., p. 90.

65. Constitution of the Republic of South Africa, 8 May 1996, paragraph 190, http://www.justice.gov.za/legislation/constitution/saconstitution-web-eng.pdf, last accessed 26 April 2019.

66. Jakkie Cilliers and Ciara Aucoin, 'South African Scenarios 2024: Politics, Violence and Growth in the Rainbow Nation', Institute for Security Studies, 20 June 2016, https://issafrica.org/research/papers/south-african-scenarios-2024-politics-violence-and-growth-in-the-rainbow-nation, last accessed 26 April 2019.

67. Van Onselen, 'Political assassinations are on the rise'.

12. THE MAKING OF PRESIDENT RAMAPHOSA

1. Ray Hartley, *Ramaphosa: Path to Power*, London: Hurst and Company, 2018, p. 17.

2. Ibid., p. 39.

3. Jeremy Gordin, 'The Ramaphosa enigma', Politicsweb, 7 May 2018, https://www.politicsweb.co.za/opinion/the-ramaphosa-enigma, last accessed 22 June 2019.

4. Martin Plaut, 'Cyril Ramaphosa', BBC Radio 4, 4 November 2007, https://www.bbc.co.uk/programmes/b0084wr0, last accessed 26 April 2019.

5. Hartley, *Ramaphosa*, p. 79.

6. Anthony Butler, *Cyril Ramaphosa*, Johannesburg: Jacana, 2007, p. 330.

7. Hartley, *Ramaphosa*, p. 84.

8. Butler, *Cyril Ramaphosa*, p. 345.

9. Siyabonga Mkhwanazi, 'Ramaphosa, Sexwale named in anti-Mbeki plot', Independent Online, 24 April 2001, https://www.iol.co.za/news/politics/ramaphosa-sexwale-named-in-anti-mbeki-plot-65207, last accessed 26 April 2019.

10. 'Sexwale, Phosa angry over Mbeki conspiracy claims', News24, 25 April 2001, https://www.news24.com/SouthAfrica/Sexwale-Phosa-angry-over-Mbeki-conspiracy-claims-20010425, last accessed 26 April 2019.

11. Chris McGreal, 'ANC veterans accused of plot to harm Mbeki', *The Guardian*, 26 April 2001, https://www.theguardian.com/world/2001/apr/26/chrismcgreal, last accessed 26 April 2019.

12. Hartley, *Ramaphosa*, p. 129.

13. City Press, 'ANC obsession with conspiracies is dangerous', News24, 16 March 2015, https://www.news24.com/Archives/City-Press/ANC-obsession-with-conspiracies-is-dangerous-20150430, last accessed 26 April 2019.

14. Hartley, *Ramaphosa*, p. 157.

15. Ibid., p. 166.

16. Nqobile Dludla and Joe Brock, 'Gordhan arrives back in South Africa after Zuma recall', Reuters, 28 March 2017, https://uk.reuters.com/article/uk-safrica-gordhan-idUKKBN16Y2Q0?il=0, last accessed 26 April 2019.

17. '#CabinetReshuffle: Ramaphosa against Gordhan's removal', Independent Online, 31 March 2017, https://www.iol.co.za/news/politics/cabinetreshuffle-ramaphosa-against-gordhans-removal-8436396, last accessed 22 June 2019.

18. Hartley, *Ramaphosa*, p. 166.

19. Marianne Thamm, 'NASREC PLOT: IPID targets senior SAPS members and former ministerial adviser in ANC vote-buying scandal', *Daily Maverick*, 7 January 2019, https://www.dailymaverick.co.za/article/2019-01-07-nasrec-plot-ipid-targets-senior-saps-members-and-former-ministerial-adviser-in-anc-vote-buying-scandal/, last accessed 26 April 2019.

20. Amil Umraw, 'Robert McBride details ANC vote-buying scandal', *Business Day*, 8 January 2019, https://www.businesslive.co.za/bd/national/2019-01-08-robert-mcbride-details-anc-vote-buying-scandal/, last accessed 26 April 2019.

21. Amil Umraw, 'ANC Balance Of Forces: Is Ramaphosa In Control?', HuffPost, 5 May 2018, https://www.huffingtonpost.co.za/2018/05/05/anc-balance-of-power-is-ramaphosa-in-control_a_23427156/, last accessed 26 April 2019.

22. Yunus Momoniat, 'President Jacob Zuma, our arch-Machiavellian', *Business Day*, 1 January 2018, https://www.businesslive.co.za/bd/opinion/2018-01-01-president-jacob-zuma-our-arch-machiavellian/, last accessed 26 April 2019.

23. News24, 'Recalling Zuma will cause havoc, Transform RSA warns ANC leaders', *Daily Maverick*, 12 January 2018, https://www.dailymaverick.co.za/article/2018-01-12-recalling-zuma-will-cause-havoc-transform-rsa-warns-anc-leaders/, last accessed 22 May 2019.

24. Setumo Stone, 'How Ramaphosa "dodged a coup"—security bosses reveal all', News24, 22 July 2018, https://www.news24.com/South

Africa/News/security-bosses-reveal-how-cyril-dodged-a-coup-20180722–2, last accessed 22 May 2019.

25. Qaanitah Hunter, 'SACP expresses great appreciation for Ramaphosa, accuses Zuma of counter-revolution', *Daily Maverick*, 4 June 2018, https://www.dailymaverick.co.za/article/2018-06-04-sacp-expresses-great-appreciation-for-ramaphosa-accuses-zuma-of-counter-revolution/#.WxTIkEgvzcs, last accessed 22 May 2019.

26. Lizeka Tandwa, '#ZumaResigns: I do not fear impeachment or no confidence vote, says Zuma', 14 February 2018, https://www.news24.com/SouthAfrica/News/zumaresigns-i-do-not-fear-impeachment-or-no-confidence-vote-says-zuma-20180214, last accessed 22 May 2019.

13. THE 2019 ELECTION LEAVES THE COUNTRY STIRRED, NOT SHAKEN

1. Cyril Ramaphosa, 'The ANC's 2019 election manifesto', Politicsweb, 13 January 2019, https://www.politicsweb.co.za/opinion/the-ancs-2019-election-manifesto, last accessed 22 May 2019.

2. Carien du Plessis, 'Ramaphosa promises to address concerns of Mqanduli residents', Eyewitness News, 28 April 2019, https://ewn.co.za/2019/04/28/ramaphosa-promises-to-address-concerns-of-mqanduli-residents, last accessed 22 May 2019.

3. Yazeed Fakier, 'There's danger in a call to vote for Ramaphosa: Imagine a landslide for the ANC's faction of corruption', *Daily Maverick*, 23 April 2019, https://www.dailymaverick.co.za/opinionista/2019-04-23-theres-danger-in-a-call-to-vote-for-ramaphosa-imagine-a-landslide-for-the-ancs-faction-of-corruption/, last accessed 22 May 2019.

4. Zingisa Mvumvu, 'Voters like Cyril Ramaphosa more than they like the ANC: survey', *Sunday Times*, 24 February 2019, https://www.timeslive.co.za/politics/2019-02-24-voters-like-cyril-ramaphosa-more-than-they-like-the-anc-survey/, last accessed 22 May 2019.

5. See Chapter Nine.

6. Ramaphosa, 'The ANC's 2019 election manifesto'.

7. 'National Assembly: 2019 National and Provincial Elections Results Dashboard', https://www.elections.org.za/NPEDashboard/app/dashboard.html, last accessed 22 May 2019.

8. Clement Manyathela, 'Magashule: Ramaphosa cannot take credit for ANC winning elections', Eyewitness News, 10 May 2019, https://ewn.co.za/2019/05/10/magashule-ramaphosa-cannot-take-credit-for-anc-winning-elections, last accessed 22 May 2019.

9. '2016 South African municipal elections', Wikipedia, https://en.wikipedia.org/wiki/2016_South_African_municipal_elections, last accessed 22 May 2019.

10. Mbuyiseni Ndlozi, 'Ramaphosa performed worse than Zuma—EFF', Politicsweb, 16 May 2019, https://www.politicsweb.co.za/politics/iec-should-modernise-its-systems-by-2021—eff, last accessed 22 May 2019.

11. Asanda Qosha, interviewed by Martin Plaut in Eastern Cape.

12. Carien du Plessis, 'Residents of flood-hit Port St Johns to get temporary IDs ahead of elections', Eyewitness News, 29 April 2019, https://ewn.co.za/2019/04/29/residents-of-flood-hit-port-st-johns-to-get-temporary-ids-ahead-of-elections, last accessed 22 May 2019.

13. SABC Digital News, 'Democratic Alliance election rally, 04 May 2019', YouTube, 4 May 2019, https://www.youtube.com/watch?v=cZoJ1eInX6Y, last accessed 22 May 2019.

14. Moipone Malefane, 'Mmusi Maimane vows to take on "white privilege"', *The Sowetan*, 8 May 2018, https://www.sowetanlive.co.za/news/2018-05-08-mmusi-maimane-vows-to-take-on-white-privilege/, last accessed 22 May 2019.

15. Dawie Scholtz, 'Demographics and disappointment: Dawie Scholtz's complete election post-mortem', News24, 14 May 2019, https://www.news24.com/Elections/Voices/demographics-and-disappointment-dawie-scholtzs-complete-election-post-mortem-20190514, last accessed 22 May 2019.

16. Pieter du Toit, 'Elections Briefs: Why the much-vaunted DA shot blanks', News24, 16 May 2019, https://www.news24.com/elections/voices/elections-briefs-why-the-much-vaunted-da-shot-blanks-20190515, last accessed 22 May 2019; Ferial Haffajee, 'White anxiety and the rise of the Freedom Front Plus', *Daily Maverick*, 14 May 2019, https://www.dailymaverick.co.za/article/2019-05-14-white-anxiety-and-the-rise-of-the-freedom-front-plus/, last accessed 22 May 2019.

17. Carien du Plessis, 'Back to the future: Tony Leon and Thabo Mbeki on the campaign trail', *Daily Maverick*, 25 April 2019, https://www.dailymaverick.co.za/article/2019-04-25-back-to-the-future-tony-leon-and-thabo-mbeki-on-the-campaign-trail/, last accessed 22 May 2019.

18. Gia Nicolaides, 'Maimane takes full responsibility for drop in DA electoral support', Eyewitness News, 14 May 2019, https://ewn.co.za/2019/05/14/maimane-takes-full-responsibly-for-drop-in-da-electoral-support, last accessed 22 May 2019.

19. Zingisa Mvumvu, 'Maimane a no-show at DA presser about his future', *Sunday Times*, 13 May 2019, https://www.timeslive.co.za/politics/2019-05-13-maimane-a-no-show-at-da-presser-about-his-future/, last accessed 22 May 2019.

20. Helen Zille, 'From the Inside: The DA and the ANC took a knock—both require some soul-searching', *Daily Maverick*, 13 May 2019, https://www.dailymaverick.co.za/opinionista/2019-05-13-from-the-inside-the-da-and-the-anc-took-a-knock-both-require-some-soul-searching/, last accessed 22 May 2019.

21. Clement Manyathela, 'Zille: Apology over colonialism tweets genuine this time', Eyewitness News, 13 June 2017, https://ewn.co.za/2017/06/13/zille-apology-over-colonialism-tweets-genuine-this-time, last accessed 22 May 2019.

22. Kaunda Selisho, 'Don't cry when you're punished at the polls for being a d***', says DA's Mbali Ntuli', *The Citizen*, 17 May 2019, https://citizen.co.za/news/south-africa/social-media/2132068/dont-cry-when-youre-punished-at-the-polls-for-being-a-d-says-das-mbali-ntuli/, last accessed 22 May 2019.

23. Du Toit, 'Why the much-vaunted DA shot blanks'.

24. 'National Assembly: 2019 National and Provincial Elections Results Dashboard'.

25. Ibid.

26. 'EFF condemns violence at Hout Bay election debate', Eyewitness News, 5 April 2019, https://ewn.co.za/2019/04/05/eff-condemns-violence-at-hout-bay-election-debate, last accessed 22 May 2019.

27. News24, 'Karima Brown wants Malema hauled to court over his tweet', *Daily Maverick*, 26 April 2019, https://www.dailymaverick.co.za/

article/2019-04-26-karima-brown-wants-malema-hauled-to-court-over-his-tweet/, last accessed 22 May 2019.

28. Ayanda Mthethwa, 'Malema's utterances offensive but not hate speech', *Daily Maverick*, 27 March 2019, https://www.dailymaverick.co.za/article/2019-03-27-malemas-utterances-offensive-but-not-hate-speech/, last accessed 22 May 2019.

29. Ibid.

30. Ngwako Modjadji and S'thembile Cele, 'In and out: Another MP dumps EFF, but former ANCYL leader jumps ship to join red berets', City Press, 22 April 2019, https://city-press.news24.com/News/in-and-out-another-mp-dumps-eff-but-former-ancyl-leader-jumps-ship-to-join-red-berets-20190422, last accessed 22 May 2019.

31. See Chapter Four, on the political opposition.

32. Times Live, 'Julius Malema's grandmother dies', *Sunday Times*, 4 May 2019, https://www.timeslive.co.za/politics/2019-05-04-julius-malemas-grandmother-dies/, last accessed 22 May 2019.

33. Keith Gottschalk and Dirk Kotze, 'Analysis: The Who, Why and What of the Freedom Front Plus', News24, 13 May 2019, https://www.news24.com/elections/voices/analysis-the-who-why-and-what-of-the-freedom-front-plus-20190513, last accessed 22 May 2019.

34. Pieter du Toit, 'Analysis: How the Freedom Front Plus ate (some of) the DA's lunch', News24, 11 May 2019, https://www.news24.com/elections/news/how-the-freedom-front-plus-ate-some-of-the-das-lunch-20190511, last accessed 22 May 2019.

35. M&G Data Desk, 'South Africa, this is your new parliament', *Mail & Guardian*, 14 May 2019, https://mg.co.za/article/2019-05-14-south-africa-this-is-your-new-parliament, last accessed 22 May 2019.

36. 'National Assembly: 2019 National and Provincial Elections Results Dashboard'.

37. 'Yes, more than 9 million eligible voters aren't registered for South Africa's 2019 elections', AfricaCheck, 15 February 2019, https://africacheck.org/fbcheck/yes-more-than-9-million-eligible-voters-arent-registered-for-south-africas-2019-elections/, last accessed 22 May 2019.

38. Phillip de Wet, 'The pens that marked voter thumbs cost millions—

here's why their secret ink may have failed', Business Insider, 9 May 2019, https://www.businessinsider.co.za/indelible-ink-pens-for-voting-from-bidvest-secret-formula-2019–5, last accessed 22 May 2019.

39. Scholtz, 'Demographics and disappointment'.

INDEX

Note: Page numbers followed by "*n*" refer to notes and page numbers marked in **bold** indicates references to the tables.

INDEX

INDEX

INDEX

INDEX

INDEX

INDEX

INDEX

INDEX

INDEX

INDEX

INDEX

INDEX

INDEX